T0377440

EXPLORING GIFTEDNESS AND AUTISM

Savant and splinter skills are seen in memory, art, music, calendar calculation and spatial skill amongst others. They can appear remarkable, but tend to be seen as 'obsessive' behaviours. *Exploring Giftedness and Autism* is based on a unique study which introduces and explores a differentiated educational curriculum and presents a combination of strategies employed in the education of gifted children and autistic children. Providing insights on the obsessive nature of savant skills, the challenging behaviours of savants and the familial link between the subject child's savant abilities and giftedness, the author highlights how the inclusion of this curriculum is critical in promoting better school performance and post-school employment opportunities.

The study has demonstrated the importance of using a 'strengths' rather than a 'deficits' approach in the education of students with a disability, and regards autistic savants as gifted students with disabilities, or as 'twice-exceptional' students with autism. With a practical section dedicated to putting the research into practice, this book is an incredibly important read for anyone working with gifted young people with disabilities in the classroom.

Trevor Clark is National Director, Education at Autism Spectrum Australia.

EXPLORING GIFTEDNESS AND AUTISM

A study of a differentiated educational program for autistic savants

Trevor Clark

Routledge
Taylor & Francis Group

LONDON AND NEW YORK

First published 2016
by Routledge
2 Park Square, Milton Park, Abingdon, Oxon OX14 4RN

and by Routledge
711 Third Avenue, New York, NY 10017

Routledge is an imprint of the Taylor & Francis Group, an informa business

British Library Cataloguing in Publication Data
A catalogue record for this book is available from the British Library

Library of Congress Cataloging in Publication Data
Names: Clark, Trevor (Special education consultant)
Title: Exploring giftedness and autism : a study of a differentiated educational program for autistic savants / Trevor Clark.
Description: Abingdon, Oxon ; New York, NY : Routledge, 2016.
Identifiers: LCCN 2015046212| ISBN 9781138839533 (hardback) |
ISBN 9781138839540 (pbk.) | ISBN 9781315733388 (ebook)
Subjects: LCSH: Autistic children—Education. | Gifted children—Education. |
Savants (Savant syndrome) | Savant syndrome.
Classification: LCC LC4717 .C527 2016 | DDC 371.9—dc23
LC record available at http://lccn.loc.gov/2015046212

ISBN: 978–1–138–83953–3 (hbk)
ISBN: 978–1–138–83954–0 (pbk)
ISBN: 978–1–315–73338–8 (ebk)

Typeset in Bembo
by Florence Production Ltd, Stoodleigh, Devon, UK

For Paul and his family

CONTENTS

FIGURES

TABLES

APPENDICES

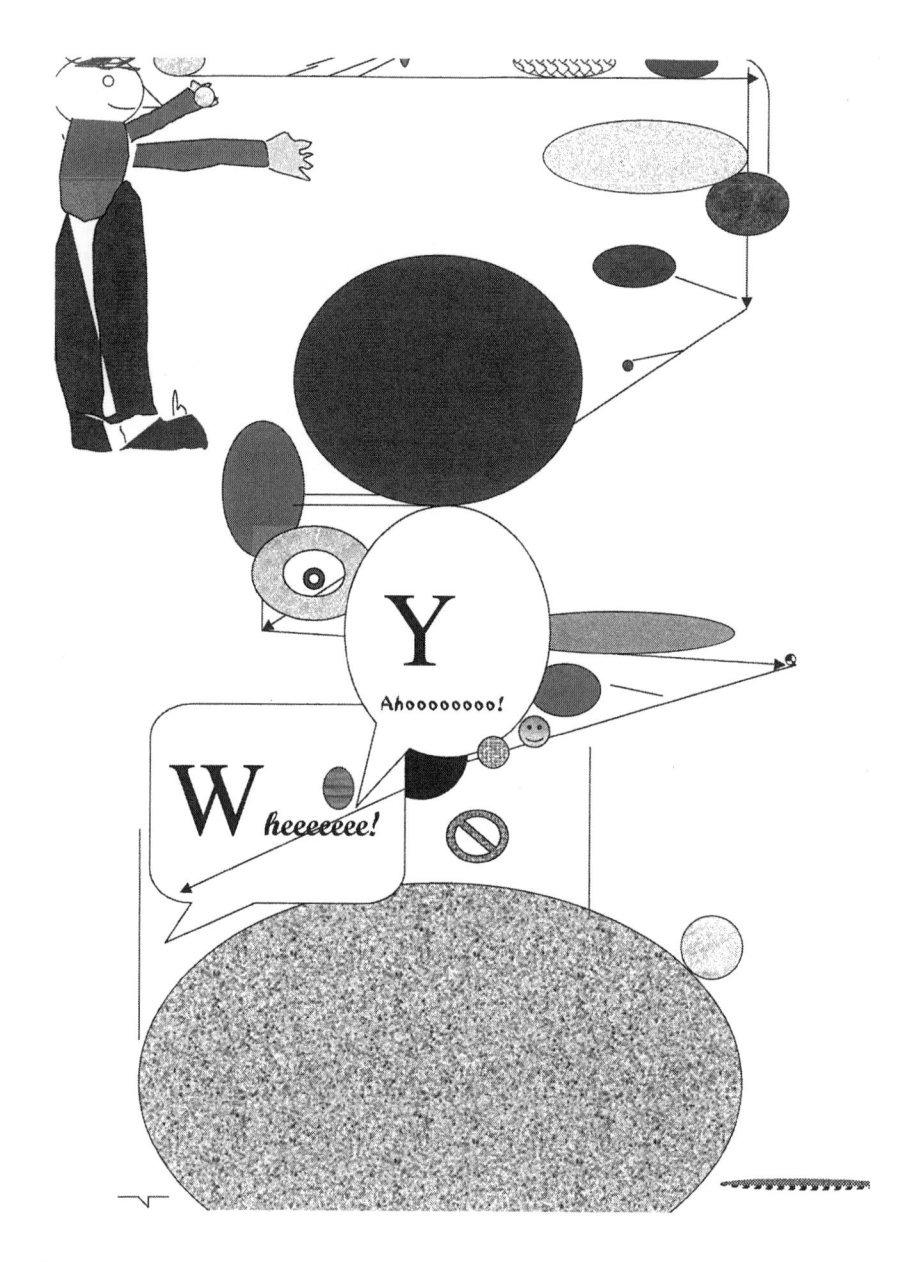

FIGURE 0.1 Marble Maze by Terry

'TRAINING THE TALENT'

A foreword

Savant syndrome raises many interesting and far-reaching questions. How is it possible for extraordinary ability and giftedness to co-exist in jarring juxtaposition with incapacitating disability in the same individual? And what might that say about dormant potential – a little Rain Man, perhaps, within us all? How does the presence of these 'islands of genius' impact on our present theories of overall intelligence? What are the brain changes that account for this remarkable condition?

Those are important questions to be sure. But for the person with savant abilities, and their families, caregivers and teachers, the more pertinent question is can this strength-based giftedness be approached and harnessed through certain education techniques in order to make these seemingly non-functional, incidental, obsessive traits and behaviours a conduit toward better communication, improved daily living skills and more independence?

It is that important task – making savant skills more functional and useful – that this book so successfully addresses.

So much has been written about the intriguing and spectacular nature of savant skills and the movie *Rain Man* has made autistic savant a household term. But essentially little, until this book, has been written about finding, formally researching and then implementing a specific education approach – the *Savant Skill Curriculum* – to make the special skills more functional and in so doing helping overcome the impact of any underlying disability.

I began studying savant syndrome after meeting my first savant in 1962 while developing a special unit for autistic children at a hospital in Wisconsin. Following that a website hosted through the Wisconsin Medical Society at www.savant syndrome.com brought many cases of this remarkable condition to my attention. Many of the emails generated from that site began, 'I've got a son or daughter who . . . ' from parents of children with savant skills. They asked 'What to do?' with these special skills. What is the best strategy toward using them to maximize overall function of the affected person and ameliorating at the same time, in some measure, the underlying disability itself?

So I was very pleased in 2001 when I was asked to review Trevor Clark's Ph.D. project: *The Application of Savant and Splinter Skills in the Autistic Population through Curriculum Design*. It was a project to formally research and apply a 'strengths'-based approach to education of the gifted and disabled rather than the usual 'deficits' approach.

How refreshing it was, and now is, to see someone formally using that strategy.

Thus, this book documents in specific detail that completed thesis now expanded into this book after much more study and research. In the meantime I have had the privilege of referring questions from many families, caregivers and teachers to Dr Clark when they raised the 'What to do?' questions to me via the website. He has always been willing to share his expertise, empathy and compassion with these many persons individually. Now this book provides the opportunity to share that practical wisdom much more widely.

The book serves two major purposes. First it provides a specific *Savant Skill Curriculum* to a number of autistic savants and a control group, and then measures what impact and success that educational strategy had on making seemingly non-functional savant skills useful ones and in so doing increasing communication, adaptive behaviours, socialization and daily living skills. This strategy does so by utilizing a number of specific techniques – acceleration, enrichment and mentorship – which have been successful in teaching non-disabled gifted and talented youngsters for many years. What occurs here is that the two fields of gifted and autistic education are merged in a most interesting and useful manner. Overall it is what I refer to as 'training the talent'.

The second major purpose of the book is to expand research on savant syndrome itself. To this point, definitions of 'savant' skills, and their quantification into levels – splinter skills, talented and prodigious – as described in my *Islands of Genius: The Bountiful Mind of the Autistic, Acquired and Sudden Savant* book, and some of my other work is admittedly subjective. In this book, Clark uses some new tailored questionnaires and scales to better standardize, document and quantify savant skills. To that end, the *Savant Skill Nomination Form,* and the *Savant Skill Questionnaires – Family and Teacher* instruments accomplish that and can be used by others in savant syndrome research. These two tools are then used to develop a *Profile of Savant Abilities* to help design each child's individual savant skill teaching program.

Analysing responses to those tools, Clark documented the obsessive nature of the savant skills; high levels of challenging behaviours as well as high levels of interest and motivation in pursuit of those skills. Interestingly, also documented was the early onset of savant skills in the absence of formal training and a familial link between the child's savant abilities and superior performance with many of the children also having gifted family members. Also there was evidence of imaginative and creative methods in some savant skills. All of the savants showed evidence of high-level memory and all showed multiple savant skills rather than a single talent. Most impressively, and important, is that savant abilities did *not* diminish as a result of the intervention; many parents fear that a loss of savant skills may occur just as suddenly as they often appear.

It has been over twenty-five years since *Rain Man* gave the term 'autistic savant' international visibility and acceptance. With it has come a tremendous availability of resources for diagnosis, treatment and education of children with autism, some of whom – autistic savants – are 'twice exceptional'. Indeed the Aspect (Autism Spectrum Australia) program, with which Clark himself is associated, is an excellent example of such a program which created the savant curriculum among other advances.

That network of autism services in most countries is impressive, but it serves mostly the under-age-eighteen population. Those children have become young adults now and in general there is a regrettable paucity of services for them. Yet, if by use of the savant curriculum and similar education strategies, autistic persons can be given functional, marketable skills, they can then enter the work world and simultaneously gain communication, social and daily living skills providing more independence for them and relief, reassurance and hope to their families.

I have seen such gains in some savants I have had the privilege of following now for a number of years. Some have put their drawing, painting or sculpting skills side by side with non-disabled persons' works in galleries and museums, and support themselves with their earnings. A number of musical savants do likewise, several of whom have gained fame internationally. Some corporations have discovered the programming skills of some savants and Microsoft recently announced a concerted effort to hire such persons working with the specialized employment agency Specialisterne, which finds and trains persons diagnosed on the autism spectrum.

Several savants have gone on to get Ph.D. degrees in mathematics or other fields and one works as a specialist in a highly sensitive position in a government agency. Another young adult who had memorized the entire Chicago Transit system was put to work as a customer services representative for lost or stranded passengers, helping to lead them to the correct terminal or safety by talking with them by telephone live and in person. A seventeen-year-old savant who began college courses at age eight is now completing his Ph.D. in theoretical physics at age seventeen and furthering his own theories in that specialty.

But not all savants will function at those high levels. Some can excel at college. Others are enrolled in programs to prepare them for a variety of work and living situations. An example of two such programs are Hidden Wings in California and the Tailor Institute in Missouri. The proliferation of such programs aimed especially at the young adult is expected, and needed. And the *Savant Skill Curriculum* as described in this book can be a frequently adopted and utilized guide for all of these programs.

In short, this book is an exceptional educational guide for persons with autism and savant syndrome, the individuals who teach them and the families who care for, and about, them. It also is a very useful contribution to better understanding savant syndrome itself and providing some manuals and measures to better define and standardize terminology and criteria for additional research into this remarkable condition.

For until we can understand and explain savant syndrome, we cannot fully understand and explain brain function, intelligence and creativity. Savant syndrome embodies all of those and better understanding, and tapping the special skills in the savant will propel us along further than we have ever been in better appreciating, comprehending and maximizing both brain function and human potential.

This book helps immensely in that important endeavour.

Darold A. Treffert, M.D.
Behavioral Health Department, St Agnes Hospital
Fond du Lac, Wisconsin 54937

www.savantsyndrome.com
www.daroldtreffert.com
email: daroldt@charter.net

FOREWORD

Can children with a severe and lifelong developmental disability also be gifted? If so, how may this affect the visibility of their gifts? Will the gift wither under the pressure of the disability or, through thoughtful educational planning, can the gift be helped to flourish in spite of it? These are questions of critical importance.

This book is, in itself, a gift to parents and teachers of children and adolescents who live with two seemingly contradictory conditions – an autism spectrum disorder and a truly astonishing level of talent which reveals itself in a single, sometimes highly unusual, field. Poignantly, Dr Trevor Clark calls these remarkable young people 'paradox children', sensitively illustrating the dilemma that confronts their parents and teachers. How do we persuade the educational community that to focus only on the young people's disability, without creating a learning and social environment responsive to their gifts, is to condemn them to a seriously unbalanced educational and social journey through childhood and adolescence?

Patrick, aged fifteen, taught himself to read by age three. He was diagnosed as autistic due to delayed speech development, hyperactivity, destructiveness and poor concentration. Yet, despite these problems, he displays truly astonishing powers of memory, a remarkable capacity for calendar calculation and mechanical/spatial and computer skills. Dr Trevor Clark believes that Patrick may be one of the world's most prodigious savants.

Natasha, aged five, can identify the flags of more than fifty countries. Her astonishing memory was evident by age two; she could recall songs, TV commercials and whole books. Like Patrick, she experiences difficulties with communication skills and she initiates conversations only to talk about her interests. Like many autistic children she becomes greatly distressed by changes to her routines.

Terry, aged five, was diagnosed at age three as suffering from Asperger's Syndrome. He displays multiple savant abilities including a quite astonishing memory. From age two he was able to recall the birthdays of other children in his pre-school and the odd and even numbers of familiar streets. By age five he could recite the twelve times table. He is able to build complex marble mazes and uses the word processor on the computer to type his words and numbers. Terry has significant problems with behaviours and social skills. If told to stop one of his savant activities, he will tantrum. He can be highly anxious and experiences difficulties changing from one environment to another.

Teachers and parents of these remarkable young people can be disturbed by the seemingly compulsive behaviours of the paradox children. The passion – indeed the obsessiveness – with which they pursue their savant talents can puzzle other children and may, indeed, seem quite incomprehensible to them.

Additionally autistic savants can often display what seem to be remarkable feats of memory retaining and recalling copious amounts of detailed information about topics that catch their attention or, indeed, about what they feel to be important issues in their area of special interest. This can sometimes lead to social difficulties. The savant may lack the capacity to discern *which* topics in his field of passionate interest may interest other children and which of the many, many facts they have acquired about these topics are of greater importance than others – and this 'information overload' which the savant may impose on listeners can lead to social wariness or rejection. Additionally, savants may form relationships between ideas or issues that may *at first* seem to be unrelated but which can turn out to be remarkable feats of synthesis of relevant (if sometimes abstruse) information. I have vivid memories of 'Kenny', a boy in a school in which I taught some years ago, who was obsessive about Enid Blyton's *Famous Five* books and who brought the characters and their stories into every conversation – regardless of the conversational topic. Unless his teachers knew about his passion for the *Famous Five* books they would be unaware that one of the characters, Timmy, is not a child but a dog – and his comments would have seemed quite irrational. Sadly, I was quite unaware, in the early years of my teaching career, of the characteristics and needs of paradox children; if only I had known, then, what I have learned since these days from my colleague and friend Dr Trevor Clark.

Like non-disabled gifted students who require differentiated educational programs if they are to make the best use of their special gifts and talents, the 'paradox children' can benefit from thoughtfully designed specialized educational programs and supports.

Mentorships

Children who display remarkable levels of aptitude in specific fields require encouragement and support to develop their abilities into achievements. This is a key principle of talent development in children and adolescents and it holds good for the translation of the savant's knowledge and skills into productive activities just as it does for any other group of gifted young people. The opportunity to work with an adult who is both knowledgeable and skilled in their field of passionate interest could be a powerful catalyst in assisting a savant child to translate his or her ability into achievement. If Natasha could be provided with an adult mentor who is an expert on the history of flag design and development, and the meaning of the symbolism in many flags, she might be encouraged to hypothesize about what beliefs or experience gave rise to the design of the flags of particular countries. If I had thought of it, all these years ago, perhaps I could have found a mentor for Kenny who might have been able to broaden his reading interests by introducing him to a range of authors of children's books in which animals play an important part in the story through their relationships with the child protagonists.

Acceleration

In 2014, with two American colleagues, Professors Susan Assouline and Nicholas Colangelo of the University of Iowa, I wrote a two-volume report on the *eighteen forms* of academic acceleration used in schools (and substantiated by research) to facilitate the development of talent in gifted and highly able children and adolescents. The report is entitled *A Nation Deceived: How Schools Hold Back America's Brightest Students*. The report has its own website (www.nationdeceived.org) and I warmly encourage you to access it. Here is a brief description of acceleration from this report.

> Acceleration is an intervention that moves students through an educational program at rates faster, or at younger ages, than typical. It means matching the level, complexity and pace of the curriculum to the readiness and motivation of the student. Examples of acceleration include early entrance to school, grade-skipping, moving ahead in one subject area or Advanced Placement (AP). Acceleration is critical to the vast majority of academically gifted children.

Perhaps Patrick, with his astonishingly early grasp of reading, could have been a candidate for acceleration – perhaps early entry to school if his parents and the school principal felt that he might be ready for this. If he was presented with material which truly challenged and excited him, he might have exhibited, to his teachers, both his remarkable powers of concentration and his motivation to work with passion and precision on the numerical calculations that excited him so much and which were so clearly visible in his passionate absorption in calendar calculation. This might have led to an individual subject-specific acceleration program in which Patrick would have taken reading with the grade above his so that he was no longer the only child who could read. This would have been an exciting, rewarding and, importantly, *validating* response to his remarkable gifts.

Miraca U.M. Gross
Emeritus Professor of Gifted Education
The University of New South Wales
Sydney, Australia

PREFACE

This book is an overview of a doctoral thesis completed in Sydney, Australia. The study explored the application of savant and splinter skills in the autistic population through a differentiated educational program, the *Savant Skill Curriculum*, over a two-year period. A longitudinal multiple-replication case study research design was used for the study, and involved a group of twenty-two children between the ages of four and sixteen diagnosed with autism, and who displayed a variety of savant and/or splinter skills. These children are 'twice-exceptional' in that they are both gifted and have a diagnosed disability. These gifted children with autism, referred to as *autistic savants*, are among the most underserved minority of all gifted children with disabilities.

They are the 'paradox children' in that they exhibit high-level skills in the context of low IQ or overall delayed developmental functioning. Savant and splinter skills are exhibited in the domains of: memory; hyperlexic; art; music; mechanical or spatial skill; calendar calculation; mathematical calculation; sensory sensitivity; and athletic ability. Although savant and splinter skills appear remarkable in contrast to the disability of autism, they are rarely viewed as functional skills, and are generally exhibited in obsessive ways.

There is a growing interest world-wide in the need to support this unique group of children and young people. With the increasing prevalence of autism, there has emerged the need to focus on the strengths and interests of people with autism, as a vehicle to improve their opportunities for employment, and post-school quality of life outcomes. As the functional application of strengths and interests (savant and/or splinter skills) is the central focus of this study, the time has arrived to share the *Savant Skill Curriculum*. Although the study was completed several years ago, there have been no further studies of a differentiated educational program for autistic savants. The study continues to be a 'world-first'.

The educational strategies and outcomes of the study are described through the stories of the children. The book also includes a practical section – the 'Guide to Practice' for teachers and carers, and which also provides an example of how research can be translated into practice; an issue identified as a significant challenge in the field of intervention research and disability.

The study has demonstrated the importance of using a 'strengths' rather than a 'deficits' approach in the education of students with a disability, and was founded on the basis that rather than regarding autistic savants as disabled students with 'freak talents', it is more appropriate to regard them as gifted students with disabilities, or as 'twice-exceptional' students with autism.

1

THE SCOPE OF THE PROBLEM – INTRODUCTION TO THE CHILDREN

Who are the 'paradox children', the challenges they face and why do they need a 'differentiated' educational program?

Rather than greeting his friends, family members and teachers with the usual 'Hello' or 'How are you?' Patrick will instead ask them, 'What is your birthday? Where do you live? What is your car registration?' The next time he meets these people he recites their personal details and laughs with joy if he is correct, which is always. Patrick has an extraordinary memory for facts and information that he finds interesting.

Patrick, a rather chubby Italian boy with an infectious smile and laugh, is fourteen years of age. He lives with his mother and five brothers, of which he is the youngest, in the western suburbs of Sydney, his father having recently passed away. Along with his remarkable memory, Patrick has had a great love of numbers from the age of two. If asked to provide the day of the week of any date between 1900 and 2010, he can give the answer accurately within a few seconds. He can also correctly calculate five-and six-digit addition, subtraction, multiplication and division equations mentally within a few seconds, often faster than his teacher using a calculator. Patrick is both a calendar and an arithmetic calculator.

Rather than speak words, Patrick prefers to spell them. He spells most words accurately (two years above his chronological age) and can spell many words in Latin and also in Italian. He displays what is known as hyperlexic skills, which is the term used to describe the ability to decode letters and words without necessarily knowing their meaning. Patrick also loves the computer and without any formal training is able to use many software programs. His brother, who is a computer 'geek', discovered Patrick had removed some of his files, and hidden others on the family computer much to their frustration.

Bradley lives with his family in the Northern Beaches of Sydney. He is six years of age and has a younger brother and sister. Like Patrick, Bradley loves words. He enjoys reading street directories, the telephone book and encyclopedias for leisure.

He is reading and spelling two years ahead of his chronological age. He could read and write the alphabet at the age of two years. When he is not reading, Bradley likes to construct electronic objects from LEGO™, in particular traffic lights, stereos, computer, video-recorders, and batteries. He is fascinated by all things 'electronic', spending many hours each day on his constructions. His mechanical or visual-spatial skills are eight years in advance of his chronological peers. Like Patrick, he is very interested in numbers and enjoys reading maths tables. He counts to 1,000 forwards and backwards often by twos, fives and tens, laughing as if he were playing a game. On a test of number concepts and skills, he scored higher than 72 per cent of his non-disabled age-peers.

Terry is an only child and lives with his parents in Sydney's Northern Beaches. He is five years of age, is small in stature and has blond hair and blue eyes. From the age of two, he was able to recall his telephone number and address, the birthdays of his pre-school friends, and odd and even street numbers of familiar streets in his neighbourhood. He would also recall the exact number of street-hole covers of every street in the greater Hornsby area of Sydney. He was able to recognize and write many words and numbers and could recite the twelve times tables by the age of five years. He takes great delight in building complex marble mazes, can calculate the age of a person when told their birthdate, draws complex street grids and mazes, and uses the computer independently. Both Terry's father and grandfather are gifted in mathematics and his father is a financial planner. His mother is an editor of children's literature.

The above descriptions highlight the exceptional abilities of three young children. All, however, have been diagnosed with the disability of autism spectrum disorder (ASD), a life-long neurodevelopmental disorder. At the time of this study, they attended special schools for children with autism. Patrick has a diagnosis of Autistic Disorder (severe autism), Bradley, a diagnosis of autism spectrum disorder (ASD), and Terry, a diagnosis of Asperger's Disorder as classified by the *Diagnostic and Statistical Manual of Mental Disorders – Fourth Edition (DSM-IV)*. Autism is identified by two primary diagnostic characteristics or markers: difficulties in social communica-tion and restricted or repetitive behaviours and interests. Examples of difficulties in social communication include challenges in social reciprocity, non-verbal social behaviours, and establishment of relationships. Restricted and repetitive behaviours include stereotypic behaviour or speech, excessive adherence to routines and highly fixated interests. Also, co-occurring conditions, such as intellectual disability or attention deficit hyperactive disorder, may also be diagnosed alongside a diag-nosis of autism. With the recent advent of the revised *Diagnostic and Statistical Manual of Mental Disorders, DSM-V* (2013), there is now only one classification, termed autism spectrum disorder (ASD). The effects of ASD are present across the lifespan. Patrick suffers also from mild intellectual delay, while Bradley and Terry are performing in the average range of intellectual functioning, in spite of both displaying a wide scatter of skills. An insight into the profile of each of these children would not be complete without a brief description of their disabilities. Although the term 'autism spectrum disorder' (ASD) is the correct diagnostic classification, some people on the autism spectrum have expressed concern that the term portrays a negative perception of people with this diagnosis. With this in mind, the term 'autism' will be used in place of 'autism spectrum disorder' (ASD) in this book.

Now that we have outlined the exceptional abilities of Patrick, Bradley and Terry, we will examine more closely the impact of autism on their lives.

Unless able to obtain access to his number and reading interests, or given an instruction to finish these high-interest activities by his teacher or caregiver, Patrick will engage in a variety of challenging behaviours; biting himself or others, tantrums and running from the class or room. On occasions he has escaped from both home and school, placing himself in grave danger by running through traffic to access newspapers, car manuals, street directories and other items related to his interests. Patrick has no road-crossing or survival skills and requires constant one-to-one care and supervision by his teachers and family, when in community settings. His communication skills are severely delayed, scoring in the lowest percentile for children his age in both receptive and expressive language. His social skills are delayed and disordered, his behaviours assessed as being in the severely disturbed range, and his self-esteem is low. He currently attends an autism-specific school operated by Autism Spectrum Australia (Aspect), where the focus of his program is to improve his language, social skills and behaviour whilst teaching him functional self-help and leisure skills. He is in a class of students with moderate to severe autism and intellectual impairment, the majority of whom are non-verbal and display severe levels of challenging behaviour. His teachers and family find Patrick a very difficult child to manage and are often at a loss how to control his outbursts.

Bradley is easily stressed when he experiences difficulty with his constructions. If a piece of LEGO™ is missing, or he has been asked to finish or move onto the next class activity, he will throw tantrums and become non-compliant. If a home or school routine is changed, he also becomes extremely anxious, crying and demanding that the routine be followed. He often needs to be distracted from his fascination with his interests to focus on other tasks. His expressive and receptive language skills are in the mildly delayed to average range, his social skills assessed as being in the moderately delayed range, and his behaviour classified as disturbed. Bradley has a moderate-to-low self-esteem. Like Patrick, he attends an autism-specific school but is in a class of students classified as high-functioning, or more able. He will soon transfer to one of Aspect's Satellite Classes for more able students with autism located in a neighbouring government mainstream school. His educational program involves the teaching of communication and social skills, appropriate behaviours and the usual mainstream curriculum subjects. His reading, writing and number skills are at a much higher level of ability than those of his autistic classmates.

Terry experiences difficulties with his social skills and behaviour. If he does not get his own way, he will tantrum, scream, refuse to cooperate and can become aggressive. If told to stop a savant activity, he will tantrum. Terry can also be highly anxious and has difficulties changing from one environment to another. His social skills fluctuate from age-appropriate to very immature and he generally engages in solitary play. He can, however, cooperate with structured interactive group games if interested, his favourite being snakes and ladders. Terry finds it difficult to accept the opinions of others and easily becomes anxious and distressed if someone disagrees with his viewpoint. Although his behaviours were not assessed as being in the disturbed range by his family and teacher, his parents find him almost twice as difficult to manage in the home as does his teacher in the school environment. His self-esteem was rated as moderate. Terry's current education program incorporates the teaching of communication, social, academic, appropriate behaviours and school-readiness skills. Although he is in an Early Childhood class of more able students with autism, he is performing academically well in advance of his classmates and, like Bradley, he too will soon transfer to one of the Aspect Schools' Satellite Classes in a mainstream school. He is considered to be a delightful but highly anxious student.

These children are autistic savants. They are three of the twenty-two children who were subjects of this study, between four and sixteen years of age, diagnosed with autism spectrum disorder (ASD), and who display a variety of savant and/or splinter skills. They all display high-level skills in association with either a low IQ, or delayed levels of developmental functioning (Goodman, 1972). Although the term 'idiot savant' was originally used to describe persons with an intellectual disability who displayed special skills or gifts, it would appear that at least half of all savants are in fact autistic (Hill, 1978; O'Connor and Hermelin, 1987; Treffert, 2012). Savant refers to 'a learned or knowledgeable person', whereas 'idiot' referred to a person with an IQ 'below 25'. Treffert (1989), the world's leading authority on savants, defined the phenomenon as savant syndrome. In his widely accepted definition, he classified the skills of savants as either Savant I or Savant II skills; exceptional or with spectacular islands of ability or brilliance which stand in contrast to the disability (Talented Savant I); or spectacular even if viewed in contrast to the non-disabled person (Prodigious Savant II).

> 'Savant syndrome' is an exceedingly rare condition in which persons with serious mental handicaps, either from developmental disability (mental retardation) or major mental illness (early Infantile Autism or schizophrenia), have spectacular islands of ability or brilliance which stand in stark, markedly incongruous contrast to the handicap. In some, savant skills are remarkable simply in contrast to the handicap (Talented Savants or Savant I). In others, with a much rarer form of the condition, the ability or brilliance is not only spectacular in contrast to the handicap, but would be spectacular even if viewed in a normal person (Prodigious Savants, or Savant II).
>
> (Treffert, 1989, p. xxv)

Although it was originally thought that all savants have a low IQ, it should be noted that individuals with savant abilities have been identified across all levels of intellectual ability (Treffert, 1989). There are a number of reports in the literature of individuals with autism who are considered to be autistic savants despite average or above-average intellectual functioning (Hermelin, Pring and Heavy, 1994; Young and Nettlebeck, 1995). Having had the privilege of teaching several high-functioning students with autism, who also displayed savant skills, I confirm this to be the case.

Patrick, Bradley and Terry display these exceptional or spectacular savant abilities as defined by Treffert (1989). They have multiple savant skills, which may be found amongst Hill's (1974) list of savant abilities: memory, art, music, mechanical, calendar, calculation, arithmetic calculation, athletic skill, sensory sensitivity and hyperlexic skills (the ability to read, write and spell). All have savant memory ability and their level of savant abilities include both Savant I (Talented) and Savant II (Prodigious) skills. Although not included in Treffert's definition of savant syndrome, splinter skills are relatively common in children with autism, and are emerging or partially developed savant skills. In my view, they warrant classification as a Savant I (Talented ability) (Clark, 2001). All three children are highly motivated by their savant interests to the point of obsession, spending many hours each day focused on their activities, to the exclusion of teachers and families. They are what I refer to as the 'paradox children', as they display high-level skills or gifts alongside their diagnosed disability of autism.

These students are both gifted and disabled. The term 'twice-exceptional' is now being used to describe students who are gifted and also have a disability (Betts and Neihart, 2010; Assouline and Whiteman, 2011). In their profiles of the gifted and talented student (2010), Betts and Neihart use the term 'twice/multi-exceptional' to describe the profiles and the educational supports required for this emerging new group of gifted disabled students.

It should be highlighted that although the autistic savant comes under the umbrella label of the 'twice-exceptional' learner with autism, they are a subset of this group. Not all gifted learners with autism are savants, and not all savants are high intellectual performers. For the classification of a student as being an autistic savant, they must have first been diagnosed as having an autism spectrum disorder (*DSM-IV/V*), and exhibit one or multiple savant skills (Hill, 1974; Rimland, 1978; Miller, 1998), which also stand in contrast to their disability as defined by Treffert (1989). For a student to be assessed as being a 'twice-exceptional' learner, they need to be identified as gifted, or talented in one or more areas whilst also possessing a learning, emotional, physical, sensory and/or developmental disability (Yewchuk and Lupart, 1988, cited in Assouline et al., 2006, p. 14).

The challenge of developing savant skills into productive talents

We now know that there are many more autistic savants in the overall autistic population than were first thought. A study by Patricia Howlin and colleagues in 2009 puts the rate of savant skills in adults with autism close to 30 per cent, rather than the 9.8 per cent we believed to be the case based upon the founding work of Rimland (1978). Along with the realization of the larger numbers of autistic savants in the autistic population comes the associated world-wide reports of the increase in the prevalence of those with autism. Recent research is pointing to prevalence rates of between 1 in 50, and 1 in 88, children (Blumberg et al., 2013).

With the increasing numbers of children and adults being diagnosed with autism is the urgent need to provide more evidence-based interventions, services and supports that will truly make a difference in the lives of these disabled people. A new attitude to the understanding, research and care of those with autism is now emerging.

Post-school life and employment outcomes for people with autism are often poor. Research into the outcomes for adults on the autism spectrum universally show poor employment, social and life outcomes (Howlin et al., 2004; Cimera and Cowan, 2009; Taylor and Seltzer, 2011; Howlin and Moss, 2012; Baldwin, Costley and Warren, 2014;). The results of the most recent study in the US, the *National Autism Indicators Report: Transition into Young Adulthood* (Roux et al., 2015), highlights the poor outcomes for young adults with autism; 28 per cent being unemployed, 26 per cent having received no services after leaving school, only 19 per cent living independently of their parents. Parents involved in this study referred to the reduction of services post-school as akin to 'falling off a cliff'. In their study of the rates of savant skills in the adult autistic population, Howlin et al. (2009) found that of the 137 adults with autism who display savant skills, only five individuals with exceptional abilities had succeeded in using these skills to find permanent employment. For the majority, the skills remained isolated leading to neither employment nor social integration.

> The practical challenge now is now to determine how individuals with special skills can be assisted, from childhood onwards, to develop their talents in ways that that are of direct practical value (in terms of educational and occupational achievements), thereby enhancing their opportunities for social inclusion as adults.
>
> (Howlin et al., 2009, p. 1365)

Despite their savant skills, the challenge for autistic savants, teachers and parents is how to apply their savant abilities in practical and functional ways, which will serve to increase the future opportunities for employment and leisure. Recent feedback from the parent of a young man who was a subject of this study serves to highlight the challenges facing many young autistic savants and their families as they transition into adult life:

> I have been disappointed that Simon has not been able to secure a more challenging work of longer duration for his skills . . . but that is the situation with persons that are savants – their opportunities are limited.
>
> (Email correspondence from parent of Simon, August 2014)

There is an urgent need to better support the education of these 'paradox children', the Patricks, the Bradleys and the Terrys of this world, with the aim of improving their outcomes as adults. The lack of differentiated educational programs for autistic savants is part of a much wider issue facing educators today. With increasing prevalence rates, the numbers of students with autism enrolled in our education systems continues to grow. Based on a survey completed by the Australian Bureau of Statistics (ABS), *Survey of Disability, Ageing and Carers, 2014*, there are approximately 81,000 students with a diagnosis of autism attending Australian schools between the ages of five and nineteen years. The education of students with autism is fast becoming one of the most significant challenges faced by teachers, schools and education providers in Australia and around the world.

Schools provide an important social environment where children and young people learn to interact with their peers – a task that people with autism often find difficult. As a result of the unique learning styles, and the impairments associated with autism, many of these students experience significant challenges in schools. They are misunderstood by educators and peers, struggle to cope and may actually leave the education system altogether. Again, in the Australian context, the ABS survey confirms the challenges faced by students with autism in schools, and reported that 95 per cent experienced some form of educational restriction. Of the 95 per cent of children that did experience some restriction, 6 per cent were not able to attend school because of their disability. For children with autism who were attending school, 86 per cent reported 'having difficulty'. Of even greater concern is the data from the survey which suggests that the difficulties experienced in gaining an education continue after school. Of the people with autism who had finished school, 81 per cent had not completed a post-school qualification, which was well above the rate for the rest of the population with a disability, and people with no disability.

Teachers and schools often feel under-equipped to successfully include and cater to the educational needs of their students with autism. A recent survey of adolescents with autism and their parents, undertaken by Autism Spectrum Australia (Aspect), *We Belong Too* (2013) found that 65 per cent of the parents of adolescents with autism did not believe educators were well-informed about autism, and 70 per cent of the adolescents with autism did not believe their educational needs were being met. There is clearly an urgent need for education providers to make available appropriate education provisions and ensure equal access for all students.

The challenges faced by students with autism and their teachers is further compounded by the fact there is currently a paucity of educational research in autism, with much yet to be achieved in translating evidence-based educational programs into classrooms (Clark, 2013; Costley, Clark and Bruck, 2014). Much of the research in autism to date has been concentrated on programs and support mechanisms for preschool-aged children, with limited peer-reviewed research available for evaluating school-based interventions (Detrich and Lewis, 2013; Dingfelder, 2011; Kasari and Smith, 2013; Parsons et al., 2013). This has left the education community with a shortage of rigorously assessed programs to implement in the classroom. This situation is further compounded by the large gap between research and practice. The lag between the development of evidence-based intervention and its integration into routine practice is estimated to be twenty years (Walker, 2004).

Within the field of gifted education, scholars and educators alike are seeking answers to the diagnostic and intervention questions required to adequately serve these students, in and out of the classroom. Yet this increasing attention has not always been matched with empirical evidence supporting students' needs, prompting some to deny even the existence of the twice-exceptional learner (Lovett and Lewandowski, 2006). Unlike other twice-exceptional students, who are now being identified and included in differentiated programs for the gifted – students with specific learning disabilities (SLD) and attention deficit hyperactivity disorder (ADHD) – this is not the case for autistic savants (Nicpon, Allmon, Seick, and Stinson, 2011). They remain the least recognized and underserved minority of all gifted students. Although Patrick, Bradley and Terry are receiving an autism-specific education related to their disability, their savant skills or gifts have largely been ignored, put on the 'back-burner' or, even worse, extinguished as they have been viewed as useless obsessions. Like many gifted students are 'out-of-sync' with their classmates (Gross, 1993; Hollingworth, 1942; Silverman, 1993) and who therefore require a differentiated educational program, these children are also 'out-of-sync' with their autistic peers.

> Identifying and nurturing gifts and talents to enable young children to actualise their potential is a way of improving the mental health and quality of life of such individuals. We know that a wide discrepancy between full potential and full utilization of potential is a breeding ground for maladjustment and unproductivity. The need for early identification and early programming is thus manifest.
>
> (Karnes and Johnson, 1986, p. 53)

Like their non-disabled gifted peers, the skills of the twice-exceptional student with autism, including those classified as autistic savants, need to be identified and nurtured. The 'paradox children' require a differentiated program to ensure they are receiving an education commensurate to their level of ability.

For many years, savants have been the subject of much debate in the fields of education, psychology and psychiatry, and their outstanding skills have been the topic of many television shows, documentaries and books. The very existence of such abilities has generated a challenge to our widely accepted views on cognition. However, little interest has been paid to the 'human' side of savant syndrome, with very few examples of differentiated programs for adult autistic savants, and none until now for school-aged savants. Given the possibility that there exist large numbers of autistic savants in schools today, I think it is time that we attended to the 'human side' of this extraordinary condition and assist the Patricks, Bradleys and Terrys of this world to use their special gifts or skills. This study was founded on the basis that, rather than regarding autistic savants as disabled students with 'freak talents', it is more appropriate to regard them as gifted students with disabilities. It is time for us to reframe our old ways of thinking about the 'paradox children'. I share the view of Darold Treffert (2012):

The special skills, even unconventional ones, seen in many persons with autism or Asperger's are not frivolous or trivial. They are instead an island of intactness, and sometimes an island of genius, that provides a ready entrée into connectedness and interaction. Fully utilised they can provide the 'conduit toward normalization'.

(Treffert, 2012, p. 9)

New possibilities

Our research efforts in autism are beginning to turn from a focus on primarily the causes of autism, and the early years, to exploring educational interventions and services. There is now emerging a focus on using the strengths and interests of those with autism, and which is beginning to drive new and innovative research and programs that aim to create better post-school employment opportunities and quality of life outcomes (Robison, 2008; Lanou, Hough and Powell, 2011; Grandin, 2012; Shore, 2012).

A young talented teacher who currently works at one of Autism Spectrum Australia's schools for children with autism in Sydney, and who is a young Apple Distinguished Educator, has developed a number of exceptional programs for his students with autism based on their student's strengths and interests (Smith, 2014). One such example is that of a young boy in his class who loves dance music. He loves the big beats, the pop singers, the history, and everything about dance music. And he had an enormous talent for music. Once, when walking past the local town public library, on a community excursion with his class, the student stopped next to a large air-conditioning unit on the side of the library, which was making a large droning hum. The student proclaimed with excitement and joy, 'That sound is an E flat.' He had perfect pitch and other savant capacities for music. However, he also had significant sensory sensitivities, so much so that playing traditional instruments was too much for him, and he couldn't stand being near them. His teacher introduced an iPad into the classroom. The student started to explore sound in a whole new way, and to use the iPad to create music. The teacher would schedule special sessions in class where the student could use music to engage in social skills lessons, to create songs about 'emotional regulation' and similar topics, and to explore numeracy and other content. From there, he started to upload his own music to the internet, and achieved a number two ranking in the national station's pop charts for one of his dance songs. Today, he is in high school and regularly performs his music at school. He also mentors other students with autism at a local music social club, where he helps them write and perform songs. A truly amazing story of success and an example of how fostering a student's special interests allowed him to access functional skills and community inclusion. The student is now a local music superstar.

Patrick Schwarz, a Professor at the National-Louis University in Chicago in the field of education, has written several books for teachers with the aim of encouraging them to think about their students' strengths and interests and, for some, their 'obsessions' as powerful positive teaching tools that calm, motivate and improve learning. In collaboration with Paula Kluth, Patrick wrote the book *Pedro's Whale* (Kluth and Schwarz, 2010), which is based on the real-life experience of a young autistic boy's first day in school. The boy, who loves whales more than anything, is heartbroken when his teacher tells him to put away his favourite toy whale. Eventually Pedro's teacher realizes that his interest in whales could actually be a strong motivator to learning, and incorporates his special interest into the class curriculum. The following excerpt from *Pedro's Whale* is, in fact, the central platform of the Savant Skill Curriculum.

> Every child has fascinations, areas of expertise, and passions he or she brings to school. As teachers, our job is to honour them! We need to exploit the 'loves' of our learners, not extinguish them.
>
> (Kluth and Schwarz, 2010, Preface)

A further example of using the strengths and interests of a young man with autism, and that resulted in meaningful employment, is that of Brad Fremmerlid, reported in the *Sydney Morning Herald* in January 2014. The twenty-four-year-old Canadian cannot speak or read, and communicates only by gestures. As a young boy with autism, Brad displayed exceptional skill in building LEGO™ and other models. His father identified his interests and skills in construction and tailored a job to suit him. He recently helped his son launch a business, 'Built by Brad', as an IKEA furniture assembler. Although not officially assessed as being an autistic savant, Brad appears to display exceptional mechanical/spatial skills, and skills that he has been supported with by his father which have led to meaningful employment. His father in fact has become Brad's mentor in relation to the application of his strengths and interests. It is indeed encouraging to know that the strengths and interests of students with autism are being to be seen as motivators to further learning and as facilitators for employment.

This book focuses on a new educational program, the *Savant Skill Curriculum*, which is leading the way in achieving better outcomes for autistic savants. The *Curriculum* is centred on the application of the strengths and interests of a group of children with autism who also display savant skills, with the aim of improving their long-term outcomes. Not every person with autism who displays savant skills will overcome the debilitating effects of this condition. However, the *Savant Skill Curriculum* may help many to make functional use of their skills, which, in turn, may help to improve their post-school opportunities for employment, socialization and quality of life.

As mentioned previously, in the field of gifted education there is a growing interest in identifying and better supporting the twice-exceptional gifted student in schools around the world. By writing this book, I would like to promote a similar interest in supporting the twice-exceptional learner with autism, including the autistic savant, in both the fields of gifted and autism education. It was only by looking through the double-lenses of these two fields of education, and the subsequent merging of successful strategies in both, that led to the design and development of the *Savant Skill Curriculum*.

I believe we are only at the very beginning of our understanding of these exceptional students and how to accommodate their skills in educational programs. A great deal more research and training for teachers and allied health professionals is required. As mentioned previously, even with attempts to identify and provide differentiated programs for the twice-exceptional student with autism, the autistic savant has been largely overlooked. There is little justification, of course, for identifying and labelling a child as twice-exceptional, unless there is a viable plan for programming for that child. This study is therefore aimed at redressing the current oversight in research and the lack of educational programming for the autistic savant.

The application of savant and splinter in differentiated educational programs may in fact be the educator's prime weapon in the fight against the debilitating effects of autism. Just as many gifted students without disabilities are receiving support through differentiated educational programs, to transform their gifts into productive talents (Gagné, 2009), the autistic savant also requires a differentiated program. Effective educational strategies for the gifted student have been adapted for this study, to assist young autistic savants to make functional use of their skills, and to improve their communication and social skills, behaviour and adaptive functioning. The long-term goal of the *Savant Skill Curriculum*, although beyond the parameters of this study, is to facilitate the use of the children's skills to improve their post-school life outcomes.

The children

Before I embarked on this study, I had the privilege of teaching Patrick. Having recently emigrated from New Zealand to live in Australia, I was appointed to a teaching position at a then small autism-specific school operated by Autism Spectrum Australia (Aspect) in Sydney's southeastern suburbs. The school was housed in a tiny three-bedroom cottage, and catered to fifteen students with autism. Given the cramped teaching and learning environment, and having been assigned a class of five severely autistic students, I admit, after my first few days at the school, to questioning whether or not I was suited to teaching students with autism. Then, Patrick was enrolled in my class. I recall the first time I met Patrick; he excitedly asked me my age, the date of my birthday, my address, my car make and number plate. From this very first meeting, my days were spent in hot pursuit of Patrick as he ran from room to room in the school, searching for books and magazines to flip through, all the while counting the number of pages and laughing loudly. On one occasion, while I was distracted by another of my students, Patrick jumped out of the open classroom window, climbed over the school fence and ran into a neighbour's house. Taking chase, I eventually found Patrick sitting in the neighbour's lounge room, much to the woman's dismay, rummaging through her book collection, and looking very pleased with himself.

I quickly became fascinated with Patrick's extraordinary memory, maths and spelling skills and came to the realization that to teach him successfully would require teaching strategies that were outside my usual repertoire. Patrick needed much more than the autism-specific education program he was currently receiving. My journey in the world of the autistic savant had begun.

At this time, I enrolled in a Masters of Education Degree at the University of New South Wales (UNSW), Sydney, Australia. As part of the degree, I undertook a subject in the field of gifted education, a departure from my previous studies in education and disability, in the hope that I would learn new strategies and skills to support my teaching of Patrick. I also completed the inaugural Certificate in Teaching Gifted Students at the UNSW as part of my degree program, which proved invaluable. And, as they say, the rest is history. I had the good fortune to study with Emeritus Professor, Miraca Gross who was then the Director of the Gifted Education Research, Resource and Information Centre (GERRIC) at the UNSW. Through her interest and encouragement in my studies, and my teaching of Patrick, I then embarked on my doctoral studies, which led to the development and trial of the *Savant Skill Curriculum*.

In 1995, my doctoral thesis proposal, *The Application of Savant and Splinter Skills in the Autistic Population through Curriculum Design: A Longitudinal Multiple-Replication Case Study*, was awarded the International Hollingworth Award for Excellence in Education and Psychology of the Gifted. To date, I am only the second person to be awarded this award outside of the United States, Emeritus Professor Gross being the first in 1987. Although the award was a great honour personally, it signalled a further step forward in the recognition of school-aged autistic savants, and the need to cater to their differing educational needs. The funding from this award gave me the opportunity to travel to the United States to interview a number of people in the fields of both autism and savant syndrome, which informed the development of the *Savant Skill Curriculum*.

The remainder of this chapter will include a brief introduction to six of the twenty-two children who were subjects of the study. To include all of the children would be exhaustive for the purpose of this book; however, the full comprehensive assessment results for all of the sixteen treatment children are included in tabular form, as they were included in the original *Savant Skill Curriculum* evaluation data analysis and results. The full assessments are available for those who may wish to view them on the Routledge website. These six children have been selected as the 'focus group' and will provide a rich descriptive overview of the challenges faced by the larger group of 'paradox children' and their families. The selected children illustrate the most commonly occurring savant skills, gender, age range, varying degrees of autism and intellectual functioning. Each of the children will be introduced in relation to their disabilities, level of cognitive ability, communication skills, behaviour, social functioning, academic self-esteem, savant abilities, age of onset of abilities, familiar background, pregnancy and birth details and educational placement at the point of referral to the study (see Routledge website Pre-Curriculum Assessments of the Children – Tables 1.1 to 1.7). Subsequent chapters will address in depth each of the children's savant abilities, their individual teaching priorities and strategies and their outcomes as a result of receiving the *Savant Skill Curriculum* over a period of two years.

The identities of all the children who participated in the study, and their families, have been concealed by the use of pseudonyms. The age of each of the children is the age at the commencement of the two-year longitudinal treatment program. All children were identified by use of the *Savant Skill Nomination Form* – Clark, 2011, designed for the study (Appendix 1) – by both teachers and families and were only selected for further investigation when agreement was reached between both the teacher and the parent as to the child's savant abilities. Accordingly, the overview of each child below describes the children as they were at the time of the study. A full overview of the methodology and procedures including a description of the pre- and post-treatment measures used will be outlined in Chapter 3.

Patrick

A brief introduction to Patrick was given at the start of this chapter. At the time of the study he was fourteen years of age. His birth was normal and no complications were experienced during pregnancy. Due to the death of his father, Patrick's eldest brother, Jack, has taken on the paternal role in the family. As Patrick's mother speaks very little English, Jack acted as the interpreter for the study.

At the age of four years, due to delayed speech development, abnormal behaviour, hyperactivity, destructiveness and poor concentration, Patrick was diagnosed as suffering from autism and developmental delay. Although initially assessed as functioning within the upper range of moderate intellectual disability, a subsequent assessment on the Stanford-Binet Revision IV in 1996 indicated that Patrick's overall level of functioning was in the mild range of delay. It should be noted that at the time of the initial diagnosis Patrick was observed as displaying 'definite islands of ability and potential to learn'.

Patrick was referred to this study by his family and teacher for displaying multiple savant abilities. His savant abilities included: memory, hyperlexia, calendar calculation, mathematics calculation, mechanical/spatial, music, and computer skills. The majority of his skills were identified as being 'exceptional in the normal population'. Patrick is quite possibly one of the world's most prodigious savants. His family reported that he developed an early interest in numbers and words, and had taught himself to read by the age of four years. Patrick is extremely obsessed with his savant interests, spending many hours per day engaged in his savant activities. Although the family reported no evidence of other family members displaying savant skills, or who might be considered gifted and talented, his eldest brother is a highly skilled executive in the computer industry.

Patrick's communication skills are severally delayed. His performance on the *CELF-3* at the age of fourteen years and six months indicates his receptive and expressive skills to be in the lowest percentile for children of his age. His communication skills are equivalent to those of a five-year-old. He rarely initiates communication with family or peers, except to indicate his 'wants' and 'needs' or 'distress'. He will on occasion, however, attempt to converse with others in relation to his savant interests.

His social skills and behaviour are similarly severely delayed and disordered. Patrick's social interactions are directed towards servicing his 'wants' and 'needs'. Unless given a savant activity or a favourite food item, or a change in his program or environment occurs, Patrick will tantrum, bite himself or become destructive. He is unable to form normal social relationships, failing to take turns or make appropriate eye contact in interactions.

His obsessive interests can result in life-threatening situations. As mentioned previously, Patrick on occasions has escaped from home or school and run across busy roads and into shops or houses in his search for reading materials. He has no survival skills. When assessed using the *Developmental Behaviour Checklist*, which measures the severity of behavioural and emotional disturbances in children with intellectual delay, Patrick scored in the severely disturbed range. He spends only about 50 per cent of his time at school engaged in productive learning, and requires an increased share of the teacher's time.

Patrick also suffers from a low academic self-esteem. On the *BASE* rating scale (Copersmith and Gilberts 1982) he scored in the low self-esteem range on all behavioural items, which includes student initiative, social attraction, success/failure, social attention and self-confidence. Again, his self-esteem appears to be in the lowest percentile for children of his age.

Currently Patrick attends a school for children with autism operated by Autism Spectrum Australia (Aspect). His educational program takes the form of an Individual Education Plan (IEP) that focuses upon the teaching of communication and social skills, behaviour support, academics and community access. Patrick's IEP fails to incorporate teaching activities related to his savant skills and interests.

Christopher

Christopher, who is thirteen years of age, is the only non-verbal subject of this study. He is the eldest of two boys and was born by Caesarean section in the fortieth week of gestation. He lives with his family in the western suburbs of Sydney and regularly attends a respite cottage to give his family relief from the constant one-to-one care he requires.

Christopher was diagnosed with autism at the age of two years and eight months. At this time Christopher presented with 'odd' behaviours, appearing to be living in a world of his own. He would engage in repetitive, ritualistic behaviours, hum to himself constantly and tantrum when interrupted from tasks, and he had not developed speech. Although initially considered to suffer from a moderate to severe intellectual handicap, subsequent assessments using the Stanford-Binet Revision IV place him in the mild range of intellectual handicap. His highest score was in the area of quantitative reasoning.

He was referred to this study by his teacher and family for displaying high memory, reading and spelling ability, visual-spatial abilities in relation to mapping or directional skills, and computer ability. Christopher's skills developed at an early age. At two years six months, he appeared to have developed a 'sense of direction' and would tantrum when his parents changed the direction or route of travel from home to a familiar destination. By five years six months, Christopher was reading television program guides, books, magazines, bus and train timetables, travel brochures and street directories. An uncle on his mother's side of the family excelled in mathematics and statistics and attended an 'Opportunity Class' for gifted students in primary school. He later became the treasurer of a large corporation. A second uncle on his father's side of the family was a gifted musician and won a scholarship to the Australian Conservatorium of Music. Christopher's mother is an avid collector of stamps.

Christopher's communication skills as tested by the *CELF-3* are significantly delayed and disordered. His receptive and expressive language skills are equivalent to those of a five-year-old. It should be noted that his low expressive language score reflects his inability to use spoken language. Christopher, however, can express himself reasonably well through non-verbal means such as gestures, body language and challenging behaviours, that is, crying and tantrums. Christopher seems unique in the field of autistic savants, in that no reports exist in the literature of a non-verbal savant who has developed hyperlexic and mechanical skills.

From an early age Christopher has displayed a variety of challenging behaviours. He constantly requests new car brochures, magazines, train timetables and visits to the local library. If these requests are not met, he will tantrum, including screaming, crying, damaging the family car or property, and running away. Although his family describe his outbursts as intense but short-lived, his teacher reports he can remain difficult all day if not given his savant materials or activities. Christopher scores in the severely behaviourally and emotionally disturbed range as assessed by the *Developmental Behaviour Checklist*. He spends less than 25 per cent of his time at school in productive learning and requires an increased share of the teacher's time when compared to other students. He also suffers from a low academic self-esteem as measured by the *BASE* rating scale.

Although he attended specific schools for children with autism (Aspect), he was recently transferred to a private Catholic Special School for students with a range of intellectual disabilities. His educational program is centred on the teaching of communication skills, functional living skills and appropriate behaviours. Christopher is considered to be difficult to manage by both his parents and teachers.

Benjamin

Ben is nine years of age and the eldest of two boys. As his parents are divorced, he lives with his mother during the week and spends each weekend with his father. Ben is about to move with his mother and brother to live in Queensland to be closer to his grandparents. Ben was born by Caesarean section at thirty-seven weeks following a difficult pregnancy. At twenty-six weeks, a premature labour was stopped by the use of IV salbutamol. He received oxygen immediately after birth.

Although his family did not report that there were family members who might be considered gifted or talented, his mother, a nurse, is an accomplished musician and singer and his father holds a law degree. Ben's younger brother suffers from ADHD and his paternal uncle and maternal great-grand-aunt both suffer from schizophrenia. His mother's late brother displayed much challenging behaviour throughout his life.

Ben was diagnosed with autism at the age of three years. From birth, he had been a difficult self-contained child, preferring to 'live in a world of his own'. Changes to routine would result in severe temper tantrums with high-pitched and persistent screaming. He displayed a variety of ritualistic behaviours including wearing his shoes to bed, lining up objects and playing counting games over and over. He also displayed an interest in words and letters and could name all the letters of the alphabet from the age of two. He appeared interested in music and nursery rhymes. Initially assessed as functioning in the moderate range of intellectual

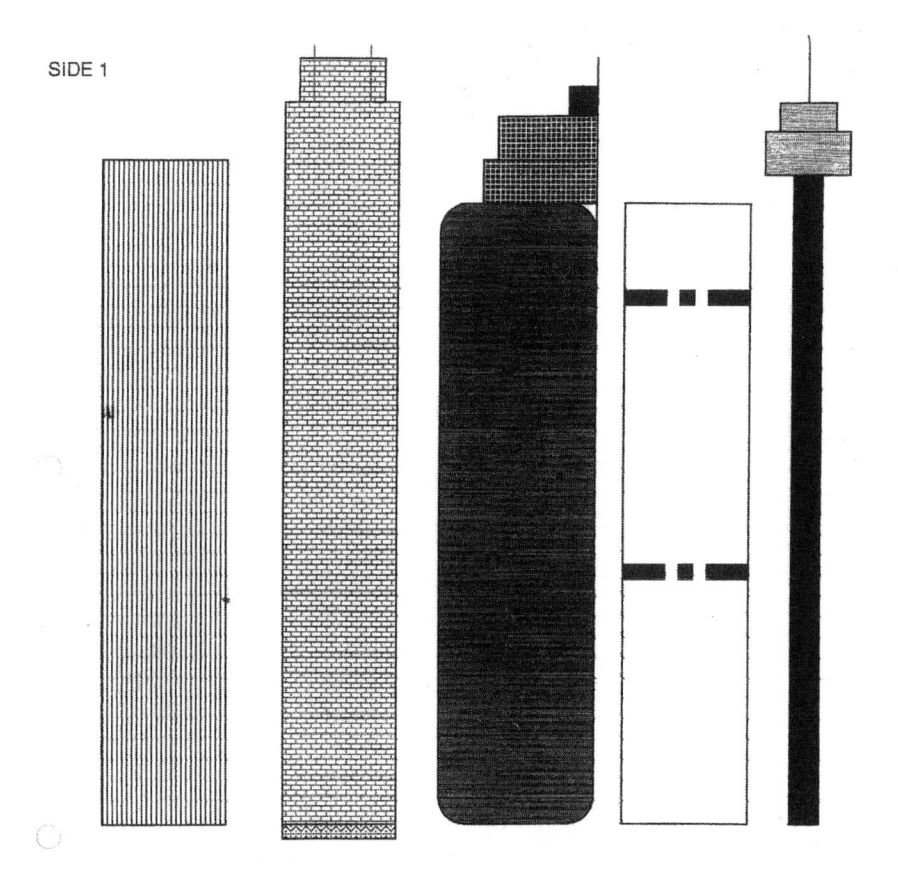

FIGURE 1.1 Sydney Tower and Opera House – computer graphic by Benjamin

delay using the Griffith Mental Developmental Scales, a more recent assessment (the Stanford-Binet IV) places him in the mild range of intellectual delay. Strengths in abstract/visual and quantitative reasoning were observed. The Woodcock Reading Mastery Test was administered at the same time. Ben scored above his chronological age on the Word Identification subtest but below average on the Passage Comprehension subtest.

His teacher and mother referred Ben to this study as he displayed memory, hyperlexic, music, computer and sensory abilities. At the age of two and a half, his family report he was able to recite TV advertisements, could read signs and posters and recite song words and jingles. He could recall the entire City Rail system. At seven months he was able to recite many letters in the alphabet. He can sing in perfect pitch and play the piano keyboard by ear. Benjamin is also able to accurately tell the time without reference to a clock, and has a highly developed sense of direction.

Ben's language skills as assessed by the *CELF-3* are severely delayed for his age. He experiences difficulties in all areas of expressive and receptive language. His age equivalent score is five years. It should be noted, however, that Ben's functional use of language indicates a higher level of language ability than his performance on the standardized test. He is able to adequately service his needs and wants, can take turns in a conversation when prompted and can follow two-step directions. He rarely initiates conversation or interaction.

Ben displays poor social skills and a variety of challenging behaviours. Although he appears to enjoy interactions with adults, these interactions are always on 'his terms'. He experiences difficulties taking turns, sharing and playing with peers. His behaviours, as assessed as by both his teacher and mother using the *Developmental Behaviour Checklist*, are in the severely behaviourally and emotionally disturbed range. His behaviours include screaming, hitting adults and peers, and throwing objects, running away and refusing to follow instructions. His academic self-esteem is low as measured by the *BASE* rating scale.

Ben has attended an Aspect school since the age of four years. He will transfer shortly to a Queensland Department of Education and Communities government school for students with intellectual disabilities in Nambour, Queensland. To date, his educational program has focused upon the teaching of communication and social skills, behaviour support and academics. His interest and strengths in reading and spelling have been partially catered for in his IEP. He is considered to be a very difficult student due to his difficult behaviours.

Natasha

Natasha, who is five years of age, is the only girl in the treatment group. She lives with her mother in central Sydney, her parents having divorced. She rarely sees her father. She is the eldest of three children. Both the pregnancy and birth were normal.

FIGURE 1.2 Self-portrait by Natasha

Natasha's mother is a gifted artist. Her mother's sister's son is also autistic and displays high-level arithmetic skills. He is able to mentally calculate arithmetic problems with a high degree of accuracy and speed.

Due to a severe delay in language and social skills, restricted interests, adherence to routines, lack of toileting skills and difficult behaviours, including tantrums and biting herself and others, Natasha was diagnosed as severely autistic and intellectually delayed at the age of three years. She is currently functioning within the mild range of intellectual disability as assessed by the WPPSI-R. Natasha displayed a relative strength on tasks requiring visuospatial skills and on these tasks scored up to the superior range of ability.

Natasha was identified by her teacher as displaying exceptional memory, hyperlexic, drawing, mechanical/spatial and sensory skills and was subsequently referred to this study. At the age of two years, she could recall numbers, colours, songs, TV commercials, whole storybooks and family events. She developed a particular interest in flags and is now able to identify the flags of over fifty countries. She loves to write and read words. Her favourite pastime is drawing and she spends many hours each day drawing people and TV characters. Natasha is also able to decipher small objects far in the distance and is acutely sensitive to certain sounds.

Although her communication skills are in the mild to moderate range of delay as assessed by the *CELF-3*, her functional use of expressive language is only mildly delayed. She is able to greet and farewell appropriately on occasions, gain attention and can communicate her needs and wants. However, she often chooses to express herself through inappropriate behaviours such as screaming, kicking and tantrums when she does not want to do something. She only initiates conversation to service her needs or talk about her interests.

Natasha experiences difficulties with her social interactions and behaviours. She prefers to work alone, does not like to share or play with others, and is very much locked into her routines and rituals. She becomes greatly distressed by changes to her routines, or by requests to undertake tasks she does not like. Her tantrums may be directed towards her peers, which results in much hair-pulling and kicking. Her behaviours as assessed by the *Developmental Behaviour Checklist* are in the severely behaviourally and emotionally disturbed range. She is a very strong-willed child. Her academic self-esteem has been measured as low by the *BASE* rating scale.

Natasha is currently enrolled at an Aspect school. Her peers range in age from four to seven years and represent all levels of the autism spectrum. Her IEP emphasizes the development of social, communication and pre-academic skills. Her drawing skill is currently used as a reward for appropriate work and behaviour in class. Natasha requires an increased level of teacher attention and is engaged in productive learning about 50 per cent of class time.

Bradley

Bradley, who is six years of age, was also introduced previously. He is one of three children. Although the pregnancy was normal, some complications occurred at birth (meconium-stained waters), which resulted in Bradley being administered oxygen for an hour in an incubator.

Bradley was assessed as having an autism spectrum disorder at two years and ten months. At this time, Bradley presented as a very anxious child who displayed a great deal of fear of any new environments. His eating was very restricted and he would only drink a specific mixture containing Kindivite and milk. He would become anxious if presented with any other food items and would watch his mother to ensure she did not add anything to the mixture. He displayed a variety of unusual behaviours, including lining up objects, spinning wheels repetitively and a fascination with watching fans and audiotapes go around and around, and he preferred to play by himself. His mother's first cousin suffers from severe autism

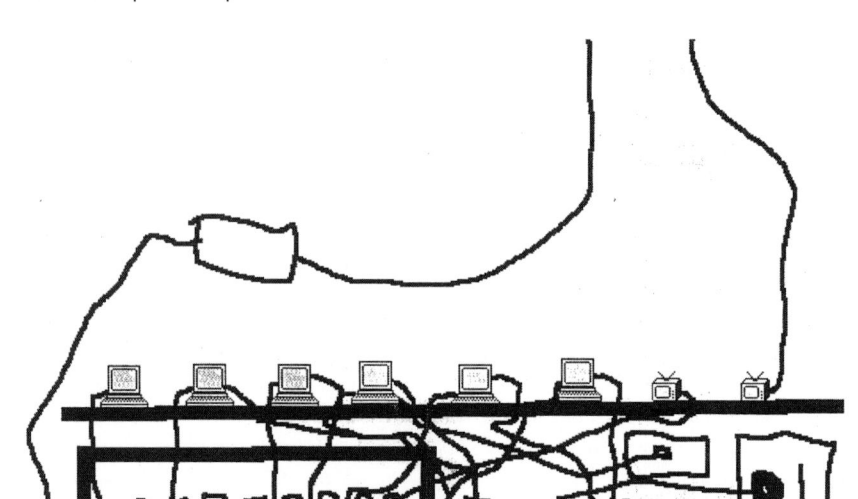

FIGURE 1.3 Computers – computer graphic by Bradley

and lives in an institution in Norway. Her brother suffers from attention deficit disorder and is manic-depressive. His father has little knowledge of his family, as he was adopted.

His initial psychological assessment using the Griffiths Developmental Scales indicated highly significant differences between his skill areas. He had a very wide scatter of skills, with some on the Personal Social Scale not achieved at the two-year level while other scale items (Performance Scale) were passed at the six-year level. His most recent assessment on the Stanford-Binet IV indicated Bradley to be functioning in the average range of intellectual ability. He scored highly on the scales for abstract/visual reasoning, quantitative reasoning and short-term memory.

Bradley was referred to this study by his mother and teacher as displaying the following savant skills: memory, hyperlexia, number, mechanical/spatial, drawing, computer and sensory skills. He recalls not only TV ads and shows but also how many days it was since they last appeared on television. He spends several hours each day reading and studying the telephone book, street directories and encyclopedias. He loves to draw detailed pictures of electronic equipment including fans, stereos and videos. He is able to build traffic lights and signs, computers and radios from LEGO™. He is particularly interested in all things electrical. Bradley is able to add and subtract and can give the square roots of familiar numbers. He loves playing counting games and can also play games on the computer, and has learned to access PowerPoint and opens and close files with ease. He appears to have a highly developed sense of both direction and smell. Bradley's father is an accomplished mechanic and auto-electrician and his mother a talented drawer and artist.

The ability to understand language and to express himself appears to be an area of strength for Bradley. In this respect, he is atypical when compared to all other children in the study. Bradley's overall language skills as tested by the *CELF-3* are at the high end of the normal range. His age-equivalent score was seven years and one month. His ability to use language expressively was above average and his knowledge and comprehension were in the average range. However, he does not always use language appropriately to express his emotions and feelings and needs to be prompted to use language in social situations.

Bradley appears to display a variety of challenging behaviours in the home but few at school. Most of his behaviours take the form of crying and tantrums if unable to access, or continue working on, a savant interest. He is an anxious boy who can become distressed at not being able to perform a task correctly. His behaviour as measured by the *Developmental Behaviour Checklist* in the school setting is not in the behaviourally disturbed range, but is classified as being severely behaviourally and emotionally disturbed in the home. Due to problems with attention, Bradley spends about 75 per cent of his class time engaged in productive learning. His academic self-esteem as assessed by the *BASE* rating scale is moderately high.

Bradley is currently enrolled in an Aspect school and attends a satellite class in a mainstream school for students with mild autism. His IEP emphasizes the development of social skills, academic and school-rehearsal skills. Bradley is considered to be a delightful but anxious boy with abilities in many areas.

Terry

Like Patrick and Bradley, Terry was introduced briefly at the beginning of this chapter. Terry is five years of age and is currently attending an autism-specific school operated by Aspect. No problems were experienced either during pregnancy or at the birth.

Terry was diagnosed as suffering from Asperger's Syndrome at the age of three years. The diagnosis was made as Terry presented with the following behaviours: a fascination and obsession for manhole covers, numbers and letters; social interaction difficulties with peers and a preference for solitary play; a restricted diet; sensory sensitivities, in particular to the textures of clothes; a sensitivity to high-pitched sounds; and a delay in social, self-help skills and toilet training. With respect to Terry's family history, his father's brother is considered to be a loner who has poor social interaction skills, and he also has a cousin from his father's side that was diagnosed as having Attention Deficit Disorder. Although his first psychometric assessment was conducted using the Griffiths Mental Developmental Scales, and these indicated overall average developmental functioning, weakness was noted in the areas of Abstract/Visual Reasoning and Short-Term Memory. The most recent assessment using the Stanford-Binet IV placed him above average in terms of intellectual functioning with his best scores in the area of Quantitative Reasoning. Terry is the only subject in this study who has an above-average IQ.

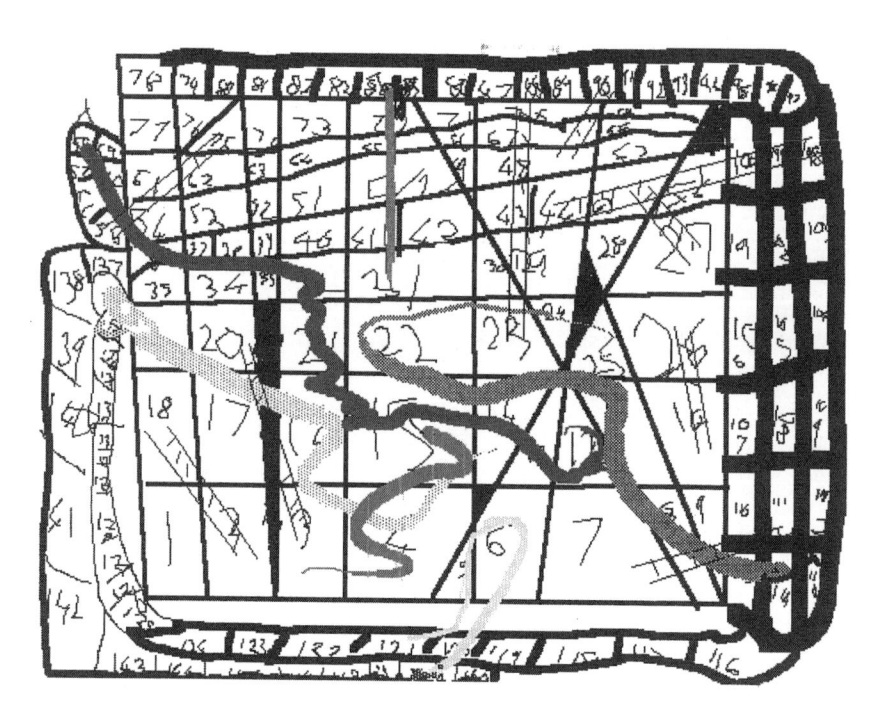

FIGURE 1.4 Snakes and Ladders – computer graphic by Terry

Referred to this study as a preschooler by his Early Intervention teacher, he was identified as displaying multiple savant abilities. These abilities included: memory, hyperlexic, mechanical/spatial, calendar calculation, arithmetic calculation and computer skills. From the age of two years, he was able to recall his telephone number and address, the birthdays of his preschool peers and odd and even street numbers of familiar streets. He would also recall the exact number of street-hole covers of every street in the greater Hornsby area. He was able to recognize and write many words and numbers and could recite the twelve times tables by the age of five years. He is able to build complex marble mazes, can calculate the age of a person when told of their birthdate, draws complex street grids and mazes, and uses the word processor on the computer to type his words and numbers. Both Terry's father, mother and grandfather are gifted in their respective fields.

Terry is the only subject to have performed well on the *CELF-3* test of language skills. His receptive and expressive language scores were well within the normal range for his age. His age-equivalent score was five years and ten months. However, difficulties were noted with Terry's speech, notably his articulation and rhythm/intonation. In the class setting, he also experienced difficulties in answering simple 'who', 'what', 'where', 'when' and 'how' questions and following non-routine three-part commands. As with most students with autism or Asperger's disorder, he is unable to express his feelings and emotions.

With respect to behaviour and social skills, Terry experiences difficulties. If he does not get his own way, he will tantrum, scream, refuse to cooperate and can become aggressive. If told to stop a savant activity, he will tantrum. Terry can also be highly anxious and has difficulties changing from one environment to another. His social skills fluctuate from age-appropriate to very immature and he generally engages in solitary play. He can, however, cooperate with structured interactive group games (snakes and ladders, noughts and crosses) if interested. Terry finds it difficult to accept the opinions of others and easily becomes anxious and distressed if someone disagrees with his viewpoint. Neither his family nor his teacher rated his behaviours in the disturbed range using the *Developmental Behaviour Checklist* (Einfield et al. 1998). However, it should be noted his family finds him almost twice as difficult to manage in the home as does his teacher in the school environment. His self-esteem was rated as moderate using the *BASE* rating scale.

Terry's current IEP incorporates the teaching of communication, social, academic, behavioural and school skills. He is in an Early Childhood class of high-functioning students with autism and will hopefully transfer to an Aspect satellite class in a mainstream school.

★

The stories of these children will continue to be told throughout the chapters to come and serve to highlight the development of the *Savant Skill Curriculum*, outline the study and the results. A 'Guide to Practice' will be outlined in Chapter 4 and will include a step-by-step guide for teachers on how to implement the *Savant Skill Curriculum* in the classroom.

References

American Psychiatric Association (1994). *Diagnostic and Statistical Manual of Mental Disorders* (4th Ed.). Washington, DC: APA.

American Psychiatric Association (2013). *Diagnostic and Statistical Manual of Mental Disorders* (5th Ed.). Arlington, VA: American Psychiatric Publishing.

Assouline, S.G., Foley-Nicpon, M., and Huber, D.H. (2006). The impact of vulnerabilities and strengths on the academic experiences of twice-exceptional students: A message to school counsellors. *Professional School Counselling, 10(1)*, 14–21.

Assouline, S.G., and Whiteman, C.S. (2011). Twice-exceptionality: Implications for school psychologists in the 'post-IDEA 2004 era'. *Journal of Applied School Psychology, 27,* 380–402.

Australian Bureau of Statistics. (2014). *Autism in Australia, 2012* (latest issue released at 11.30AM (Canberra time) 04/06/2014. Retrieved from www.abs.gov.au/ausstats/abs @.nsf/Latestproducts/4428.0Main%Features52012?opendocument&tabname=Summary& prodno=4428.0&issue=2012&num=&view.

Autism Spectrum Australia (Aspect). (2013). *We Belong Too.* Retrieved from www. autism.spectrum.org.au/content/we-belong-key-findings.

Baldwin, S., Costley, D., and Warren, A. (2014). Employment activities and experiences of adults with high-functioning autism and Asperger's disorder. *Journal of Autism and Developmental Disorders,* 1–10.

Betts, G.T., and Neihart, M. (2010). *The revised profiles of gifted and talented: A research-based approach*. In Keynote Address at *11th Asia Pacific Conference on Giftedness*.

Blumberg, S.J., Bramlett, M.D., Kogan, M.D., Schieve, L.A., Jones, J.R., and Lu, M.C. (2013). Changes in prevalence of parent-reported autism spectrum disorders in school-aged U.S. children: 2007 to 2011–12. *National Health Statistics Reports, 64*, 1–12.

Cimera, R.E., and Cowan, R.J. (2009). The costs of services and employment outcomes achieved by adults with autism in the US. *Autism, 13*, 285–302.

Clark, T.R. (2001). *The application of savant and splinter skills in the autistic population through Curriculum design: A longitudinal multiple-replication case study*. A thesis in partial fulfilment of the Doctor of Philosophy Degree, University of New South Wales.

Clark, T. (2013). *Education and the* Student *with an Autism Spectrum Disorder – Where is the research? Where is the evidence?* Keynote paper presented to the Asia Pacific Autism Conference, 2013. Adelaide, Australia.

Coopersmith, S., and Gilberts, R. (1982). *BASE. Behavioural Academic Self-Esteem. A Rating Scale*. CA: Consulting Psychologists Press, Inc.

Costley, D., Clark, T., and Bruck, S. (2014). The Autism Spectrum Disorder Evaluative Education Model: A school-based method of assessing and selecting interventions for classroom use. *Sage Open, 4*.

Costley, D., Keane, E., Clark, T., and Lane, K. (2012). *A Practical Guide for Teachers of Students with an Autism Spectrum Disorder in Secondary Education*. London: Jessica Kingsley Publishers.

Detrich, R., and Lewis, T. (2013). A decade of evidence-based education: Where are we and where do we need to go? *Journal of Positive Behaviour Intervention, 15*, 214–220.

Dingfelder, H. (2011). Bridging the research-to-practice gap in autism intervention: An application of diffusion of innovation theory. *Journal of Autism and Developmental Disorders, 41*, 597–609.

Einfield, S.L., Tonge, B.J., and Parmenter, T. (1998). *Developmental Behaviour Checklist. Teachers Version (DBC-T)*. Melbourne and Sydney: University of New South Wales, Monash University, and University of Sydney.

Gagne, F. (2009). Building gifts into talents: detailed overview of the DMGT 2.0. In B. MacFarlane and T. Stambaugh (Eds.), *Leading Change in Gifted Education: the Festschrift of Dr. Joyce Van Tassel-Baska* (pp. 61–80). Waco, TX: Prufock Press.

Goodman, J. (1972). A case study of an autistic savant. Mental function in the psychotic child with markedly discrepant abilities. *Journal of Child Psychology and Psychiatry, 13*, 267–278.

Grandin, T. (2012). Learning basic skills helped me succeed. In L. Perner (Ed.), *Scholars with Autism. Achieving Dreams* (pp. 158–170). Arizona: Auricle Books.

Gross, M.U.M. (1993). *Exceptionally Gifted Children*. London: Routledge.

Hermelin, B., Pring, L., and Heavey, L. (1994). Visual and motor functions in graphically gifted savant. *Psychological Medicine, 24*, 673–680.

Hill, A.L. (1974). Idiot savants: A categorization of abilities. *Mental Retardation*, December, 12–13.

Hill, A.L. (1978). Savants: Mentally retarded individuals with special skills. In N. Ellis (Ed.), *International Review of Research in Mental Retardation, 9* (pp. 277–298). New York: Academic Press.

Hollingworth, L.S. (1942). *Children above IQ 180*. New York: World Books.

Howlin, P., Goode, S., Hutton, J., and Rutter, M. (2004). Adult outcomes for children with autism. *Journal of Child Psychology and Psychiatry, 45*, 212–229.

Howlin, P., Goode, S., Hutton, J., and Rutter, M. (2009). Savant skills in autism: Psychometric approaches and parental reports. *Philosophical Transactions of the Royal Society B, 364,* 1359–1367.

Howlin, P., and Moss, P. (2012). Adults with Autism Spectrum Disorders. *Canadian Journal of Psychiatry, 57(5),* 275–283.

Karnes, M.B., and Johnson, L.J. (1986). Identification and assessment of gifted/talented handicapped children. In J.R. Whitmore (Ed.), *Early Childhood Intellectual Giftedness in Young Children. Recognition and Development* (pp. 35–55). London: Haworth Press.

Kasari, C., and Smith, T. (2013). Interventions in schools for children with autism spectrum disorder: Methods and recommendations. *Autism, 17,* 254–267.

Kluth, P., and Schwarz, P. (2010). *Pedro's Whale.* Baltimore: Brookes.

Lanou, A., Hough, H., and Powell, E. (2011). Case studies on using strengths and interests to address the needs of students with autism spectrum disorders. *Intervention in School and Clinic, 20(10),* 1–8. Hamill Institute on Disabilities. New York: SAGE.

Levy, M. (2014). The autistic man with a talent for building furniture. *Sydney Morning Herald.* http://m.smh.com.au/lifestyle/life/the-autistic-man-with-a-talent-for-building-furniture-20140120–31448.html.

Lovett, B.J., and Lewandowski, L.J. (2006). Gifted students with learning disabilities: Who are they? *Journal of Learning Disabilities, 39,* 515–527.

Miller, L.K. (1998). Defining the savant syndrome. *Journal of Developmental Physical Disability, 10,* 73–85.

O'Connor, N. and Hermelin, B. (1987). Visual and graphic abilities of the idiot savant artist. *Psychological Medicine, 17,* 79–90.

Nicpon, M.F., Allmon, A., Seick, B., and Stinson, R.D. (2011). Empirical investigation of twice-exceptionality: Where have we been and where are we going? *Gifted Child Quarterly, 55(1),* 3–17.

Parsons, S., Charman, T., Faulkner, R., Wallace, S., and Wittemeyer, K. (2013). Commentary – Bridging the research and practice gap in autism: the importance of creating partnerships with schools. *Autism, 17,* 268–280.

Rimland, B. (1978). Inside the mind of the autistic savant. *Psychology Today, 12,* 68–80.

Robison, J.L. (2008). *Look Me in the Eye: My Life with Asperger's.* New York: Three Rivers Press.

Roux, A., Shattuck, P., Rast, J., Jessica, E., Rava, J., and Anderson, K. (2015). *National Autism Indicators Report: Transition into Young Adulthood.* Philadelphia, PA: Life Course Outcomes Research program, A.J. Drexel Autism Institute, Drexel University.

Semel, L., Wiig, E.H., and Secord, W.A. (1995). *Clinical Evaluation of Language Fundamentals – 3rd Edition.* San Antonio: The Psychological Corporation. Harcourt Brace and Co.

Shore, S. (2012). Observations on education from within the autism spectrum. In L. Perner (Ed.), *Scholars with Autism. Achieving Dreams.* Arizona: Auricle Books.

Silverman, L.K. (1993). *Counselling the Gifted and Talented.* Denver: Love Publications.

Smith, C. (2014). *Reaching All Learners: Utilising Student Interests to Empower Accessibility* [iBook]. Retrieved from https://itunes.apple.com/au/book/reaching-all-learners-utilising/id870422846?mt=11.

Taylor, J.L., and Seltzer, M.M. (2011). Employment and post-secondary educational activities for young adults with autism spectrum disorders during transition to adulthood. *Journal of Autism and Developmental Disorders, 41,* 566–574.

Treffert, D. (1989). *Extraordinary People.* London: Bantam Press.

Treffert, D. (2012). Scholars with autism. Achieving dreams. In L. Perner (Ed.), *Introduction: Oval Souls on a Round Planet* (pp. 1–15). Sedona, AZ: Auricle Ink Publishers.

Walker, H.M. (2004). Commentary: Use of evidence-based interventions in schools: Where we've been, where are we, and where we need to go. *School Psychology Review, 33,* 398–407.

Young, R.L. and Nettlebeck, T. (1995). The abilities of a musical savant and his family. *Journal of Autism and Developmental Disorders, 25,* 231–248.

2

WHERE ARE WE NOW? – THE PREVIOUS RESEARCH

What do we know, what don't we know about savant skills? How can autistic savants be helped to 'apply' their special abilities?

To teach a student with autism, either in a mainstream or a special education class, can be a challenging business. As mentioned previously, due to the unique learning styles and the impairments associated with autism, many of these students experience significant challenges in schools. They are misunderstood by educators and peers, struggle to cope and may actually leave the education system altogether. Add to this scenario those students who are also gifted and require additional supports due to them being 'out-of-sync' with their autistic peers. The challenging behaviours exhibited by Patrick, Bradley, Terry, and the other young savants, was not due to the impact of their autism alone, but also to the frustration and boredom of not having their special education needs met. Teachers of these students need assistance to provide an appropriate differentiated program, to help reduce the challenges faced by their twice-exceptional students with autism. The brief overview of the literature that follows will provide an insight into this condition, as well as highlight the critical factors that have influenced the successful application of the skills of some savants, that have been documented to date. This will shed light on the reason for the inclusion of the strategies employed in the *Savant Skill Curriculum*, which offers a way forward for educators, professionals, students and families alike. The study also sought to answer a number of research questions related to the nature of savant skills, a topic that requires further exploration, and a number of questions related to new areas of enquiry, not yet documented in the literature.

Savant syndrome: nature and etiology of savant skills

Savant skills present a paradox to the notions of talent and disability; on one hand, they are reported to be self-taught, while on the other hand, they sometimes are dismissed as nothing more than the product of relentless practice and over-learning. Savant skills have garnered attention and amazement, not only because of the paradoxical presence of a well-developed skill in the context of disability but also because of the nature of the emergence of these skills.

(Wallace, 2008, p. 232)

Research in the field has primarily focused upon such questions as 'What is savant syndrome?', 'How do savants do the extraordinary things they do?' and 'What implications does savant syndrome have for our understanding of human neurological functioning and/or human intelligence?' Although the phenomenon of savant syndrome has intrigued professionals for a long time, with many cases being documented in the literature, relatively little is still known about the organization or development of savant abilities, or the nature of the mental functioning involved. Wallace, in his 2008 overview of neuropsychological studies of savant skills, provides a well-documented history of the research in pursuit of finding answers to these important questions.

Savant skills

Savant and splinter skills develop within a fairly narrow range of activities or domains (Heaton and Wallace, 2004; Hill, 1974; Miller, 1998; Treffert, 1989; Tredgold, 1914; Rimland, 1978; Young, 1995). Although Hill's original list of savant skills included seven categories of abilities, this has been increased over the past two decades and now includes: *memory ability* which is generally related to narrow fields of interest, e.g. postcodes, birthdays, telephone numbers and addresses, public transport routes and timetables, sports teams/players/results, capital cities, states; *hyperlexia or pseudo-verbal skill* evidenced by an ability to decipher and recall language either spoken or written, and/or reading ability, however the reading ability is generally related to word-identification and not comprehension of what has been read; *artistic ability* generally restricted to either drawing and painting, and on rare occasions sculpting; *musical ability* expressed by an ability to play an instrument, or to sing with relative ease, to play or sing melodies upon a single hearing, has very good pitch; *mechanical (visual-spatial) ability* which is often exhibited by computer skills, an ability to dismantle and assemble such mechanical objects as video players, vacuum cleaners, clocks, televisions, radios with only anecdotal examples in the literature; *calendar calculation*, which involves naming of the day of the week on which a given date has fallen or will fall; *mathematical calculation*, mostly arithmetic ability and occasionally the ability to identify prime numbers; and *athletic or coordination ability* as evidenced by superior balance (e.g. walking on the tops of fences, cribs and clothes lines) and/or swimming, skating, basketball free throws, bicycle riding and unspecified ball skills. It is not uncommon for multiple savant skills to be exhibited by the savant and at different levels – Talented Savant I or Prodigious Savant II (Treffert, 1989, 2012). In their review of savant syndrome, a comprehensive historical overview of the research related to each of these savant skill categories was undertaken by Nettlebeck and Young (1999).

Hill (1974) originally expressed concern about the inclusion of fine sensory discriminations as a savant ability. Hyper- and hypo-sensitivity across all sensory domains have been observed among persons with autism, which, in fact, may be due to a failure in sensory processing or a sensory abnormality (Leekham et al., 2001; O'Neill and Jones, 1997; Tomchek and Dunn, 2007). Some anecdotal reports of enhanced sensory perception have appeared in the savant literature including: the case of a child who could hear conversations out of range of hearing, the child who could correctly state the time of day without referring a clock or watch, and a report of a young blind musical savant who, on hearing the horn sound of her school bus on arrival at her home, announced 'new horn' without knowing that indeed the driver had bought a new school bus (Treffert, 1989). Although an earlier quantitative test for a sensitivity to smell failed to confirm a superior ability (Horwitz et al., 1965), recent studies have demonstrated superior sensory processing in those with autism (Bertone et al., 2003; Heaton et al., 2008; Mottron et al., 1999; O'Riordan and Passetti, 2006). It has been suggested that talent in autism is associated with systemizing, defined as the drive to analyse or construct systems. The domains in which savants typically excel are those that are highly systemizable. Strong systemizing, or hyper-systemizing, therefore requires an excellent attention to detail, a characteristic often associated in those with autism and which may result in sensory hypersensitivity across a number of sensory modalities (Baron-Cohen, Ashwin, Ashwin, Tavassoli and Chakrabarti, 2009). Whilst teaching students with autism, including those with savant skills, I observed many examples of sensory abnormalities (hyper- and hypo-sensitivities). I am of the view that savant-like sensory performance is better explained by sensory abnormalities, and, in particular, sensory hypersensitivity.

All of the above-mentioned savant abilities or skills are exhibited by the sixteen treatment children in the study who received the *Savant Skill Curriculum* – see Table 2.1. The remaining six of the twenty-two children who participated in the study formed a small control group and will be discussed in the methodology section in Chapter 3.

The most frequently occurring savant skills in the treatment children are memory (100 per cent), hyperlexia (87 per cent) and mechanical/spatial skills (81.25 per cent). Calendar calculation (25 per cent), number (18.25 per cent) and athletic (6.25 per cent) skills occurred with the least frequency. It should be noted that most children displaying mechanical/spatial skills do so in relation to the use of computers. More than 50 per cent of the children also displayed sensory abilities. This figure may have been influenced by the fact that many students with autism display sensory sensitivities, which are generally considered to be deficits rather than skills. Patrick displays the greatest number of savant skills (seven), with the least number of skills (three) being displayed by John, Jack, Martin and Timothy.

To further illustrate the range, level and nature of the savant skills of the children in the study, a comprehensive 'Profile of Savant Abilities' was developed for each of the children. A copy of Patrick's profile is included (Table 2.2) with copies for

TABLE 2.1 Frequency of savant skills of treatment children

Child	Memory	Hyperlexia	Art	Music	Mechanical/ spatial	Calendar	Number	Sensory	Athletic
Patrick	X	X		X	X	X	X	X	
Christopher	X	X			X			X	
Benjamin	X	X		X	X			X	
Natasha	X	X	X		X			X	
Bradley	X	X			X		X	X	
Terry	X	X			X	X	X		
Anthony	X	X		X		X		X	
John	X			X	X				
Jeremy	X	X	X		X				
Warren	X	X		X	X				
Timothy	X	X						X	
Zane	X	X		X	X			X	
Joseph	X	X	X		X				
Martin	X	X	X						
Simon	X	X			X	X		X	
Jack	X				X				X
Percentage	100%	87%	25%	37.5%	81.25%	25%	18.75%	56.25%	6.25%

the remaining five focus children, and a summary of the range of measures used to assess the savant skills of the children, available on the Routledge website (Profiles of Savant Abilities; Summary of Savant Skill Assessments; Level of Savant Skills – Tables 2.3 to 2.11). Information regarding savant skills was drawn from family interviews, the *Family and Teacher Savant Skill Questionnaires* (Clark, 2011, Appendix 2 and 3) designed for the study, a variety of standardized tests as outlined in Chapter 3, along with observations, documents and artefacts. The level of each child's individual savant skills is presented using Treffert's (1989) classification of savant skills as either Talented (Savant I) or Prodigious (Savant II) skills.

Patrick's memory, maths and calendar calculation savant skills were assessed at the prodigious Savant II level. He is without doubt one of the world's most prodigious savants. The full breadth of the savant abilities of the 'paradox children' can only be truly identified by using a combination, and wide range of both standardized and non-standardized measures.

Given the paradox nature of savant abilities, there has been a great deal of debate as to the underlying neuropsychological basis of savant skills. Hill (1978) proposed the view that savant skills are independent of IQ based on the fact that a person with an intellectual disability, and/or in this case autism, can also display a number of high-level abilities. O'Connor and Hermelin undertook a number of studies (thirty in total) to investigate the range of savant skills. In doing so, they made comparisons between savants and appropriate non-intellectually impaired controls, and came to the conclusion that savant activities are largely independent of IQ. They also speculated, however, that IQ may play a supporting role in the development of these skills (O'Connor and Hermelin, 1987). This debate continues today with complete agreement yet to be reached.

Memory

Early explanations for the possible development of savant skills favoured a rote memory viewpoint (Hill, 1978). More recent studies, however, have indicated the role of rule-based memory. O'Connor and Hermelin (1984) demonstrated that savant skills are frequently based on the application of rules whereby an extensive knowledge is organized. They found that the reaction times of calendar calculators were slower to remote dates, either past or future, than to proximate dates; and they established that the calendar calculators were aware of, and could use, structural regularities within and across calendars.

The association of exceptionally good memory has been made for most savant skills; for musical skills (Hermelin et al., 1989; Young and Nettlebeck, 1995), mathematics (Stevens and Moffit, 1988), artistic ability (O'Connor and Hermelin, 1987), calendar calculating (Hermelin and O'Connor, 1986; Young and Nettlebeck, 1994) and hyperlexia (Goldberg, 1987). Treffert (1989) also supported the notion of superior memory in savants. Howe (1989), on the other hand, discounted the role of superior memory because savants were found to perform poorly on standardized memory tests. This was also the experience of Young (1995),

TABLE 2.2 Profile of Patrick's savant abilities

PROFILE OF PATRICK'S SAVANT ABILITIES		
NAME: Patrick AGE: 14 RESULTS OF PRE-TESTS		
PROFILE OF SAVANT SKILLS		
SAVANT ABILITY AND LEVEL	STANDARDIZED MEASURES	NON-STANDARDIZED MEASURES / INFORMATION
Memory Savant II	**WRAML – Wide Range Assessment of Memory and Learning** The WRAML assesses a child's ability to use short-term memory and retrieval skills in a variety of ways. It also measures the ability to develop a 'learning curve' with repeated trials. (Average Score – 100). **Index Percentile** (i) General Memory 48 0.05 (ii) Verbal Memory 57 0.5 (iii) Visual Memory 54 0.2 (iv) Learning Index 62 1 P. performed best on the Number/Letter Subtest. The overall WRAML scores are not high, which may have been due to P's inability to comprehend the verbal/language instructions of the test. Many test items were context based and required a developed degree of receptive comprehension. These results confirmed by the Stanford-Binet Intelligence Scale (4th Edition). He scored relatively well in the Short-Term Memory domain but primarily due to his superior performance in the Memory for Digits Subtest. He was able to repeat up to 9 digits forwards and 7 digits in reverse (Short-Term Memory Score – 79).	**Family/Teacher Savant Skill Questionnaire and Informal Memory Checks Designed for the Study** P. can recall the following items with a high degree of accuracy on informal testing (i.e. informal verbal tests of memory items designed for the study). **Birthdays** – familiar people (present and past) – 95% accuracy. **Car Number Plates** – family and staff (present and past) – 95% accuracy. **Telephone Numbers** – familiar people and organizations (present and past) – 80% accuracy. **Postcodes** (Australian) – State, city, suburbs throughout Australia – 95% accuracy. **Life Events –** (home and school) e.g. weddings, deaths, places visited, excursions, beginning/end of school terms (present and past) – 90% accuracy. **Names of People** – familiar people (past and present) – 95% accuracy. **Country/Capital City and City Names** – recalls and matches cities to countries and vice versa – 99% accuracy. **Street Directories** – can locate streets, suburbs rapidly (within seconds) upon request using the street directory. He can locate the appropriate map number for the required location. On occasions he can immediately state the correct map number of a street from memory.

<table>
<tr><td></td><td>

Songs – recalls all lyrics and tunes of favourite songs. He imiates his favourite singers.

American Presidents – recalls all Presidents' birth dates, deaths, time in office, their order e.g. 'The 21st President is –?' (100% accuracy).

Recipes – recalls each ingredient in familiar recipes.

Note: According to family and teachers, P. can recall most information following only one reading or exposure to the material. He currently is reading encyclopedias at home. He is also studying the computer program – 'World Atlas'.

It should be further noted that P. responded rapidly to all of the above memory items when tested.

Reading

P. can identify most familiar words in his home/school environment (people, places, events, objects, etc.), i.e. words he has read or been exposed to in the past. He has an advanced ability to 'decode' words. However, his general comprehension of words/books/phrases remains well below his chronological level.

Spelling/Writing

P. can write/spell most familiar words in his environment (people, places, objects, events). His ability extends to spelling and writing 'Latin' words. Again this spelling ability may be related to his exposure to words previously seen in books (a memory skill). P. writes quickly when writing – he has low muscle tone.

P. spends a great deal of time in reading books/magazines, etc. obsessively. He has been interested in letters and words since 4 to 5 years of age.

</td></tr>
<tr><td>

Hyperlexia

(Reading/Spelling/Writing)

Level I/Splinter Skill

</td><td>

A. Reading/Woodcock Reading Mastery Tests – Revised G. 1987

Results:

Subtest:

i)Word Identification

Age Equivalent = 11.5

Grade Equivalent = 5.7

Percentile Rank = 24

Subtest

ii) Passage Comprehension

Age Equivalent = 7.7

Grade Equivalent = 2.3

Percentile Rank = 0.1

B. Spelling/Westwood Test of Spelling – Westwood, 1979

Date of Testing : 21.2.96

Results:

i) Approximate spelling age is 15 years 6 months.

Average Score for age as at 14 years 4 months = 51

(P.'s Raw Score was 55).

</td></tr>
</table>

TABLE 2.2 Profile of Patrick's savant abilities—*continued*

SAVANT ABILITY AND LEVEL	STANDARDIZED MEASURES	NON-STANDARDIZED MEASURES / INFORMATION
Music **Savant I/Splinter**	No standardized measures undertaken due to time constraints of the study. Music was not included in P.'s Curriculum Program.	P.'s music ability takes the form of : • Memory for popular songs (home and school). P. watches TV Music Video hits each week and listens to Top 40 songs on the radio daily. He memorizes songs easily. • Sings in almost perfect pitch most of the time, i.e. when in the mood. • Spends a great deal of time listening to songs (home and school). P. particularly enjoys singing using the microphone. • P. has not yet demonstrated an interest or ability in playing musical instruments. **Favourite Songs/Artists** Phil Collins • 'You Can't Hurry Love' • 'Another Day in Paradise' • 'Say You, Say Me!' Tina Arena – all her songs Liza Minnelli – 'New York, New York' Peter Allen – 'I Still Call Australia Home' Most Top 10 hits – enjoys popular hits
Mechanical/Spatial Skill **Computer** **Savant I**	**WRAVMA Wide Range Assessment of Visual Motor Abilities.** The WRAVMA assesses visual motor functioning in children and adolescents. The Matching test measures 'visual-spatial ability'	P. is able to: (i) Complete 60-piece jigsaw puzzles. (ii) Operate computer and use software with ease. (iii) P. taught himself independently to use the following programs; DOS, 'Body Works' and 'The World Atlas'. His family reports

	Results: Raw Score = 33 Standard Score = 86 Percentile = 18th Age Equivalent = 10 years, 3 Months P. performed well below his chronological age on this test. The test failed to highlight his abilities as outlined in the Family and Teacher Savant Skill Questionnaire.	he has moved Microsoft Works from the menu of their home computer. He is able to access and remove files. (iv) P. can connect/disconnect and operate (without being shown) the following; • Video Recorder • Galaxy Paye TV • CD Player • Stereo • Kitchen Stove. He is able to follow the instructions in the operation manuals.
Calendar Calculation **Savant II**	*No standardized measures available.*	**Four Calendrical Experiments**. Robyn Young, 1994 (based on Hermelin and O'Connor's 1986 experiments). **Aims of the Experiments**: **Test 1**: – To test the rule that the date in a given month may fall on the same day as the same date in another month. **Results**: – 100% accuracy (one second average response time for each item). **Test 2**: – To test knowledge of the 14 configurations at the Calendar (#s 1 to 14) **Results**: – 85% accuracy. **Test 3**: – To test the rule that in non-leap years the day of a date in one year will be the following day in the next year and the previous day in the preceding year. **Results**: – 92.5% accuracy. **Test 4**: – To test the range of ability with respect to both past and future dates.

TABLE 2.2—*continued*

SAVANT ABILITY AND LEVEL	STANDARDIZED MEASURES	NON-STANDARDIZED MEASURES / INFORMATION
		Although the aim of Robyn Young's (1994) experiments was to explore the use of rule-based strategies in calendrical calculations with 'speed response' being a primary measure, the tests were used for this study to determine the 'range' of calendrical knowledge and accuracy.
		Results: – 47% accuracy. Robyn Young was present for this experiment and suggested P.'s poor result may be due to his having access to a perpetual calendar with the range of years limited to 1901 to 2100.
		P. became frustrated and upset with his performance, appearing confused. When asked how far his calendar at home reached or how he could answer the items, he was unable to respond.
Mathematical Calculations **Savant II**	A. Nottingham Number Test – **W. Gilllham and K. Hesse (9.0 to 11.0)**	**Informal tests of mental calculation ability were undertaken including +, –, ×, ÷ equations.**
	Note: Although P. was 14 years at time of testing and beyond the age range of this test, the test was used as instructions are given orally by the examiner, and the complexity of verbal instructions has been reduced. (P. has poor reading comprehension.) The test is still not ideal as it also relies heavily on verbal comprehension.	P. on most tests was 100% accurate and would mentally calculate the answers with rapid speed. Where he was unable to calculate the answer rapidly and correctly, he would ask to use a calculator. Examples of mental calculations correctly answered and response times.
	Results: Percentile Rank i) Number Concepts 37 ii) Number Skills 98 Overall Percentile Rank 81	**Equation Response Time** 248 1.75 sec + 486 734

	P. achieved significantly higher in 'number skills' (+, −, ×, ÷ equations). He performed poorly in 'number concepts' due to higher verbal component and abstract concepts.	12,742 (4.4 sec) +11,959 24,701
		131,212 (2.9 sec) +85,391 216,603
		5,941 (4.8 sec) −825 5,116
		975,305 (6.6 sec) −189,823 788,482
		72 (3.3 sec) ×12 864
		175 (4.9 sec) ×15 2625
		$100 \div 4 = 25$ (1.3 sec) $307 \div 12 = 25.5$ (6.4 sec) $534 \div 18 = 29.6$ (5.1 sec) $10,455 \div 52 = 201$ (6.1 sec)
		P. is unable to calculate square roots at present. His teacher had noted P. learned to calculate × and ÷ after a single teaching session.
		Although P. demonstrates prodigious savant skills in basic maths calculation, his understanding of, and performance across, a broad range of mathematical concepts is extremely poor.
		P. is only just beginning to use money appropriately. He is able to calculate the time when presented in digital form.

who tested fifty-one savants and found, in fact, memory performance to be consistent with IQ scores.

Jordan (2008), in *Memory in Autism*, makes the point that the narrow and rigid nature of these skills provides evidence of memory processes in autism that are significantly different from those found in typical development. She also compares processing in people with autism more akin to artificial intelligence, and while that has some advantages it is not geared to everyday problem solving. People with autism who display savant memory skills may do so at the expense of efficiently accessed and coherent memories. Jordan also makes reference to this study (Clark, 2005), in that all of the children displayed savant memory skills (see Table 2.1). As memory testing was administered as part of the assessment of each child's savant abilities, this allowed me to observe first-hand superior memory ability in all of the children.

Inherited skills – innate gifts or talents

Some have suggested that savant skills are, in fact, innate talents or gifts (Fein and Obler, 1988; O'Connor, 1989; Snyder and Mitchell, 1999). The view that savant skills depend upon domain-specific skills is becoming more widely accepted (Feldman, 1993; Gardner, 1983; Heaton and Wallace, 2004; O'Connor, 1989; Sacks, 1985; Spitz, 1995; Strauss, 2013; Treffert, 1989, 2012). From converging anecdotal evidence it would appear these domain-specific skills typically emerge at a very early age and in a manner that seems different from the usual longer learning curve (Rimland, 1978; Rosen, 1981). The skills seem to 'just appear' as in the case of Nadia (Selfe, 1977), whose exceptional drawing skills appeared at age three and a half years. In his review of musical savants, Miller (1989) found evidence of an early interest in music. Young (1995) also found the early onset of savant skills to be common among most of her subjects. This early onset of skills, coupled with the fact of little or no formal training, supports the view that savant skills may have a genetically determined basis, and are in fact inherited skills.

Treffert, in the book *The Complexity of Greatness* (2013, pp. 103–118), makes a strong case for the existence of innate talent which is linked to 'genetic memory'. Genetic memory is, by definition, the inherited transfer of specific talents and actual knowledge in addition to all other physical characteristics and traits, including instincts that our inherited genes carry forward in each of us. Genetic memory goes far beyond height, eye colour and facial features, in other words the usual heritability (Ericsson, Roring and Nandagopal, 2007). Neuroscientists working on the Blue Brain project discovered that neurons make connections independently of a subject's experience (Perin, Berger and Markram, 2011). This finding further supports the view that some of our fundamental basic knowledge is inscribed in our genes.

There is evidence of a genetic link in the appearance of domain-specific gifts in the non-disabled gifted population. Evidence of similar interests and talents or gifts has been also noted in the families of savants (Brink, 1980; Hermelin and

O'Connor, 1990b; Rimland, 1978; Young, 1995). A family study by Baharloo et al. (2000) suggests that 'absolute pitch' (AP), a skill over-represented among individuals with autism, and seemingly universal among savant musicians (Miller, 1989), is highly familial and heritable. Again, this study questioned families as to their interests and skills to explore the view that savant skills may have a hereditary basis.

Practice

Rather than savant skills having a hereditary or innate basis, some have suggested the development of the skills may in part be linked to practice or concentration (Anastasi and Levee, 1960; Comer, 1985; Ericsson and Faivre, 1988; Hoffman and Reeves, 1979; Howe, 1989; Miller, 1989; Treffert, 1989). Where individuals spend a great deal of time at an activity, they are likely to become more proficient at it, and savants are no exception to this. As mentioned previously, savant talent or gifts may be innate and therefore not dependent on rehearsal or practice. Observations of the behaviours of savants, and anecdotal reports from caregivers, highlight the intense concentration and hours of practice that is typically involved in savant activities (Charness et al., 1988; Comer, 1985; Hill, 1978; Treffert, 1989, 2012; Young, 1995). This was indeed my experience working alongside the children in this study, all of whom would spend hours each day focused on their savant interests. It should be noted, however, that the practice of the savant in essence involves long periods of performing or engagement, which is not directed to anything much other than just playing the instrument, or repeating the savant task over and over. This engagement of the savant may be more akin to obsession or motivation and may be seen as a possible explanation for the development of savant skills.

Nadia, a child savant artist, was reported to have lost her skills when she no longer practised her drawing at the time of her enrolment in a special school (Treffert, 1989). Alternatively, I think it more likely that her reported loss of skills may have been due to the lack of a differentiated program and support for her drawing abilities at her new special school. In summary, although practice may play an important role in talent development (savant or non-savant), it is insufficient to account for most, if not all prodigious skill, especially in rare cases when the skills suddenly emerge with no previous hint of their existence. Evidence of the rehearsal or practice of savant skills, and the loss of skills, were also explored by this study.

Motivation

Motivation has also been viewed as an explanation for the development of savant skills. The high levels of interest and motivation of each of the children in this study were used as a catalyst to facilitate the children's communication, social skills and behaviour support in the *Savant Skill Curriculum*. Some consider motivation or the capacity to concentrate to be a personality trait, or an integral aspect of the savant ability itself (Charness et al., 1988; Treffert, 1989). Many savants do follow extremely demanding routines to the point of obsession. O'Connor and Hermelin (1989, 1991a) also suggested that a tendency to repetitive behaviour and/or preoccupations with a restricted area of interest were crucial features of individuals with savant syndrome. Wallace (2008) concluded that the importance of the role of motivation, although difficult to quantify, cannot be overstated in the expression of savant-like skills. The lines between what is termed *motivation* and what is called a *restricted interest* in autism are unclear. Without doubt, the strong drive to pursue one's interest(s) only serves to maintain and possibly expand skill development. Having observed the intense motivation and concentration of Patrick, Bradley and Terry at first hand, this study also set out to examine the motivation traits of each of the children.

Executive functioning

The idea that the development of savant skills may be a result of the individual's inability to 'make sense of the world', to deal with 'abstractions', was first put forward by Scheerer, Rothman and Goldstein (1945). It has been suggested that a weak central coherence, or executive functioning, which leads to a predisposition to repetitive behaviours, may in fact play a role in the development of savant skills (Pring, Hermelin and Heavey, 1995). They proposed that the cognitive style of focusing on separate elements, rather than the whole picture, typical of autism itself, provided autistic savants with the building blocks from which musical, calendrical, artistic, numerical and other typical savant skills could be built up and extracted. Hermelin (2001) in her book *Bright Splinters of the Mind* refers to this those with autism tending to 'not see the wood for the trees' (p. 45). 'Overall, within the domain where they are talented, autistic savants appear to use the strategy of taking a path from single units to a subsequent extraction of higher-order patterns and structures' (p. 175). The savants' apparent reliance on these lower-level mental processes may be due to a failure in executive functioning (Frith, 1989; Happé, 1995; Pring et al., 1995; Snyder and Thomas, 1997). The phenomenon of weak central coherence is deemed to be central to both autism and savant syndrome.

Creativity

Whether or not savants display creativity in their fields of endeavour is also widely debated and should be discussed in relation to executive functioning. Creativity, as defined by Torrance (1974), involves flexibility, fluency, originality and elaborate quality of thought. Although Hill (1978) and Young (1995) found little evidence of creativity in savant performance on tests of creativity, others have classified the works of some savants as displaying creative elements (Sacks, 1995; Selfe, 1977; Treffert, 1989). Both Treffert (1989) and Sacks (1995) concluded however, that, although prodigious savant individuals in music and art do achieve an originality of personal expression, the quality of this is limited and repetitive. Some studies have found that creativity is correlated with IQ (Hermelin et al., 1987, 1989; Ho, Tsang and Ho, 1991; Young, 1995). A more recent study exploring creativity in savants was that of Pring, Ryder, Crane and Hermelin (2011). This study assessed savant artists relative to art students, adults with autism, and other adults with mild/moderate learning difficulties (MLD) on standardized tests of creativity, that were either related or unrelated to their domain of expertise. The results were mixed with the art students producing more creative outputs on the drawing task than the savant, autistic and MLD groups. However, the savants did produce more elaborate responses than the autistic and MLD groups. On the non-drawing construction task, the savant group produced more original outputs than the ASD and MLD groups and scored similarly to the art students. As this issue of whether or not savants display creativity remains unresolved, questions as to creativity in savant performance were also included in this study.

Other more recent theories as to 'how savants do what they do'

Pathological events/neurological functioning

Treffert (1989, 2012) suggests that savant skills are the result of pathological events involving the formation of exceptional neural structures during prenatal brain development. He postulates that neurological rewiring results in certain *cognitive* patterns including impaired abstract thinking, thought processes restricted to a narrow band, obsessiveness, practice and repetition (Treffert, 2012). Following evidence from autopsies, electroencephalographic and computer assisted tomography (CAT) scan data, and neuropsychological tests to support his theory, he found a number of cases with right hemisphere imbalance. Although these cases are small and more are needed to establish the significance of his explanation, initial reports are promising.

Functional brain activity has also been reported using positron emission tomography associated with calendar calculation (Boddaert et al., 2005). During calendar calculation as compared to rest, an adult with autism activated brain regions previously associated with memory. These findings reiterate the importance of memory processing for savant performance. Similar studies should also be undertaken of arithmetic mental calculation given that arithmetic skills are related to calendar calculating.

Another study by Pesenti et al. (2001), using positron emission tomography, compared brain activation patterns between typically developing (TD) controls and an arithmetic prodigy (RG), as they performed mental calculations. When completing simple equations they both showed activation in the brain bilaterally. However, RG accurately and quickly completed more complex calculations, in contrast to controls including recruiting a system of brain areas implicated in episodic memory. This study is important, as it suggests that the prodigy is relying on some special memory recruitment when performing his skill, as may be the case for other savants.

Brain-based imaging technologies I believe are shedding new and very important light on our previous conceptions of savant skill development and performance, and hold great promise for unravelling the mysteries of this phenomenon in the future. However, it is important to note that, from the perspective of exploring the 'human side' of the condition, little attention has been directed toward how savants can be assisted to make functional use of their special skills, and how this may impact long-term quality of life outcomes.

Cases of applied savant skills

> Talented individuals tend to be valued in our society – unless they have an intellectual disability, when respect can be replaced by curiosity. A few well-publicised savants have been able to profit financially from their skills. There is also anecdotal evidence that some savants have used their skills in paid positions within libraries and mechanical workshops. Research is required to determine the longer-term prospects for such individuals.
>
> (Nettelbeck and Young, 1999, p. 38)

In the design and implementation of the *Savant Skill Curriculum*, the aim was to not only improve the longer-term prospects of each subject, as suggested by Nettelbeck and Young (1999), but to replace society's curiosity about the savant with the respect they by right deserve. With this in mind, I reviewed the documented case studies of savants who have been helped to make functional use of their skills, to see if there were any particular strategies that could be adopted for use in the *Savant Skill Curriculum*. It should be noted that the majority of cases described in the literature are generally those that have gained recognition, through the spectacular nature of their abilities, and are often those who would receive the classification of Prodigious Savant II (Treffert, 1989). It is rare to find mention of savants whose performance is not quite so spectacular, and as a result have not been well publicized. This review is limited to a small number of cases of applied skills in savants commencing with several of the earliest cases, and concluding with more recent ones. For a more comprehensive and complete historical review of savants, I recommend Darold Treffert's book, *Extraordinary People* (1989).

Some early cases

Alonzo – the sculptor

Alonzo Clemons, a savant sculptor, was born in 1956. Alonzo's mother described him as a precocious child as he seemed to learn quickly. As a toddler, he showed

FIGURE 2.1 Alonzo Clemons – 'Sledge Hammer'

remarkable ability with and an interest in play dough. A fall at age three resulted in brain injury and a subsequent slower development, poor speech and an IQ of 40. He entered a special education facility at age four and currently lives in a group home as an adult. Although not diagnosed as autistic, Alonzo is a savant whose life's story provides an excellent example of 'applied' savant skills.

His interest in sculpting appeared before his injury and was almost obsessional. At one point, while he was in a residential facility at age twelve, it was felt that his obsessional interest was interfering with other aspects of learning so his clay was taken from him, only to use as a reward for other learning. Soon after, staff discovered sticky black animals in his bedding which he had modelled by scraping tar from the pavement with his fingernails.

Today, that obsessive attachment is to microcrystalline wax, which he transforms into remarkable sculptures of horses, gorillas and wildebeest in a very short space of time. He is able to recall objects from a single viewing and then transforms these mental images into models. In 1984, his work was featured in the National Art Festival for the Handicapped in Washington, DC where he met Nancy Reagan, following which he appeared on a television show.

In 1986, he was sponsored to hold a world premiere of thirty of his bronze sculptures, which quickly led to him establishing a national and international reputation. His works now sell for an average of $350 to $3,000 each, with some prices going as high as $45,000. Alonzo has never had a formal art lesson, as his parents, who have steadfastly encouraged him and now handle his sculptures, believe his technique or style should not be tampered with lest it be lost or destroyed. In spite of no artistic training, his work showed progression after his mother began taking him to the zoo to see animals in real life.

As his work has taken on greater dimensions, so have his vocabulary and also his self-help skills. Those who care for him report he is less shy and more spontaneous and able to adapt to new situations. He is still unable to read and write. In 1995 Alonzo moved into his own apartment in Boulder, Colorado, and has the support of a carer. He has a part-time job as janitor at the local YMCA and participates in weightlifting events and has competed in the Special Olympics. According to Treffert in his book, *Islands of Genius, The Bountiful Mind of the Autistic, Acquired, and Sudden Savant* (2012, p. 115), as his art skills have broadened and improved, so too have his speech and vocabulary, and social and living skills. His special art abilities have in fact become a 'conduit to normalization'. He also now teaches his art skills by doing demonstrations of his art in schools.

The case of Alonzo is extremely enlightening. It demonstrates the positive effect of the parent as a mentor to further his artist ability, and also the gains (reported anecdotally) in other areas of adaptive functioning, self-help, language skill, and confidence in Alonzo's case, that may result from the functional application of savant skills.

Richard Wawro – a savant artist

Richard began drawing at the age of three when first given drawing materials. This is also the age at which Richard's parents were told their son was moderately to severely intellectually retarded with an estimated IQ of 30. Blind and diabetic,

FIGURE 2.2 Richard Wawro – 'Benidorm'

he also displayed the autistic characteristics of an obsession for sameness, withdrawal and bizarre mannerisms. He exhibited challenging violent behaviours combined with hyperactivity and ritualistic spinning and twirling of objects endlessly, again characteristics of autism.

At the age of six years he was enrolled in a centre for emotionally disturbed children where he was introduced to crayons. Immediately his drawing abilities increased, and by the age of twelve years his work had been described by an accomplished artist as an 'incredible phenomenon rendered with the precision of a mechanic and the vision of a poet' (Treffert, 1989, p. 89).

Richard continues to use oil-based crayon for his pictures that are remarkable in depth and colour. Because he is so near-sighted, his blindness reduced due to the removal of cataracts, he draws only centimetres from the paper. His drawings can take a few moments or several days to complete. Over 1,600 of Richard's drawings have been exhibited world-wide, all of which capture lights and shadows masterfully. He had his first exhibition at seventeen years old. One of his exhibitions in London was opened by Margaret Thatcher, who purchased several of his works. Pope John Paul II also owned several of Richard's drawings. Richard, like other savant artists, draws from his memory often having only seen the object once. He has also mentally dated each of his drawings, which sell for between $100 and $2,000.

Much of Richard's growth as an artist and as a person has been due to the unconditional support and acceptance from his parents as they nurtured his drawing ability. An award-winning documentary film entitled *With Eyes Wide Shut*, produced by Dr Becker in Texas, which featured Richard and his skill, emphasized that, as his art developed, so too did his language and socialization. There had been no trade-off of savant ability as Richard was encouraged to excel.

This case is similar to that of Alonzo, in that, following the support and mentorship given by his parents, to make the fullest use of his drawing skill Richard also appeared to make gains in other areas of functioning. His family noted qualitative improvements in his language and social skills.

Stephen Wiltshire – a contemporary savant artist

Stephen's savant artist abilities have been described in full by both Treffert (1989) and the late Oliver Sacks (1995). On several occasions, Sacks travelled with Stephen to observe at close hand his savant drawing abilities. He is quite possibly the most famous of all contemporary savant artists, having had several books published of his exceptional drawings, often depicting landmark buildings. He has been the subject of a number of television documentaries in Britain and the United States, and the subject of studies by Hermelin and O'Connor (1990a).

Stephen, born in 1974, was diagnosed with autism at the age of three. He entered a special school for developmentally delayed children at the age of four where staff soon began to notice his increasing fascination with pictures. He soon began to scribble, which he would do for long periods at a time. His initial scribblings were of cars and occasionally people and animals. He was noted for his clever caricatures of teachers. His special interest, indeed his fixation which developed when he was seven, was to draw buildings in London he had seen on school trips, or on television or in magazines. A fascination with sudden calamities, and earthquakes in particular, also developed at this stage. When drawing these, he became very excited and upset.

In 1982, a new young teacher, Chris Marris, started teaching at Stephen's school, and soon became astonished by Stephen's drawings. Chris noted that Stephen appeared to have an innate grasp of drawing techniques and perspective, along with a prodigious visual memory. Stephen was able to view the most complex buildings, or cityscapes, and retain these images and reproduce them in fine detail. Although he would draw incessantly, he appeared not to take any interest in his drawings upon completion. He would take Stephen and his class on outings in London to increase the range of topics from which to draw. These trips encouraged Stephen's verbal skills and he soon learned to name all of his favourite London landmarks.

In 1986, Chris entered some of Stephen's pictures in the National Children's Art Exhibition, with one winning a prize. Soon after, he was filmed for a BBC program on savants, and become famous throughout England. The former president of the Royal Academy of Arts, Sir Hugh Casson, described Stephen as being 'possibly the best child artist in Britain' (Sacks, 1995, p. 194). At this time, Margaret Hewson, a literary agent, took an interest in Stephen's work, publishing his first of several books of his works, *Drawings* (Wiltshire, 1987, London). She was to become a long-time advocate. Following the departure from his life of Chris Marris, his teacher, friend and mentor in 1989, Stephen appeared to lack the initiative to draw on his own. This period passed, however, once Margaret Hewson started taking Stephen on outings to help develop his works further.

Stephen's fame continued with the publication of several more books, as well as further television appearances. He travelled extensively to the United States, and Europe, with both Oliver Sacks and Margaret Hewson. In 1993, he suddenly developed savant musical skills, playing the piano and singing with exceptional ability. His music teacher described Stephen as having extraordinary powers of harmonic identification, analysis and reproduction. Whilst singing and playing, he would take on the whole range of emotions with great 'gusto' and appeared to lose his impaired affect. Sacks (1995, p. 229), who witnessed his musical performance, stated, 'It was as if Stephen, for a brief time, had become truly alive.'

Although not formally tested, it was felt that Stephen over the years has made gains with his communication and interaction skills. However, these are still limited due to his autism. He commenced art school in 1995 and continued to go out with Margaret Hewson on drawing expeditions, still requiring this personal support to continue his work. Once again, the role of the mentor (Chris Marris and Margaret Hewson) appears central to the development and practical application of the skill of the savant. This case also illustrates the use of the savant interest to teach language and interaction skills. It should also be noted that the savant appears reliant on the ongoing support of a significant person to assist with their application of their skills. Independence is rarely achieved.

In October 2006 Stephen, with the support of his family, opened the Stephen Wiltshire Gallery at the Royal Opera Arcade in Pall Mall. He is resident two days a week at the gallery producing his extraordinary drawings. He is, without doubt, a world-famous artist. I had the privilege of accompanying Stephen during his visit to Sydney in 2010 as part of Autism Spectrum Australia's Autism Month 2010 celebrations. Following a visit to the famous iconic Sydney Tower, Stephen then drew a detailed picture of the city of Sydney after viewing the city for only thirty minutes (see Figure 2.3).

It should be noted that Stephen now prefers to be known as an acclaimed artist in his own right, rather than a person with a disability with special skills. I fully support representing Stephen as an artist in his own right, which is central to the rationale for this study. Stephen provides a very positive role model for other young artist savants and what is possible with the right support and encouragement from 'mentors'. For many savants, unfortunately their savant skills or gifts go unrecognized, and they are not supported to apply their skills functionally.

FIGURE 2.3 Stephen Wiltshire – 'Sydney'

Young Australian savants

Ping Lian Yeak – 'I want to be artist'

Ping Lian is a twenty-one-year-old man with autism who displays considerable artistic savant skill. Although initially his drawing skill was not obvious, at eight years of age Ping Lian became obsessed with drawing. His mother, Sarah Lee, who was not initially aware of his artistic special skills, decided to tap into his interests and to develop his skills in drawing further.

Although he experienced fine motor difficulties as a young child, Ping Lian was immersed in a home schooling program designed to improve these skills. His mother embarked upon a dream to develop Ping Lian's skills to become an artist. Ping Lian would often use the phrase, 'I want to be artist.' Understanding the importance of nurturing and encouraging the development of Ping Lian's skills in art, Sarah Lee immersed Ping Lian in the art world and employed three different art teachers to foster his skills.

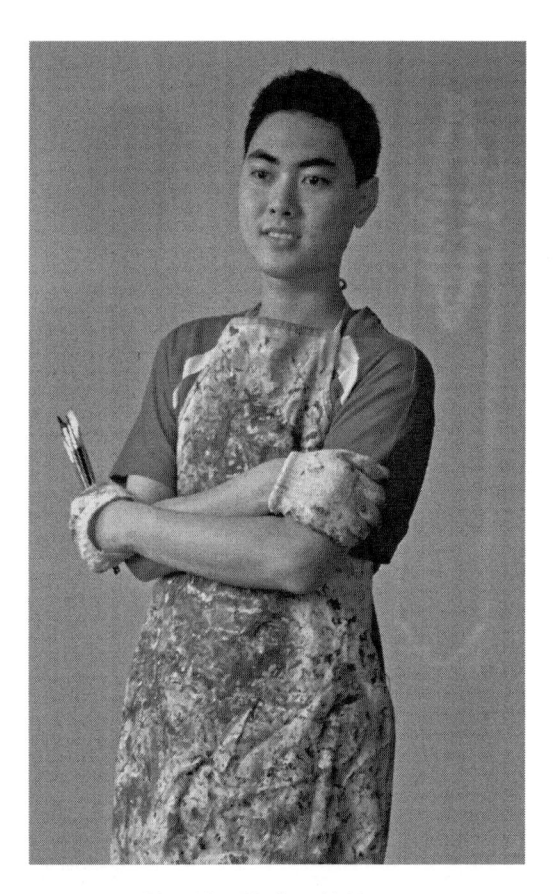

FIGURE 2.4 Ping Lian Yeak – 2014

FIGURE 2.5 Ping Lian Yeak – 'Sydney Opera House – Lunar Park'

Sarah Lee worked tirelessly to nurture the skills of her autistic son. She researched the relationship between autism and art, eventually making contact with Dr Treffert, who confirmed that Ping Lian displayed considerable artistic skill. Dr Treffert supported Sarah Lee's dream to develop Ping Lian's skills to become an artist, which inspired her to continue to shape and cultivate his love of drawing and painting. She encouraged art teachers to further assist Ping Lian to develop more sophisticated drawing and painting skills. In a very short period of time, Ping Lian's talent in art increased and was marked by his first art exhibition in 2006, in New York City, when he was just twelve years of age.

I recall several years ago receiving a call from Sarah Lee whilst the family was still living in Malaysia. She explained that the family was planning to move to Sydney and needed to find a school for Ping Lian. In May 2006, he was enrolled in one of Autism Spectrum Australia's (Aspect's) eight schools for children with autism. After moving to Sydney, based on what she had learned from Ping Lian's art teachers, Sarah Lee continued mentoring Ping Lian to further enhance and advance his savant skills.

Today, Ping Lian is renowned as an 'international prodigious artist'. His artwork ranges from flowers to animals and people to buildings from around the world. His latest exhibition in New York City is entitled 'Architectural Impressions', showing Ping Lian's imaginative and colourful interpretation of various architectural structures throughout the world. Ping Lian has now exhibited his works in a number of countries, including Australia, the United States, UK, Germany, Japan, Korea, Singapore and Malaysia. At only fifteen years of age, Ping Lian opened his personal gallery in Malaysia – 'Ping Lian @ The Art Commune' – which features a permanent showcase of his works in Malaysia. Ping Lian's art and story has been featured in several books including Darold Terfferts's *Island of Genius*, 2012.

With the support, guidance and encouragement he and his mother received from both Dr Treffert and Dr Rosa C. Martinez, Ping Lian also participated in an art exhibition, 'Windows of Genius: Artwork of the Prodigious Savant' in 2007, at the Windhover Center for the Arts in Fond du Lac, which displayed over one hundred artworks from eleven savant artists from around the world. Some of his works were also featured at the United Nations Headquarters in New York in honour of the inaugural ceremony in 2008 for World Autism Awareness Day in perpetuity, organized by Dr Rosa C. Martinez. It is important to note the mentoring role that both Dr Treffert and Dr Martinez provided to Ping Lian's mother, which she believes helped her to become a strong mentor and advocate for her son.

Through his art, Ping Lian has inspired a great deal of hope for other young savants and highlights the very important role of a mentor, in this case his mother, in nurturing and supporting the autistic savant to make functional and productive use of their skills. Ping Lian still lives with his family in Sydney, where he continues to produce his very unique artworks. For further information about Ping Lian's remarkable talent, view his website at www.pinglian.com.

Tim Sharp

Tim is twenty-six years old and is an accomplished artist. In his own words, Tim refers to himself as being 'a world-famous artist', which is indeed the case, with his many joyful artworks and drawings, involving his superhero creation, Laser Beak Man, now exhibited around the world. From the Powerhouse Museum in Brisbane, to the Museum of Contemporary Art in Sydney, to the Museum of Modern Art in New York, some of the world's best galleries have showcased Tim's artworks. His superhero Laser Beak Man has gone on to inspire an eight-part animated children's TV series and, very recently, a Broadway play in New York. The story of Tim and his mother Judy's journey, from autism diagnosis to world-renowned artist, will provide further insight into how savants can be assisted to apply their special abilities.

Having just been diagnosed with autism at the age of three years, the diagnosing specialist told Judy and her husband that Tim would be a burden for the rest of his life and that he would end up in an institution. He suggested that they put their son away and forget about him as there was no hope. Like many parents of children with autism, Judy decided to do anything and everything for her son. With the support of Tim's paediatrician, Judy embarked on a program of speech and occupational therapy after it was confirmed that Tim had severe autism of the low-functioning kind.

Tim was enrolled in a specialist Autism Centre at four years of age. Following further specialist advice, which indicated that in fact Tim may not be autistic but instead developmentally delayed with mild autistic characteristics, Judy enrolled him part-time in a regular mainstream kindergarten as a trial rather than enrol him in a special pre-school or school. It was at this time that Tim first showed an interest in watching his mother draw pictures. Although he refused to draw himself, Judy used drawings as a form of communication to explain to Tim everything he did in a day, everywhere they would go, what he was to do, and how he was to behave. It would take almost one year before Tim did his very first drawing. From then on, art became a daily activity in their home, which made Tim very happy.

Tim commenced his schooling in a special-education unit located in a mainstream school.

From the beginning Tim showed considerable talent in drawing. His mother reports he was meticulous at colouring and quickly became known for his hand-drawn Christmas cards. From the moment he started to draw, he has not stopped. As a boy, Tim drew Transformers and Pokémon characters and Thomas the Tank Engine. He started to develop characters of his own, and by the age of nine or ten he started to develop stories about these characters, making them come to life. Like most boys, Tim liked superheroes and became infatuated with Batman cartoons. When he drew superheroes, he would have them acting out scenes and his drawings always portrayed a definite sense of humour.

When Tim was eleven years old, he informed his mother that he was going to be Laser Beak Man when he grew up. He began drawing his humorous Laser Beak

FIGURE 2.6 Tim Sharp – 'A Large Sunburnt Country'

Man all the time, and quickly moved to adding a cast of characters including a villain called Peter Bartman, Concrete and Tomato Man, and a vehicle that drilled under the earth called Thriller Driller. Tim's characters were originally borrowed from film and television but gradually developed their own personalities through Tim's drawings. It was clear that Tim's talent for drawing was well in advance of his school-age peers.

Tim's artistic skills continued to develop during his teenage years. His high-school art teacher, Megan Kerr, encouraged and supported Tim's very individual style of drawing although it did not fit the requirements of the school art curriculum. Art began to open up a whole new world for him and, although he tried a range of different mediums including sculpture, lino printing and painting, he still continued to draw obsessively with half his drawings being of things and places he was interested in, like the ancient ruins of Greece, and the other half were pictures of Laser Beak Man. At this time, and due to the family's lack of money, Tim began drawing homemade birthday cards featuring Laser Beak Man, which were quickly recognized for their artistic skill by friends and family. The director of a local arts organization that supports artists with disabilities, Access Arts, was shown one of Tim's birthday cards. He contacted Judy immediately, announcing that 'Tim is a talented artist. We need to promote him.'

Tim's journey to becoming a fully-fledged artist had begun. In March 2003, Tim – or, to be accurate, Laser Beak Man – received an invitation to the Very Special Arts Festival, known as the VSA in Washington, DC, which was to be held in June 2004. The VSA was an international non-profit organization founded by Jean Kennedy Smith, the sister of John F. Kennedy, in 1974. It should be noted that Tim was also fascinated by America and displayed a considerable savant memory for all the presidents of the United States, their dates of birth, dates of death and the years they were in office. Although Judy could not afford to pay to take Tim to the VSA, she was determined that Tim would not miss out on this very important step in his artistic career. Through her determination, she eventually raised the funds and Tim, Judy and his brother Sam attended the VSA. Tim was given the honour of being the Australian flag bearer at the official opening ceremony, which was one of the most important milestones in his life. Given the huge honour of being the only Australian to be invited to show his artworks at the VSA, Judy thought it only fitting that Tim deserved some media coverage. She contacted the Australian Broadcasting Corporation's television program *Australian Story*, who immediately agreed to make a story of Tim and his family. As a result, a television crew accompanied Tim and his family to the United States and the subsequent story was shown on Australian television in 2004.

Tim continued to make more and more art and his reputation as an artist continued to grow. He had his first art exhibition in Brisbane's Hands on Art gallery, which was opened by the then Governor of Queensland, Ms Quentin Bryce, who later became the Governor-General of Australia. On finishing high school in 2005, Tim continued to draw with his pictures becoming increasingly adventurous. He was invited to exhibit his art in a number of galleries and travelling exhibitions, the result being that Tim's artworks were in great demand. As soon as Tim finished an artwork, it was purchased by an eager buyer. His pictures, with their obvious sense of humour and wit, appeared to be not only an expression of his great drawing skills, but Tim's way of communicating his own view of the world, given his life-long struggles with communication and language as a result of his autism.

During an exhibition of Tim's art at the Brisbane Powerhouse Museum in 2009, Laser Beak Man was noticed by two television animators who were in the process of developing ideas for submission to the Australian Broadcasting Corporation (ABC) for a an animated series for a new ABC children's channel. The series went to air in 2009 with resounding success. By 2011, the series had been sold to cartoon Network Asia Pacific and was shown throughout the Asia-Pacific region. Tim was the first person in the world with autism who had made a television series, paving the way for other artists and animators with autism.

Tim and Laser Beak Man went on to further acclaim, with a play being made based on his character in 2011 in collaboration with Cate Blanchett, the Sydney Theater Company and an interstate theatre, that specialized in making theatre with people with disabilities. The US band the Ghost Ballerinas produced a song inspired by the titles of one of Tim's artworks, with Tim doing the artwork for their album cover. In 2014, through the efforts of two hard-working members of the Dead Puppet Society, the Laser Beak Man show opened in New York at the New Victory Theater on Broadway.

Tim's incredible journey, starting with his diagnosis of autism at three years of age, to that of 'world-famous artist', has been the result of the very strong mentoring and advocacy by his mother, and also from a number of other significant people in Tim's life. Although not officially classified as an autistic savant, his mother preferring not to define her son by his condition, Tim's remarkable drawing abilities, and also his memory for information about topics that interest him, are similar to the abilities of the young savants described above. The underlying factor in Tim's success, and indeed the very productive application of his artist skills, has been the important role of mentor, in Tim's case his mother Judy.

As awareness grows of the skills and abilities of those with autism, so too does the number of examples of applied skills emerge. The cases overviewed in this chapter merely serve to illustrate what can be achieved by nurturing, appreciating and celebrating the 'strengths' of this extraordinary people. The future may just be looking brighter for the autistic savant.

Several key elements or factors appear to have served as catalysts in the transformation of savant abilities or gifts into productive talents. It is clear from the stories of Alonzo, Richard, Stephen, Ping Lian, and also of Tim, that what is required to support young autistic savants to achieve, and to become accomplished in their area of skill, is a differentiated approach to their support and skill development, which also includes the incredibly important role of mentor. Mentors, whether they be parents, teachers or other significant people in the lives of the savant, act as powerful environmental catalysts to transform the savant skill into a productive talent (Gagné, 2009). The majority made gains in language and social functioning, according to anecdotal reports. Many seemed to gain a great deal of reinforcement and pleasure from their savant performances, showing signs of increased self-confidence.

The fact that the majority of these cases of applied savant skills were arts based, being either musical or drawing or sculpting abilities, may suggest that these types of skills are more easily applied than other skills, such as calendar calculating. All skills, however, appeared to have a superior memory basis and developed early on in the life of each savant.

Any differentiated program for savants should therefore be inclusive of mentors, further training, and opportunities to both engage in their interests and to receive praise and reinforcement for their achievements. Adaptive functioning should be the aim of such programs, to remove savant abilities from what Treffert (1989) refers to as the 'Gee Whiz' category.

> The time has come to take out the 'Gee Whiz' category and learn what we can about them, and from them, not just about memory and brain function, but about human potential and possibilities as well. Beyond any scientific significance is the inspiration and hope that these stories provide for other handicapped persons and their caretakers.
>
> (Treffert, 1989, p. xiv)

The research questions

Both the rationale for the study and the review of the literature, as outlined in both Chapters 1 and 2, have informed the development of the research questions. The research questions have been divided into three separate areas of inquiry:

A) the *nature of savant skills* which aims to add to the existing literature on savant skills;
B) *change for the better* as a result of the differentiated curriculum;
C) *change for the worse or no change* as a result of the curriculum.

A. The nature of savant skills

Obsessiveness and savant skills

Q.1. How much time do subjects spend involved in their area(s) of skill?

Q.2. Do subjects become distressed if unable to access their savant interests?

Development of skills

Q.3. Is the development of savant skills related to the child's motivation and interest in their skill area(s)?

Q.4. Did the savant skills develop at an early age?

Q.5. Have the savant skills of the subjects developed through formal training?

Q.6. Is there any evidence of giftedness or superior ability in other family members?

Level and types of savant skills

Q.7. Are there different levels of savant abilities?

Q.8. Can all savant skills be classified according to Treffert's (1989) Savant I and II classification?

Q.9. Do all subjects display multiple savant skills?

Q.10. Do all subjects demonstrate memory abilities?

Q.11. Do subjects employ imaginative and creative methods in their savant skill interests and activities?

Behaviour and savant skills

Q.12. Do all subjects display challenging behaviours?

B. Change for the better

Functional application of skills

Q.13. Has the often unproductive (of limited or no functional use) savant/splinter skills found in the autistic population 'been applied' in a functional manner through the implementation of a differentiated curriculum that focuses upon these skills or gifts?

Q.14. Are the savant skills represented in this study able to be 'applied' successfully in a teaching/mentoring program?

Communication skills

Q.15. Has an improvement in the communication skills of the subject's occurred as a result of the Savant Skill Curriculum intervention?

Social skills and behaviour

Q.16. Has an improvement in the social skills and behaviour of the subjects occurred as a result of the Savant Skill Curriculum intervention?

Self-esteem

Q.17. Has there been an increase in the academic self-esteem of the subjects as a result of the study?

Degree of autism

Q.18. Has there be a change in the degree of autism of each subject as a result of the study?

C. Change for the worse or no change

Savant skills

Q.19. Have the subject's savant skills remained the same, been reduced or lost over the period of the Savant Skill Curriculum intervention?

References

Anastasi, A., and Levee, R. (1960). Intellectual defect and musical talent: A case report. *American Journal of Mental Deficiency, 64*, 695–703.

Baharloo, S., Service, S.K., Risch, N., Gitschier, J., and Freimer, N.B. (2000). Familial aggregation of absolute pitch. *American Journal of Human Genetics, 67*, 655–658.

Baron-Cohen, S., Ashwin, E., Ashwin, C., Tavassoli, T., and Chakrabarti, B. (2009). Talent in autism: Hyper-systemizing, hyper-attention to detail and sensory hypersensitivity. *Philosophical Transactions of the Royal Society, 364*, 1377–1383.

Bertone, A., Mottron, L., Jelenic, P., and Faubert, J. (2003). Motion perception in autism: a 'complex' issue. *Journal of Cognition and Neuroscience, 15*, 218–225.

Boddaert, N., Barthelemy, C., Poline, J.B., Samson, Y., Brunelle, F., and Zilbovicius, M. (2005). Autism: Functional brain mapping of exceptional calendar capacity. *British Journal of Psychiatry, 187*, 83–86.

Brink, T.L. (1980). Idiot savant with unusual mechanical ability: An organic explanation. *American Journal of Psychiatry, 137*, 250–251.

Charness, N., Clifton, J., and MacDonald, L. (1988). Case study of a musical 'mono-savant': A cognitive-psychological focus. In L. Obler and D.A. Fein (Eds.), *The Exceptional Brain* (pp. 277–293). New York: Guilford.

Clark, T.R. (2005). Autistic savants: educational strategies for the functional application of savant and splinter skills in children with autism and Asperger's disorder. Paper presented at the Autism Spectrum Australia Research Forum, 23–24/07/2005, Sydney, Australia: Autism Spectrum Australia (Aspect).

Comer, D. (1985). Musical talent brightens life in a blind severely retarded man. *The Toronto Star*, 16 May, p. 6.

Ericsson, K.A., and Faivre, I. (1988). What's exceptional about exceptional abilities? In L. Obler and D.A. Fein (Eds.), *The Exceptional Brain* (pp. 436–473). New York: Guilford Press.

Ericsson, K., Roring, R., and Nandagopal, K. (2007). Giftedness and evidence for reproducibly superior performance: An account based on the expert performance framework. *High Abilities Studies*, *18*, 3–56.

Fein, D., and Obler, L.K. (1988). Neuropsychological study of talent: A developing field. In L. Obler and D.A. Fein (Eds.), *The Exceptional Brain* (pp. 3–18). New York: Guilford Press.

Feldman, D.H. (1993). Child prodigies: A distinctive form of giftedness, *Gifted Child Quarterly*, *37*, 188.

Frith, U. (1989). *Autism: Explaining the Enigma*. Oxford: Blackwell.

Gagné, F (2009). Building gifts into talents: Detailed overview of the DMGT 2.0. In B. MacFarlane and T. Stambaugh (Eds.), *Leading Change in Gifted Education: The Festschrift of Dr. Joyce VanTassel-Baska* (pp. 61–80). Waco, TX: Prufock Press.

Gardner, H. (1983). *Frames of Mind: The Theory of Multiple Intelligences*. New York: Harper and Row.

Goldberg, T.E. (1987). On hermetic reading abilities. *Journal of Autism and Developmental Disorders*, *17*, 29–44.

Happé, F.G.E. (1995). The role of age and verbal ability in the theory of mind task performance of subjects with autism. *Child Development*, *66*, 843–855.

Heaton, P., Davis, R.E., and Happé, F.G. (2008). Research note: Exceptional absolute pitch perception for spoken words in able adult with autism. *Neuropsychologia*, 46, 2095–2098.

Heaton, P., and Wallace, G.L. (2004). Annotation: The savant syndrome. *Journal of Child Psychology and Psychiatry*, *45(5)*, 899–911.

Hermelin, B. (2001). *Bright Splinters of the Mind: A Personal Story of Research with Autistic Savants*. London: Kingsley.

Hermelin, B., and O'Connor, N. (1986). Idiot savant calendrical calculators: Rules and regularities. *Psychological Medicine*, *16*, 1–9.

Hermelin, B., and O'Connor, N. (1990a). Art and accuracy: The drawing ability of idiot-savants. *Journal of Child Psychology and Psychiatry and Allied Disciplines*, *31*, 217–228.

Hermelin, B., and O'Connor, N. (1990b). Factors and primes: A specific numerical ability. *Psychological Medicine*, 20, 163–169.

Hermelin, B., O'Connor, N., and Lee, S. (1987). Musical inventiveness of five idiot-savants. *Psychological Medicine*, *17*, 79–90.

Hermelin, B., O'Connor, N., Lee, S., and Treffert, D. (1989). Intelligence and musical improvisation. *Psychological Medicine*, *19*, 447–457.

Hill, A.L. (1974) Idiot savants: A categorization of abilities. *Mental Retardation*, December, 12–13.

Hill, A.L. (1978). Savants: Mentally retarded individuals with special skills. In N. Ellis (Ed.), *International Review of Research in Mental Retardation*, *9* (pp. 277–298). New York: Academic Press.

Ho, E., Tsang, A., and Ho, D. (1991). An investigation of the calendar calculation ability of a Chinese calendar savant. *Journal of Autism and Developmental Disorders*, *21*, 315–327.

Hoffman, E., and Reeves, R. (1979). An idiot savant with unusual mechanical ability. *American Journal of Psychiatry, 136,* 713–714.

Horwitz, W.A., Kestenbaum, C., Person, E., and Jarvick, L. (1965). Identical twins – 'idiot savants' – calendar calculators. *American Journal of Psychiatry, 121,* 1075–1079.

Howe, M.J.A. (1989). *Fragments of Genius: The Strange Feats of Idiot Savants.* London: Routledge.

Jordan, R. (2008). Practical implications of memory characteristics in autism spectrum disorders. In J. Boucher and D. Bowler (Eds.), *Memory in Autism* (pp. 203–308). Cambridge: Cambridge University Press.

Leekham, S.R., Neito, C., Libby, S.J., Wing, L., and Gould, J. (2001). Describing the sensory abnormalities of children and adults with autism. *Journal of Autism and Developmental Disorders, 37,* 894–910.

Miller, L.K. (1989). *Musical Savants: Exceptional skill in the Mentally Retarded.* Hillsdale, NJ: Erlbaum.

Miller, L.K. (1998). Defining the savant syndrome. *Journal of Developmental Physical Disability, 10,* 73–85.

Mottron, L., Burack, J.A., Stauder, J. E., and Robaey, P. (1999). Perceptual processing among high-functioning persons with autism. *Journal of Child Psychology and Psychiatry, 40,* 203–211.

Nettlebeck, T., and Young, R.L. (1999). Savant syndrome. In L. Masters Glidden (Ed.), *International Review of Research in Mental Retardation, 22,* 137–173.

O'Connor, N. (1989). The performance of the 'idiot savant': Implicit and explicit. *British Journal of Disorders, 24,* 1–20.

O'Connor, N., and Hermelin, B. (1984). Idiot savant calendrical calculators: Maths or memory? *Psychological Medicine, 14,* 801–806.

O'Connor, N., and Hermelin, B. (1987). Visual and graphic abilities of the idiot savant artist. *Psychological Medicine, 17,* 79–90.

O'Connor, N., and Hermelin, B. (1989). The memory structure of autistic idiot savant mnemonists. *British Journal of Psychology, 80,* 97–111.

O'Connor, N., and Hermelin, B. (1990). The recognition failure and graphic success of idiot savant artists. *Journal of Child Psychology and Psychiatry and Allied Disciplines, 31,* 203–215.

O'Connor, N., and Hermelin, B. (1991). Talents and preoccupations in idiot-savants. *Psychological Medicine, 21,* 959–964.

O'Neill, M., and Jones, R.S.P. (1997). Sensory perceptual abnormalities in autism. A case for research? *Journal of Autism and Developmental Disorders, 27(3),* 283–293.

O'Riordan, M., and Passetti, F. (2006). Discrimination in autism within different sensory modalities. *Journal of Autism and Developmmental Disorders, 36,* 665–675.

Perin, R., Berger, T.K., and Markram, H. (2011). A synaptic organising principle for cortical neuronal groups. *Proceedings of the National Academy of Sciences, 108(13),* 5419–5424.

Pesenti, M., Zago, L., Crivello, F., Mellet, E., Samson, D., Duroux, B., et al. (2001). Mental calculation in a prodigy is sustained by right frontal and medial temporal areas. *Nature Neuroscience, 4,* 103–107.

Pring, L., Hermelin, B., and Heavey, L. (1995). Savants, segments, art and autism. *Journal of Child Psychology and Psychiatry, 36,* 1065–1076.

Pring, L., Ryder, N., Crane, L., and Hermelin, B. (2011). Creativity in savant artists with autism. *Autism, 16,* 45–57.

Rimland, B. (1978). Inside the mind of the autistic savant. *Psychology Today, 12,* 68–80.

Rosen, A.M. (1981). Adult calendar calculators in a psychiatric OPD: A report of two cases and comparative analysis of abilities. *Journal of Autism and Developmental Disorders, 11,* 285–292.

Sacks, O. (1985). The twins. *New York Review of Books*, *32*, 16–20.

Sacks, O. (1995). *An Anthropologist on Mars*. London: Picador.

Scheerer, M., Rothman, E., and Goldstein, K. (1945). A case of 'idiot savant': An experimental study of personality organization. *Psychological Monographs*, *58(4)*, 1–63.

Selfe, L. (1977). *Nadia: A Case of Extraordinary Ability in an Autistic Child*. New York: Academic Press.

Snyder, A.W., and Mitchell, D.J. (1999). Is integer arithmetic fundamental to mental processing? The mind's secret arithmetic. *Proceedings of the Royal Society. Biological Sciences*, *266(1419)*, 537–647.

Snyder, A.W., and Thomas, M. (1997). Autistic artists give clues to cognition. *Perception*, *26*, 93–96.

Spitz, H.H. (1995). Calendar calculating idiot savants and the smart unconscious. *New Ideas in Psychology*, *13*, 167–182.

Stevens, D.E., and Moffitt, T.E. (1988). Neuropsychological profile of an Asperger's syndrome case with exceptional calculating ability. *Clinical Neuropsychologist*, *2*, 228–238.

Strauss, V. (2013). Howard Gardner: 'Multiple intelligences' are not 'learning styles'. *Washington Post*. Retrieved from www.washingtonpost.com/blogs/answer-sheet/wp/2013/10/16/howard-gardner-m.

Tomchek, S.D. and Dunn, W. (2007). Sensory processing in children with and without autism. a comparative study using the short sensory profile. *American Journal of Occupational Therapy*, 61, 190–200.

Torrance, E.P. (1974). *Torrance Tests of Creative Thinking*. Bensenville, IU: Scholastic Testing Service, Inc.

Tredgold, A.F. (1914). *Mental Deficiency*. New York: William Wood.

Treffert, D. (1989). *Extraordinary People*. London: Bantam Press.

Treffert, D. (2012). *Islands of Genius: The Bountiful Mind of the Autistic, Acquired, and Sudden Savant*. London: Jessica Kingsley Publishers.

Treffert, D. (2013). Savant Syndrome. A compelling case for innate talent. In S.B. Kaufman (Ed.), *The Complexity of Greatness. Beyond Talent or Practice* (pp. 103–118). New York: Oxford University Press.

Wallace, G.L. (2008). Neuropsychological studies of savant skills: Can they inform the neuroscience of giftedness? *Roeper Review*, *30*, 229–246.

Witshire, S. (1987). *Drawings*. London: J.M. Dent & Sons.

Young, R.L. (1995). Savant syndrome: Processes underlying extraordinary abilities. Unpublished doctoral dissertation: University of Adelaide, South Australia.

Young, R.L., and Nettlebeck, T. (1994). The 'intelligence' of calendrical calculators. *American Journal of Mental Retardation*, *99*, 186–200.

Young, R.L., and Nettlebeck, T. (1995). The abilities of a musical savant and his family. *Journal of Autism and Developmental Disorders*, *25*, 231–248.

3

A SOLUTION – THE *SAVANT SKILL CURRICULUM*

Advancing knowledge of rare phenomena – a unique research design for a unique population

Meeting the exceptional needs of autistic pupils often means adopting strategies that are outside the normal repertoire of teaching techniques'
(Powell and Jordan, 1992, p. 417)

The *Savant Skill Curriculum* is an example of the use of alternative strategies that are often required in the education of the student with autism. By looking through the double-lenses of gifted and autism education, and the subsequent merging of successful strategies from both, the design and development of the *Savant Skill Curriculum* was possible. An overview of the conceptual framework follows which will help to explain the thinking behind the merging of these two distinct but interlinked fields of gifted and autism education.

Savant syndrome and models of giftedness and talent

Although many definitions of what constitutes giftedness and/or intelligence have been put forward in the literature, with some leading to the identification and differentiated curricula for the gifted student, few in fact are able to accommodate the savant (Davis and Rimm, 2004; DeHaan and Havighurst, 1961; Feldhusen, 1986; Gagné, 1995, 2009; Gardner, 1983; Marland, 1972; Renzulli, 1978; Sternberg, 1981; Sternberg and Davidson, 2005; Tannenbaum, 1983). Where definitions include 'high intelligence' as one of the ways someone may be classified as gifted, the savant, who may present with a 'low general intelligence', is therefore excluded. A definition that is more inclusive of the savant is Gagné's 2009 Differentiated Model of Giftedness and Talent (DMGT), revised from his original 1995 version (see Figure 3.1). For talent to emerge, causal contributions from many sources are required, among them high natural abilities (gifts), motivation, perseverance, supportive parents and teachers, as well as long-term investment in

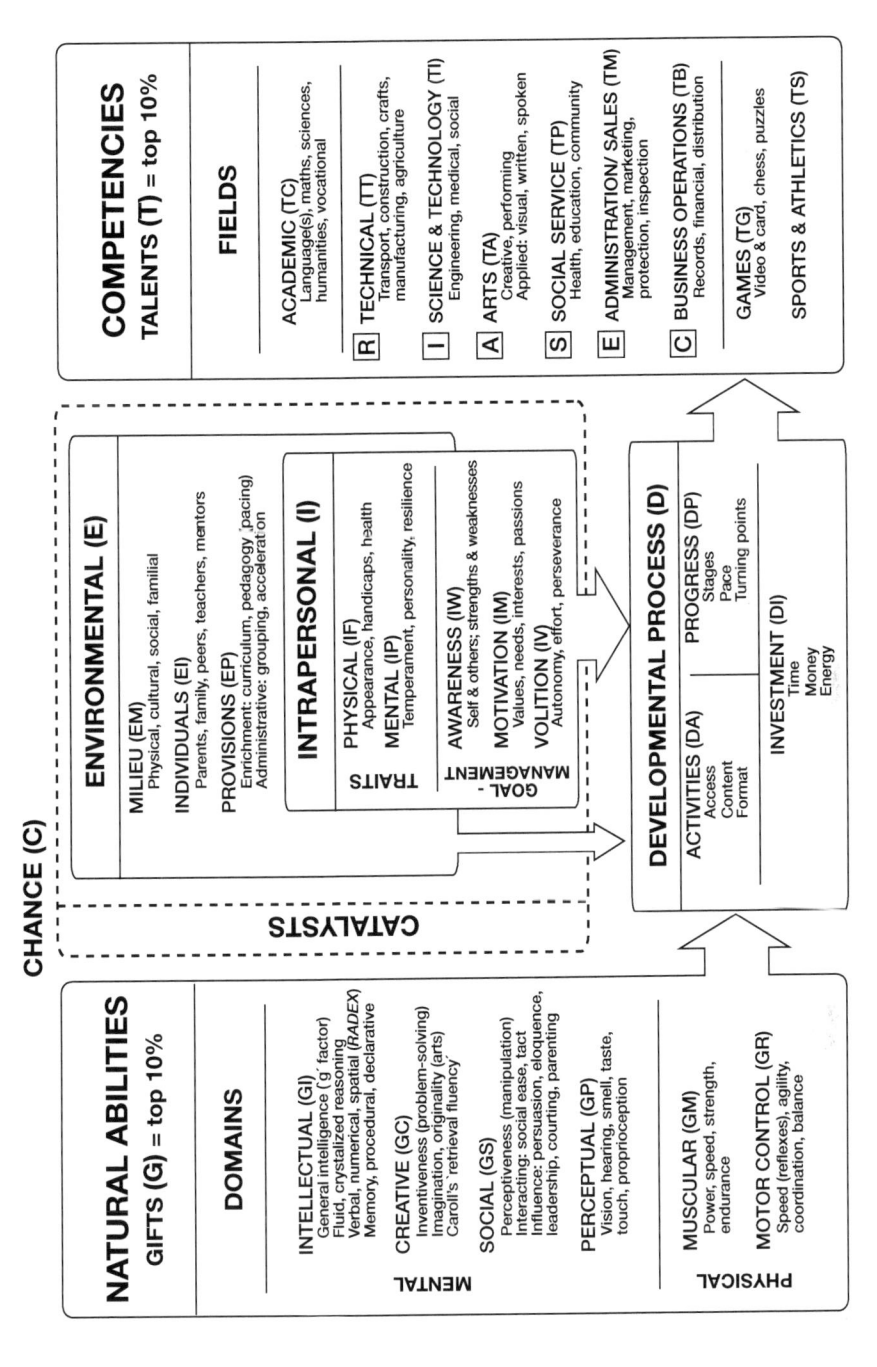

FIGURE 3.1 Gagné's Differentiated Model of Giftedness and Talent (2009)

learning, training and practising. These causal contributions form the basis of Gagne's DMGT and equally apply to the case of the autistic savant.

It is this model of giftedness and talent that underpins the conceptual framework of the *Savant Skill Curriculum*, which is primarily focused on applying the sometimes unproductive savant gift or skill, in a functional and meaningful manner. Gagné's view of giftedness and talent associates giftedness with untrained natural human abilities called 'gifts' or 'aptitudes' in at least one ability domain, to a degree that places an individual at least among the top 10 per cent of age peers. Talent designates the superior outstanding mastery of systematically developed abilities or skills (competencies) and knowledge, in at least one field of human activity, to a degree that places an individual within at least the top 10 per cent of age peers who are or have been active in that field or fields, which constitute expertise in a particular field of human activity or endeavour (Gagné, 1995, 2009). From these definitions of giftedness and talent, a simple definition for talent development (D) is extracted.

These three components, giftedness (G), talent (T) and the talent development process (D), constitute the trio of components of the DMGT. Two additional components complete the structure of the DMGT theory: intrapersonal catalysts (I) and environmental catalysts (E). The DMGT proposes six subcomponents of 'natural abilities' or 'gifts' (see Figure 3.1), four of them mental: intellectual (GI), creative (GG), social (GS) and perceptual (GP). The last two are physical abilities – muscular (GM) abilities devoted to larger physical movements, and abilities associated with fine motor control (GR); both contribute to physical activities, e.g. tennis, gymnastics. These natural abilities are controlled by the individual's genetic endowment or are considered to be 'innate' abilities. The fields in which talents or 'competencies' may be expressed are extremely diverse, highlighting many talent fields relevant to school-age youth. Nine talent subcomponents or 'competencies' are included, most of which are easily assessed.

Talent development (D) is defined as the systematic pursuit by talentees, over a significant period of time, of a structured program of activities leading to a specific excellence goal. Talent development has subcomponents: activities (DA), investment (DI) and progress (DP). Talent development begins when a child gains access through identification or selection to a systematic, talent-oriented program of activities. These may include a specific content (DAC), the curriculum, offered within a specific learning program (DAF). His model proposes a clear distinction between the two basic concepts of giftedness and talent.

This differentiation between giftedness and talent may be applied to the education of the savant. All savants display particular 'natural gifts' or 'aptitudes' in one or more savant skill domains (memory, art, music, mechanical, calendar and/or arithmetic calculation, athletic skill, hyperlexic skill, sensory sensitivities), but these remain largely undeveloped, being essentially 'rigid and obsessive' by nature and more often than not remain unproductive (Treffert, 1989). My experience teaching autistic savants has led me to believe that savants who are able to have their savant skills or talents assessed by standardized measures would in fact meet the criteria for inclusion as performing among the top 10 per cent of age peers. The deficits associated with autism, however, combine to impact negatively on performance on standardized testing. Rarely, however, are the savant's gifts or skills transformed through either intrapersonal or environmental catalysts, or by means of the talent development process (D) into productive and meaningful talents (Treffert, 1989, 2012). As discussed in the literature review in Chapter 2, there have been very few cases of savants who have achieved meaningful careers. Given that we now know that 30 per cent of adults with autism display savant skills, this is concerning. Few would, in fact, have mastered their field of human activity to a degree that places them within the top 10 per cent of age peers, or be classified as fully talented or competent. The term 'quasi-talent' could in fact be used to describe cases of savant achievement, or performance, as more often than not the skill fails to develop into a complete talent (Sacks, 1995). The term 'fragments of genius', akin to 'quasi-talents', is used by Howe (1989) to describe savant abilities.

The *Savant Skill Curriculum* has therefore been planned as an environmental catalyst (E), involving the significant factors of individuals (EI) – parents, teachers and mentors; a provision (EP) – the *Savant Curriculum* which included gifted and autism educational strategies; and chance, the chance factor of this study having been developed, and the students identified as subjects. The *Curriculum* also has acted as an intrapersonal catalyst by harnessing the intrapersonal catalyst of motivation (IM) of the child in their savant interest and passions to develop the savant natural gifts or skills into talents or competencies. The motivation the autistic savant displays when engaged in their savant area of interest has also been harnessed to attempt to teach both communication and social skills; the primary deficits of autism, as well as a 'reinforcement' for appropriate behaviours. This was the secondary aim of the *Savant Skill Curriculum*: to improve the adaptive functioning of the savant, which would then support the facilitation of the savant skills into talents.

In this model, rather than viewing performance in the top 10 per cent of the age-peers, it is more appropriate to instead make reference to Treffert's levels of savant ability – Savant I (Talented Savants) and Savant II (Prodigious Savants) as a more suitable performance indicator. The Developmental Process (D) has also been given a greater emphasis in the model as it is the most crucial element in the process of translating gifts into talents for these disabled students. It should be stressed that the implementation and the degree of success of the *Savant Skill Curriculum*, for any student, requires a great deal of investment (DI) in time and energy. Any attempt to support the development of savant skills into talent will take a long-term commitment from teacher, parents, families and mentors beyond the period of the *Curriculum* itself. As in the talent development of the non-disabled gifted student, the development process is long term, and is what will make a difference, in translating savant skills into productive talents. To further explain the thinking behind the *Savant Skill Curriculum* and the facilitation of savant skills into productive talent, a new model was developed based upon the DMGT – the Model for Savant Skill and Talent Development (Clark, 2011). The model goes further than the DMGT by including the disability of autism and its impact on adaptive functioning,

Model for Savant Skill and Talent Development – Clark, 2011

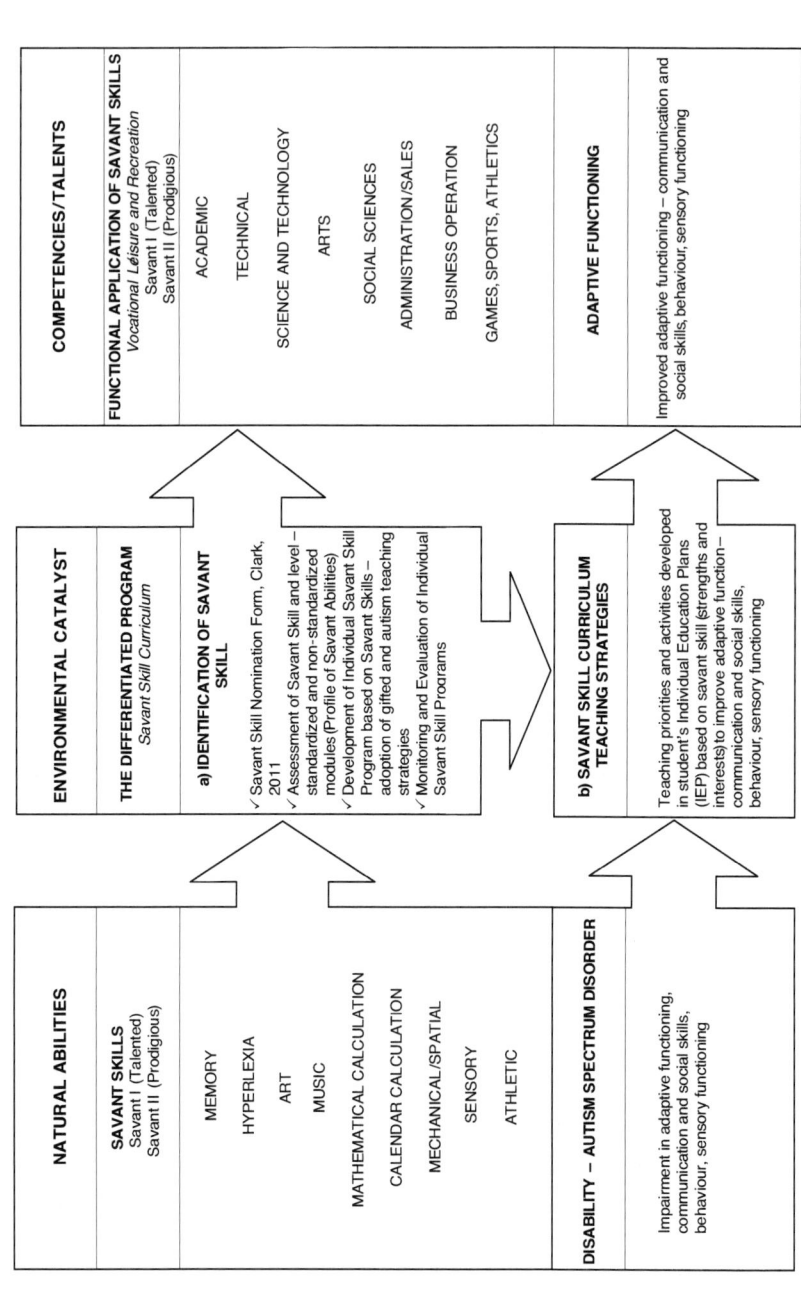

FIGURE 3.2 Model for Savant Skill and Talent Development – T.R. Clark, 2011

and includes savant skill teaching strategies directed towards improved adaptive functioning: communication and social skills, and behaviour. Improvements in adaptive functioning will further facilitate the functional application of savant skills into competencies and/or talents – see Figure 3.2, Model for Savant Skill and Talent Development (Clark, 2011).

The *Savant Skill Curriculum* explained

The *Savant Skill Curriculum*, which serves autistic savants regardless of the degree or level of their savant ability, has been developed by merging a range of educational strategies which are appropriate for both the non-disabled gifted student, and also for the student with autism. Many educational strategies have been proposed for the education of the gifted student (Renzulli, 1977; Maker, 1982; Siegle, 2007a, 2007b; VanTassel-Baska and Wood, 2009; Sak, 2011). However, only three key such strategies were selected or 'borrowed' for inclusion in the *Savant Skill Curriculum*. They include: acceleration, enrichment and mentorships (see Chapter 4). The fourth strategy, based upon the commonly accepted educational practices in autism of facilitating the communication, social skills and appropriate behaviours, is unique in that activities have been designed to this purpose, based upon the savant skills and interests of the children. The synthesis of these educational strategies from the fields of gifted and autism education has never been used before and is therefore unique to the *Curriculum*.

The use of one-to-one 'mentors' has been incorporated as a key strategy as the student with autism is more likely to benefit educationally from an individualized teaching program. It should be noted that, currently, the Individual Education Plan, which involves a structured teaching program, is the generally accepted model of educational programming in the field of special education, including autism (Lansing and Schopler, 1978; Schopler and Mesibov, 1992; Aspect Comprehensive Approach for Education, 2012). The use of individualized learning for the gifted, particularly in relation to gifted programs in the regular classroom, is also considered to be an important educational strategy (Feldhusen and Baska, 1989).

Although a variety of interventions and therapies are available to those with autism, a great deal of controversy still exists as to which intervention or program is the more successful in overcoming the deficits of autism (National Autism Centre, 2009; National Research Council, 2001; Odom, Boyd, Hall and Hume, 2010; Rutter, 1998; Wong et al., 2013). It is reassuring, however, to see the growing numbers of evidence-based interventions in the field of autism. Only autism-specific support strategies commonly accepted as successful for the student with autism were included in the fourth component of the *Curriculum*. These strategies include: the use of social stories (Barry and Burlew, 2004; Campbell and Tincani, 2011; Gray and Garand, 1993); visual supports for communication and behaviour (Angell et al., 2011; Blum-Dimaya et al., 2010; Hogdon, 1995); and the use of obsessions and stereotypes as positive reinforcement and motivators to learning (Charlop-Christy and Haymes, 1996; Grandin, 1992; Howlin and Rutter, 1987). As mentioned previously, the fourth component of the *Curriculum* involved the use of the savant skill interests and activities to teach communication, social skills and appropriate behaviours. Activities were designed from each of the children's current Individual Education Program, based upon their savant and splinter skills. Up until now, there have been only a few examples in the literature of the use of savant skills to teach adaptive behaviours (Bryant, 1993; Sacks, 1995; Treffert, 2012).

The *Curriculum* was also designed to act as a facilitator for transition to less restrictive educational environments (mainstream classes), particularly for those autistic savants with a higher level of cognitive functioning, and who may be enrolled in special education schools or classes. The integration of students with autism into mainstream environments is a major focus of autism educational programming today (Carter et al., 2014; Costley et al., 2012; Roberts et al., 2008).

Methodology and procedures of the study

A longitudinal multiple-replication case study design was chosen to explore the effectiveness of the *Savant Skill Curriculum* in developing savant skills in the autistic population in functional ways, and to improve adaptive functioning in communication, social skills and behaviour. The study further sought to explore key issues related to savant syndrome and the nature of savant skills: memory ability as central to the development of all savant skills; the role of practice, motivation, training and creativity; whether skills may be inherited; age of onset; and the extent of challenging behaviours. Various standardized and non-standardized measures of each subject's savant abilities and adaptive functioning were taken as pre- and post-measures, to determine the effectiveness of the *Savant Skill Curriculum*.

The subjects of this study were students between the ages of four and sixteen years, diagnosed with autism spectrum disorder (ASD), and who also displayed savant or splinter skills at either the Savant I or II level (Treffert, 1989). Subjects formed two groups, one an experimental group, the other a control group, and were tracked over a two-year period during the implementation of the *Savant Skill Curriculum*. A comparison of the pre- and post-measures of the two groups was made.

Case study methodology in gifted and savant research

An example of a thorough and comprehensive multiple case study, which compared and contrasted the educational and psychological development of exceptionally and profoundly gifted children, is that of Gross (1993, 2004). Her longitudinal study examined the origin, development and school histories of forty Australian students of IQ 160+. In her book *Exceptionally Gifted Children* (2nd ed., 2004) which reports her study, Gross also provides a comprehensive literature review of multiple case studies of children of exceptional intellectual potential. Moon (1991, p. 165) recognized both the usefulness of, and the demanding nature of, multiple case study research in gifted education.

> Multiple case studies are a demanding undertaking, but they have tremendous power to advance knowledge in the field of gifted education. The multiple case-study method of developing and testing theory is particularly powerful in areas where methods based upon sampling logic are difficult or impossible to use because of rarity of the phenomena.
>
> (Moon, 1991, p. 165)

Although Moon recommended the use of the multiple case studies as particularly appropriate for advancing knowledge of rare phenomena, in this case, in the field of gifted education, it equally applies to the study of another extremely rare group of 'twice-exceptional' children, autistic savants. Isolated case studies have dominated this area of research in the past with only a few examples of multiple case studies. Treffert, in his books *Extraordinary People* (1989) and *Islands of Genius: The Bountiful Mind of the Autistic Savant, Acquired, and Sudden Savant* (2012), reviewed case studies of idiot and autistic savants from around the world, from the past one hundred years through to the present; with his 1989 book being possibly the first example of a multiple case study of savants. Howe (1989) also reviewed several cases of savants in the book *Fragments of Genius*.

Case study methodology is a sound approach for developing specific knowledge about the savant syndrome in current time. It enables the researcher to observe and describe intensively the particular and idiosyncratic features of a child's development (Foster, 1986). It provides a holistic view of the person being studied and allows the researcher to develop and validate theories that are grounded in direct observation of an individual's behaviour and development (Frey, 1978; Merriam, 1988). This 'human need study' study is such an example, examining not only the functional application of savant skills, but also changes to behaviour, communication, social skills and self-esteem, over a two-year period. Prose and literary techniques were used to describe the cases under study.

Multiple case studies

To compare the educational and psychological development of the group of children with autism displaying savant skills, the multiple case research design was employed. The study, which includes a wide range of both quantitative and qualitative data-gathering procedures, has followed Yin's (2009) replication logic; each case is treated as if it were a 'whole' study in which evidence is sought and analysed from a variety of sources. All sixteen children were treated with the *Savant Skill Curriculum* using the same observation procedures, data collection and analyses as employed in the first case, replicated for each case in the study. A control group of six children was also used to assist in determining the effectiveness of the *Savant Skill Curriculum*. These children were treated with the *Savant Skill Curriculum*, following the conclusion of the experimental study. The control group was subjected to the same observation and data-gathering procedures but did not receive the *Savant Skill Curriculum*.

A quasi-experimental design

Although this study, as outlined above, is a qualitative case study design, it also employs aspects of a quantitative quasi-experimental investigation. Often in educational research, it is simply not possible to undertake true experiments. True experimental designs (the pre-test, post-test control group designs) involve the use of two groups that have been constituted by randomization. At best, they may be able to employ something approaching a true experimental design in which they have control over 'the who and to whom of measurement', but lack control over 'the when and to whom of exposure', or the 'randomization of exposure'. Such designs are referred to as quasi-experimental designs. Kerlinger (1970) refers to quasi-experimental situations as 'compromise designs', where, as in this study, the random selection or random assignment of subjects or schools and classrooms is quite impracticable. It is also not morally ethical to use a true control group for a study involving disabled students where the control group does not receive the experimental group treatment.

This study, by using a comparison group who are subjected to the same pre- and post-observations and data collection as the experimental group but not the intervention (the *Savant Skill Curriculum*), is in essence enlisting the use of a form of limited control group. One of the most commonly used quasi-experimental designs in educational research is employed for this study (Cohen and Marion, 1989), and can be represented as:

(Experimental)	O_1	X	O_2
(Control)	O_3	X	O_4

The dashed line separating the parallel rows in the diagram of the non-equivalent control group indicates that the experimental and control groups have not been equated by randomization – hence the term 'non-equivalent'. Where matching is not possible, the researcher is advised to use samples from the same population that are as much alike as possible.

Identification instruments

To assist with the identification of students with autism displaying savant or splinter skills, a nomination form was designed for the study: *The Savant Skill Nomination Form* – T.R. Clark (2011) Appendix 1. Upon notification of a possible subject, a *Savant Skill Nomination Form* was sent to both the child's family and his/her teacher (family and teacher versions). Each nomination form was accompanied by a letter describing the study and including a definition of savant syndrome (Treffert, 1989). Although standardized tests were administered when available, non-standardized measures were developed and used to assess some savant abilities; calendar and computer skills. To assist with both the identification and assessment of subjects, and to also gather information on the profile and nature of each subject's savant abilities, a questionnaire was also developed, *The Savant Skill Questionnaire* – Appendix 2 and 3 (Teacher and Family versions). An overview of all tests of savant skills were discussed in Chapter 2 and are available on the Routledge website: Profiles of Savant Abilities – Table 2.8. *Summary of Savant Skill Assessments.*

Assessing the level of savant skill

As mentioned previously, Treffert's (1989, p. xxv) attempt to define and classify skills as either the Savant I or Savant II skills has been employed for this study. Savant I or Talented savants are those assessed as displaying savant skills which stand in contrast to the individual's disability. Savant II or Prodigious savants are those who display skills that would be considered spectacular even if viewed in a normal person. Where a savant or splinter skill appeared to be less highly developed than a Talented Savant (I) level skill, but is apparent or emerging, I also made the additional classification of Talented/Splinter skill (I/S). Each of the subject's savant skills were then assessed as being a Savant I/S, I or II skill. When skills were assessed using standardized measures and the subject performed above chronological age level, the Savant II level skill was awarded. For those who did not reach levels of performance appropriate for chronological age, and non-standardized information from the *Savant Skill Questionnaires* (Clark, 2011) indicated savant ability, a Savant I classification was awarded. It is important to note that each savant skill was assessed using both standardized and non-standardized measures to accurately portray each subject's abilities. The results of both the standardized and non-standardized measures were recorded on the *Profile of Savant Abilities Form* (see Chapter 2) designed for the study. These profiles were then used to design each subject's individual savant skill teaching program.

Pre-test and post-test measures

The measures outlined below relate to the adaptive functioning of each subject and were employed both pre and post the *Savant Skill Curriculum* to determine whether or not the *Curriculum* resulted in change:

1) functional application of the savant skill
2) communication ability
3) social skills and behaviour
4) academic self-esteem
5) degree of autism.

The functional application of savant skill

To examine the degree to which the savant skills of each of the children were applied in functional and meaningful ways, a variety of qualitative measures were employed. As discussed earlier, two questionnaires were designed for the study: the *Savant Skill Questionnaire (Family and Teacher versions)* – T.R. Clark, 2011 (Appendix 2 and 3), and also the *Savant Skill Post-Study Family/Teacher Questionnaire* – T.R. Clark, 2011 (Appendix 5). It should be noted that all questionnaires designed for the study were revised in 2011. *The Savant Skill (Family and Teacher) Question-naires* were designed to gather information on the current state of functional application of each savant skill prior to the curriculum. Each question was framed as a statement with the following instructions – 'To explore more *fully* your child's savant skills or gifts, please indicate *how much* you think your child *is like* the item by using the scale to the right of each item. Mark on the scale of 1 to 11 whether you STRONGLY AGREE (SA) to STRONGLY DISAGREE (SD). Circle the *appropriate number*. If you are unclear or haven't observed the skill in your child, put a tick in the UNSURE or DON'T KNOW box.' A scale of 1 (SD) to 11 (SA) was used. A response between '7 and 11' indicated 'agreement' with the statement above and a response between '1 and 5' indicated 'disagree-ment'. A response of '6' indicated 'ambivalence'. The same questions were also included in the *Savant Skill Post-Study Family/Teacher Questionnaire* to allow a comparison of functionality before and after the study. A combination of both open (verbal) and scale structured questions (Youngman, 1986 cited in Bell, 1987) were used in both questionnaires with the aim of extracting knowledge of savant syndrome.

To examine more closely the application of skills, a teacher/mentor evaluation form of the teaching objectives (Annual Priorities) was developed to be used during the implementation of the *Savant Skill Curriculum*. The *Curriculum Strategy Annual Priorities Evaluation – Form D* was designed for each subject and included all of the teaching or mentoring activities or priorities, and the curriculum strategies (see copy of Christopher's form in Appendix 6). The evaluation form again used the same eleven-point scale as the *Savant Skill Questionnaires*, against which teachers and mentors were asked to rate whether: 1) the skill had *been achieved* and 2) the skill had *been applied functionally*. Respondents were also asked to indicate the level of support the subject required to both achieve the skill and to functionally apply the skill by indicating I = Independent, and S = With Support. It was necessary to include the level of support classification as used in the education of students with autism. Progress for a student in fact may be viewed as a reduction in support from the caregiver. All Annual Priorities from each subject's program were included to ensure that at least one evaluation of these activities took place during the two-year curriculum program. Artefacts were collected for each subject as examples of the functional application of savant skills where appropriate – e.g. drawings for art skill, computer printouts for computer skill.

Communication ability – Clinical Evaluation of Language Fundamentals (3rd Edition)

Communication or language ability was assessed using the *CELF-3* (Semel, Wiig and Secord, 1995 – *Clinical Evaluation of Language Fundamentals – 3rd Edition)*. The *CELF-3* is designed to identify children, adolescents and young adults who lack the basic foundations of language content and form that characterize mature language use: word meanings (semantics), word and sentence structure (morphology and syntax), as well as the recall and retrieval of spoken language (memory). The test examines both receptive and expressive language skills in a variety of subtests and was administered before and after the *Savant Skill Curriculum* by Aspect's speech pathologist, to illustrate quantitative changes in language skills. Questions relating to qualitative information of change in language skills were included in the *Savant Skill Post-Study Family/Teacher Questionnaire* (Appendix 5).

Social skills and behaviour – Developmental Behaviour Checklist (DBC)

The *Developmental Behaviour Checklist* (Einfield, Tonge and Parmenter, 1998) was administered before and after the *Savant Skill Curriculum* to establish behavioural and social change. The DBC is an instrument for the assessment of a broad range of behavioural and emotional disturbances in children and adults with mental retardation. The instrument was designed as a standardized screening tool to identify cases and non-cases of behavioural problems as well as to act as a screener for a particular diagnosis, for example autism. According to Einfield (1992), behavioural and emotional problems are two to three times more common in people with mental retardation (MR) compared with those without MR. Both teacher and family (primary carer) versions of the *Developmental Behaviour Checklist* were used for this study. The instrument (*Manual for the Developmental Behaviour Checklist*, p. 56, Enfield et al., 1998) is considered useful for research purposes to determine if an intervention has assisted in the amelioration of behavioural symptoms. The *Developmental Behaviour Checklist* can be interpreted at three different levels. The first is the Total Behaviour Problem Score (TBPS), which gives an overall measure of behavioural/emotional disturbance. The second level is that of the subscale scores, which give a measure of disturbance in six dimensions – disruptive, self-absorbed, communication disturbance, anxiety, social relating and anti-social. The third level is the score of individual items. Again additional questions regarding the development of social skills and behaviour are included in the *Savant Skill Post-Study Family/Teacher Questionnaire* (Appendix 5).

Academic self-esteem – Behavioural Academic Self-Esteem (BASE)

To determine change in self-esteem, the *Behavioural Academic Self-Esteem Rating Scale* (Coopersmith and Gilberts, 1982) was administered. Due to their communication and social impairments, children with autism would be unable to complete the majority of self-esteem inventories which generally involve self-reports. The *BASE* was selected as it is completed by teachers, parents or other observers who have first-hand experience of the student. The *BASE* measures a child's academic self-esteem by using direct observation of their classroom behaviours. The factors examined by the *BASE* include: student initiative, social attention, success/failure, social attraction and self-confidence.

The *BASE* total score (the sum of the five factors) indicates a student's overall level of academic self-esteem as inferred from an observer's judgement about the child's behaviour in school.

Autism – Autism Behaviour Checklist

To establish a level or measure of autistic behaviour in subjects, the *Autism Behaviour Checklist (ABC)* (Krug, Arick and Almond, 1988) was used. The *ABC* is a functional screening tool consisting of a checklist of behavioural characteristics that have been used in the diagnosis of autism. Although other more detailed instruments are available to diagnose autism, for example, the *Childhood Autism Rating Scale* (Schopler, Reichler and Renner, 1986), they are generally lengthy, time-consuming assessments and beyond the time constraints of this study. The *ABC* can be completed by parents, caregivers or professionals, who should have at least three to six weeks' experience with the subject.

The *ABC* incorporates weighted scores to assist in quantifying the data obtained. Numbers 1 to 4 follow each behavioural descriptor. A behavioural characteristic with a weighted score of 4 is the highest predictor of autism. The behavioural characteristics, for purposes of developing a behaviour profile, have been separated into five diagnostic categories: sensory, relating, body and object use, language, and social and self-help. Based on the specific behaviours, a behavioural profile is plotted. This profile accurately differentiates individuals who have been diagnosed autistic from all other handicapping conditions. It should be noted that, for the purposes of this study, the overall total scores that indicate a level of autism and/or a different diagnosis, before and after the *Savant Curriculum*, were compared to determine any change in the behavioural symptoms of autism.

Interviews, school/psychological/medical records, training

A single initial family interview – *Family Interview (Pre-Treatment)* (Appendix 7) was conducted by the author to add to the information derived from the initial identification and assessment of subjects. Telephone interviews were also conducted throughout the study to clarify issues relating to their child's Savant Skill Program and to maintain a monitoring contact to ensure continuation of the Program. A variety of records and documents were consulted to also gather data for the study. To establish diagnosis of autism and intellectual functioning for each subject previous medical and psychological reports were consulted. Information sessions centred on savant syndrome, and the *Savant Skill Curriculum*, were provided for teachers, families and mentors.

Procedures to increase reliability and validity

To increase the internal validity of the research findings, a number of procedures were used. The use of multiple methods and sources of data collection is termed 'triangulation' (Denzin, 1970). Methodological triangulation combines dissimilar methods such as standardized tests, questionnaires, interviews, observations, documents and artefacts to study the same topic or unit. Hollingworth (1942) and Gross (1993, 2004) both used triangulation in their multiple case studies of extremely gifted children. Data were collected over the course of the *Savant Skill Curriculum*, a two-year period. Information from parents, teachers and mentors was recorded continuously on a monitoring form. Artefacts were gathered continuously over this period. Communication, social skills and behaviour assessments were repeated at the conclusion of the study along with the repetition of some questionnaire items. The author observed each subject many times throughout the course of the study.

Data analysis

The data have been presented according to three separate areas of inquiry, that is, A) the nature of savant skills, B) change for the better as a result of the *Savant Skill Curriculum*, and C) change for the worse or no change. A variety of data analysis techniques were employed and included the Wilcoxin T Test for two dependent samples, the Mann–Whitney U Test for two independent samples, and directional t-tests for dependent samples. Means for the data for most questions are included for interest, although due to the non-parametric nature of the statistical analyses they were not used to calculate levels of significance. The results have been presented in both tabular and narrative form. Non-parametric statistical analyses were employed due to the small numbers of subjects in both the treatment and control groups. The Mann–Whitney U Test for two independent samples and the Wilcoxin T Test for two dependent samples are commonly used when populations cannot be assumed to be normally distributed with equal variances.

Individual savant skill programs

Teaching priorities and activities were developed that incorporated a range of gifted education teaching strategies, including the use of enrichment, acceleration and mentorships to facilitate the functional application of each subject's individual savant skills. A variety of communication, social and/or behavioural priorities were also designed and included in each program, which are based upon the savant interests and skills of the subjects.

Each savant skill program is divided into three separate sections:

1) *Curriculum Strategy Annual Priorities – Form A* (Appendix 9) which outlines the twelve-month broad teaching priorities (goals);

2) *Curriculum Teaching Activities and Strategies – Form B* (Appendix 10), which contains the specific teaching activities that relate to each of the Annual Priorities (Form A); and

3) *Curriculum Teaching Activities – Form C* (Appendix 11), which incorporates the communication, social or behavioural priorities (goals) to be taught.

It should be noted that the same educational strategies (enrichment, acceleration and mentorships) were used for all the research children but in varying combinations. Not all savant skills were suitable for the use of the mentorship strategy. Each program contained a 'smorgasbord' of teaching activities for the teachers to select from over the period of the study. The Individual Savant Skill programs served as 'working documents' for both families and teachers and were presented at each subject's Individual Annual Education Plan meeting. Patrick's Individual Savant Skill teaching program is included in Table 3.1. Copies for the remaining five focus children – Bradley, Terry, Christopher, Benjamin and Natasha – are available on the Routledge website: Individual Savant Skill Programs – Focus Children.

To assist with the evaluation and monitoring of the Individual Savant Skill Programs, the *Curriculum Strategy Annual Priorities Evaluation – Form D* (Appendix 12) was used at the completion of each individual program.

The savant skills of each of the selected children that were used in the *Savant Skill Curriculum* have been summarized in Table 3.2. Due to the time constraints on the teachers, not all of the savant skills of each subject were incorporated in the individual programs. The most highly developed skills of each subject were used to maximize the use of high-level motivational influences as well as building upon pre-existing strengths rather than weaknesses.

The results

Did the differentiated educational program make a difference for the 'paradox children'?

The results of the *Savant Skill Curriculum* study are outlined in this section as responses to the Research Questions (see Chapter 2). The data have been presented according to three separate areas of inquiry, that is, A) the nature of savant skills, B) change for the better as a result of the differentiated curriculum, and C) change for the worse or no change. It should be noted that it is not uncommon for children with autism to respond differently in the home environment from the school environment. A lower level of performance or underachievement was noted also by Gross (1993, 2004) among the highly non-disabled gifted child in the school setting. This difference in behaviour and performance may impact upon the perceptions of teachers and families and subsequently their responses to the questions in the *Savant Skill Questionnaires*.

TABLE 3.1 Patrick's Individual Program

PATRICK'S CURRICULUM STRATEGY ANNUAL PRIORITIES – FORM A						
NAME: Patrick AGE: 14						
		CURRICULUM ANNUAL PRIORITIES				
Savant Skill and Level (I or II)	H/S	ENRICHMENT	ACCELERATION	MENTORSHIP	COMMUNICATION/ SOCIAL	COMMENTS
Calendar Calculations (Savant II)	S & H	**Written Language** To use existing c.c. skills to broaden P.'s knowledge of world events (e.g. history) and to increase his awareness of the concept of time (past, present, future) P. to be responsible for school excursion calendars/schedules.	**Research Skills** Teach P. research skills to access high interest information (as for Enrichment).			
Mathematical Calculation (Savant II)	S & H	**Mathematical** To use calculation skills for home and school activities e.g. budget keeping.	**Mathematical** To teach higher-level maths concepts (based on DSE Maths Curriculum).			
Mechanical / Computer (Savant I)	S & H	**Computer** To introduce different types of software using existing computer.	**Computer** To teach the use of variety of advanced computer software (as for enrichment).	(As for Acceleration.) Brother to be mentor.		

TABLE 3.1 —*continued*

PATRICK'S CURRICULUM TEACHING STRATEGIES – FORM B						
NAME: Patrick		AGE: 14				
		CURRICULUM ANNUAL TEACHING ACTIVITIES				
Savant Skill and Level (I or II)	H/S	ENRICHMENT	ACCELERATION	MENTORSHIP	COMMUNICATION/ SOCIAL	COMMENTS
Calendar Calculations (Savant II)	S & H	**Written Language** Compile lists of historical events using encyclopedias, computer programs of European events, monarchs, wars, etc. P. to research the answers. **Present/Future Info** Record school/family events and birthdays in personal diary, e.g. holidays, birthdays, excursions.	**Research** P. to be taught to use the computer Dewey system in local and school library.		Refer to Form C.	
Mathematical Calculation (Savant II)	S & H	**Mathematical** Class Bank. Keep accounts for class spending and home shopping skills.	**Mathematical** P. to be taught higher-level maths concepts; divisions, square roots, geometry and trigonometry, etc.			

		CURRICULUM ANNUAL TEACHING ACTIVITIES				
Savant Skill and Level (I or II)	H/S	ENRICHMENT	ACCELERATION	MENTORSHIP	COMMUNICATION/ SOCIAL	COMMENTS
Mechanical Computer (Savant I)	S & H	**Computer** Use the following programs independently: World Atlas, Word, Excel, Kid Pix, Clipart etc.	As for Enrichment.	**Mentor** Use word processor, printer for budget keeping (family and personal with own pocket money). Typing of staff meeting agenda and minutes. Family letters/business, recordkeeping, etc. (as for enrichment).		

TABLE 3.1 —*continued*

PATRICK'S CURRICULUM TEACHING ACTIVITIES – FORM C				
NAME: Patrick		**AGE: 14**		
ANNUAL PRIORITY	**E/ment H/S**	**CALENDAR CALCULATION**	**MATHEMATICAL CALCULATION**	**MECHANICAL/COMPUTER COMMUNICATION**
To perform a non-routine task independently with visual cues, i.e. make a pizza, doing washing, ironing clothes, etc.	H & S	Plot 'non-routine' tasks 'Monthly/Work calendar' (i.e. P.'s individual calendar)	1) Number visual augmentative sequences. Get P. to do calculations e.g. How many steps to go?, etc. 2) Measure own quantities of ingredients for cooking etc.	Computer. Teach to use Boardmaker (Visual Communication Software). P. to write the above 'Self-Care Activities' on own computer disc ('a diary').
P. to follow two and three-part unrelated commands with visual cues (fade to gestural prompts).	S	On 'Monthly Work Calendar' plot P.'s. class jobs/responsibilities (e.g. toys away, putting up chairs, cleaning white board). Ensure 'two and three-part jobs assigned visually on the above days in sequence.	Number the instructions, i.e. 'P. 1) get your bag' 2) put your books in bag' 3) sit down', etc.	Type two and three-part commands on computer (word processor) and P. to follow the 'Number Sequence' if necessary.
P. to recall and comment on past and future events.	S	Record all class excursions, major school events, holidays, etc. on 'Monthly Calendar'. Use these past/future events to prompt conversation (i.e. comment on).	Number and date all events. Prompt discussion by relating a number to the event to be discussed. Discuss class budget and shopping lists (past).	Record/document on personal diary on computer program/software. Use as a discussion point.

ANNUAL PRIORITY	E/ment H/S	CALENDAR CALCULATION	MATHEMATICAL CALCULATION	MECHANICAL/COMPUTER COMMUNICATION
SOCIAL / BEHAVIOUR				
To greet unfamiliar people appropriately.	S	On 'Monthly Calendar' identify social excursions. For each excursion rehearse appropriate greeting (record greeting as a 'Social Story') P. to take on excursions. Reward appropriate greeting with a book/magazine (token economy reinforcer).	After five (or ten) appropriate greetings (P. to add up) then he is able to purchase a magazine.	Type 'Social Story greetings' on computer.
To improve turn-taking skills.	S	Take turns with guessing historical dates and mental calculations.	Bingo – make bingo games using the above information.	Take turns with P. typing on word processor word lists, events, dates, etc. Play computer games.
To receive and deliver messages within the school.	S	Daily P. to go to office and collect daily school roll (absences, etc.). Record on P's own Personal School Roll/Calendar on computer, i.e. date number absent number present totals, etc.	As for Calendar Calculation.	As for Calendar Calculation.

TABLE 3.2 Savant skills of treatment children – Individual Savant Curriculum Programs

Child	Memory	Hyperlexic	Art	Music	Mechanical/ spatial	Calendar	Number	Sensory	Athletic
Patrick					X	X	X		
Christopher	X	X			X				
Benjamin		X		X	X				
Natasha	X	X	X						
Bradley		X			X		X		
Terry	X	X			X	X	X		
Anthony	X				`	X			
John	X				X				
Jeremy	X	X			X				
Warren	X	X			X				
Timothy	X	X							
Zane	X	X							
Joseph		X	X		X				
Martin		X	X						
Simon	X				X	X			
Jack	X				X				

The results for each of the three areas of inquiry are summarized below. A complete copy of the results are available on the Routledge website in both narrative and tabular form: The Results – Tables 3.5 to 3.15; 3.18 to 3.26.

The nature of savant skills

Data relating to the nature of savant skills have been collated under the following areas that relate to specific topics in the literature on savant syndrome. They include: obsessiveness and savant skills, the development of skills, levels and types of skills, and behaviour and savant skills. Data were acquired in this area from responses to the *Savant Skill Family/Teacher Questionnaires* (T.R. Clark, 2011; Appendix 2 and 3), initial interviews, documents, artefacts and the standardized tests of skills. Data on the nature of savant skills were collected before the *Curriculum* program and are in no way related to the effects of the *Savant Skill Curriculum* treatment.

Obsessiveness and savant skills

The parents and teachers of both the treatment and the control groups agreed that their student/child spent a great deal of time involved in their area(s) of skill. The majority of parents of both groups reported that their children would, in fact, 'spend up to four hours per day working on their savant tasks'. Several parents commented that their children 'spend all their waking time on their interests'. No significant differences in the reported amount of time spent by the children on their savant areas were found in the parent or teacher ratings between the treatment and control groups.

The children in this study also appear to display the intense concentration and hours of practice with savant interests that were previously reported by Charness et al. (1988), Comer (1985), Hill (1978), Treffert (1989) and Young (1995). This intense interest by the savant has been referred to as an 'obsessional preoccupation' (Rimland, 1978). Many parents involved in this study similarly described their children as having an 'obsessional interest' in their activities to the exclusion of all others.

Although it has been suggested that the intense practice or concentration of the savant in their skill area(s) may be primarily responsible for the development of savant ability (Anastasi and Levee, 1960; Ericsson and Faivre, 1988; Hoffman and Reeves, 1979; Howe, 1989; Miller, 1989; Treffert, 1989), it would appear from this study that the large amounts of time spent, and concentration on, savant activities are obsessional in nature and an integral feature of savant skills. It is the fixation on savant activities that leads to the disproportionate amounts of time the child spends on these activities, rather than the amount of practice resulting in the development of the skills.

High levels of distress were exhibited by their children when unable to access their savant interests, according to reports by teachers and parents of the treatment group with the parents of the control group in agreement. Many subjects, if unable to engage in or finish their activities, would become so distressed as to 'bite', 'hit others' and 'tantrum for hours'. Although the teachers of the control group reported lower levels of distress than the control group parents, this difference may have been due to differences between the home and school settings. There may in fact be more opportunity within the home to engage in savant activities, and thus increased opportunities for conflict, than in the mainstream classroom, where time may be extremely limited for the inclusion of savant activities due to an emphasis on the regular mainstream curriculum. It should be noted that, at the end of the study, 83 per cent of the control children were enrolled in mainstream regular classrooms.

The high levels of distress exhibited by the savants when their tasks are not accessible, are interrupted or changed may also be related to the obsessive nature of savant interest and concentration. Charness et al. (1988) made reference to the extremely demanding routines that savants follow that are consistent with obsessional aspects of personality. The children in this study also followed demanding routines in their savant activities and became very distressed if these routines or schedules were interrupted. Obsessions and routines are also a feature of autism and, if changed or interrupted, may also result in displays of inappropriate behaviours (Jolliffe et al., 1992). Autistic obsessions are thought to play a crucial role in reducing anxiety or in providing some control over what is otherwise a very confusing world. Perhaps the obsessive nature of savant activities is fulfilling a similar role by helping the autistic savants in this study to make sense of their world and to reduce their levels of anxiety.

Development of savant skills

The inquiry into the development of savant skills was divided into levels of a) interest in skill areas, and b) level of motivation of the children. The mean scores for level of interest by the children indicated agreement with the statement, 'displays a great deal of interest in skill area(s)' by teachers and parents for both the treatment and control groups. A significant difference was found, however, between parent and teacher ratings of the treatment group. The parents of the treatment group reported higher levels of interest than did the teachers. This difference may again have been attributed to the differences between home and school settings in relation to the amount of time or scope available for savant activities. It can be assumed that there are greater opportunities and time available for the children to engage in savant interests in the home than in the school. This view is supported by the results outlined in Question 1, in relation to the large amounts of time the children engage in their savant activities in the home. However, no significant difference was found between parent and teacher ratings of the levels of interest in skill areas for the control group. Again, this result may be a reflection of the very small n and the prevalence of the same rankings (2 × 10, 2 × 11; 3 × 9), as reliance on observational data indicates a substantial difference in mean scores between the parent and teacher ratings. Both the control group and the treatment groups displayed similar levels of interest in their savant skill areas as rated by both their teachers and parents.

The high mean scores for the level of motivation indicated high levels of agreement with the statement 'Is highly motivated when working on savant skills' for parents and teachers in both the treatment and control groups. Although a difference appeared between the parent and teacher ratings of the level of motivation for both the treatment and control children, this may again have occurred as a result of the difference in home and school settings. If there is less opportunity to engage in savant interests in the classroom, fewer opportunities also exist to observe savant interest and motivation in savant skill areas. As no significant differences were found with the ratings of teachers and parents between the treatment and control groups, the observed levels of motivation were in fact similar in both groups.

The high levels of interest and motivation in savant skill areas displayed by the children in this study supports the anecdotal observations of savant interest and involvement in savant activities reported in the literature by Charness et al. (1988), Comer (1985), Hill (1978), Treffert (1989), Wallace (2008) and Young (1995). The intense interest and motivation in savant activities and subsequent practice by the savant has been viewed as causal or central to the development of savant skills (Anastasi and Levee, 1960; Hoffman and Reeves, 1979; Howe, 1989; Miller, 1989; Treffert, 1989; Wallace, 2008). When individuals are interested in a subject or activity, and are motivated to spend a great deal of time concentrating upon that activity, they are more likely to develop proficiency in their area of interest. It has also been suggested that savant interest and motivation is in fact a personality trait (Charness et al., 1988; Treffert, 1989) and may possibly be an inherited trait (Young, 1995). Whether a causal factor in the development of savant skills or an inherited personality trait, it would appear from the results of this study that interest and motivation are important characteristics of savant activity and feature in the development of savant abilities.

The findings from this study supported the view that savant abilities develop at an early age. Both the treatment and control group children developed an interest and showed signs of ability in savant skill areas at an early age. The mean age of onset of savant skills for the treatment group was two years and six months, and two years and five months for the control group. No significant difference was found between the two groups. The early age of onset of savant skills of all the children in this study support the anecdotal evidence of Rimland (1978) and Rosen (1981) that savant skills typically emerge at an early age, and in a manner that seems different from the usual longer developmental learning curve. As in the case of Nadia, whose drawing skills were said to have 'just appeared' at the age of three and a half (Selfe, 1977), the drawing skills of Natasha, Joseph and Simon, all subjects of this study, emerged at an early age. The results of this study are also similar to those of Young (1995), who found that the early onset of skills was common among the subjects of her study.

Many families reported their children displayed an early 'intense interest in' particular objects or activities related to their savant domains. Typically, the families of children with mechanical abilities reported an early interest in fans and electrical equipment, whilst children with hyperlexic skills were reported to be fascinated by letters and words. Miller (1989) also found evidence of an early interest in music in relation to the musical savant, Eddie. It would appear that, not only did the children in this study display high levels of interest in their savant skill areas, as discussed previously, but that this interest developed at an early age.

Formal training as a possible characteristic and causal factor of the development of savant skills was examined. Responses from teachers and parents for both the treatment and control groups indicated overall disagreement with the statement that their child/student 'Has received some formal training in their skill area(s)'. A significant difference was found, however, between the parent and teacher ratings for both the treatment and control groups. Although the teachers generally disagreed with this statement regarding formal training, their ratings were higher than those of the parent groups, indicating perhaps an uncertainty or lack of knowledge as to the impact of formal training in relation to their students' savant skills. This difference may have also been influenced by the possible differences in home and school environments. An inherent emphasis on teaching and training in the school setting may have influenced the ratings of teachers when compared to the ratings of parents in the non-formal-educational setting of the home. Teachers of children with hyperlexic skills (87.5 per cent of the group) may have associated their teaching of reading, writing and spelling with the notion of formal training or teaching and would not have always been aware of the early onset of these skills in their students, as reported previously. In spite of this difference, no parents or teachers agreed that their child/student had received formal training in the area of their savant skill. No differences were found in the parent and teacher ratings between the treatment and control groups.

The question of whether savants have received formal training in the area(s) of their abilities is central to the discussion of the etiology of savant skills. The viewpoint that savant skills have a hereditary basis (Ericsson, Roring, and Nandagopal, 2007; Fein and Obler, 1988; O'Connor, 1989; Perin, Berger, and Markram, 2011; Snyder and Mitchell, 1999; Treffert, 2012) is in fact supported by the findings of this study, in that the subjects received no formal training in relation to their savant skills. The hereditary/innate basis of savant skills is further supported by the early age of onset of savant skills by the children in this study in the absence of formal training.

Evidence of savant abilities, giftedness or superior ability in other family members was also explored given the converging research evidence to a genetic link in the families of non-disabled gifted students. Although there appeared to be more family members of the treatment group than the control group, who displayed evidence of skills in the child's area of savant ability, giftedness or superior ability, the majority of the families of the two groups combined reported such skills amongst relatives (72 per cent). It is interesting to note the high levels of incidence of similar gifts or skills in the subject child's area of savant ability among the families of the savants in the combined groups (62.5 per cent). Several children who were assessed as having computer skills, for example, Patrick, John, and Jeremy, had brothers, sisters or fathers who were also highly skilled with computers.

The high incidence of familiar skills in the child's area of savant ability found in this study supports the previously reported evidence of similar interests and talents or gifts in the families of savants (Brink, 1980; Grandin, 1995; Hermelin and O'Connor, 1990; Rimland, 1978; Treffert, 2012; and Young, 1995). These results, in fact, suggest strongly that there is a genetic link in the appearance of domain-specific gifts among the children in this study.

These children are in fact 'twice-exceptional' or gifted students who suffer from the disability of autism. The full development and application of each child's skills are masked or inhibited by their disability of autism. The present study has indeed strengthened the view that these children are in fact 'twice-exceptional' students, and warrant differentiated educational programs and services.

Levels and types of savant skills

All of the treatment and control group children were assessed, using a combination of standardized and non-standardized measures, as displaying different levels of savant abilities. The levels of ability varied according to different savant skills, with no one child assessed as having the same level of ability for all their savant skills.

As different levels of giftedness and talent are found in the non-disabled gifted population (Gross, 1989), differing levels of savant skills also exist in the savant population. Savants do not form a homogenous group and, like the gifted, perform at different levels of ability. Although Treffert (1989), in his definition of savant syndrome, recognized that savants' skills are performed at different levels of ability (Talented Savants, Savant I; Prodigious Savants, Savant II), it should be noted that if this classification of savant skills is to be used, it should be used to describe each individual savant skill and not used as an overall descriptor to label for the individual savant. A prodigious musical savant may also display other or multiple savant skills which may in fact be performed at a lower level, for example at the Talented Savant I level (Treffert, 1989).

In spite of the attempt by this study to assess and categorize savant skills into levels of savant abilities for each child, except where the skill was able to be assessed using a standardized measure, the classification of a savant skill into various levels of ability retains an element of subjectivity. The issue of subjectivity, in relation to the classification of savant skills, will continue for those savant skills (e.g. memory) that are difficult to assess using standardized tests. However, by using both standardized and non-standardized measures to assess savant skills, a more accurate measure of savant ability is possible.

Each savant skill was rated according to Treffert's (1989) Talented Savant I and Prodigious Savant II levels of savant performance, outlined in his definition of savant syndrome. Although the majority of the skills were able to be classified as either a Level I or a Level II savant skill, some skills did not fall clearly into either level.

As mentioned previously, emergent or sensory type savant skills (for example, a heightened awareness of sounds or smells, or the ability to read and write words and letters at a very early age) were not so easily classified. These types of skills the author classified as a Talented/Splinter skill (I/S) as they were exhibited as not yet a fully developed, or as apparent as, Talented or Savant I skill. It should be noted that although splinter skills are associated with the autistic population, not all individuals diagnosed with autism display splinter skills (Applebaum et al., 1979; Howlin et al., 2009; Rimland, 1978; Rutter, 1978; Schreibman and Mills, 1983; Treffert, 2012; Wing, 1976). If splinter skills were associated with all persons diagnosed with autism they would be included in the *DSM-V* (American Psychiatric Association, 2013). However, no mention of splinter skills is made in either diagnostic instrument. For this reason, as splinter skills tend to stand in stark markedly incongruous contrast to the handicap of autism, they have been classified as Talented or Savant I skills in this study. For children whose scored well in advance of their non-disabled chronological age peers on standardized testing (e.g. Terry, Bradley, Jack, Joseph, Timothy, Natasha and others), their savant skills were classified as being at the Prodigious or Savant II level (Treffert, 1989), in that these skills would be considered spectacular even if viewed in a normal person. However, several children (Daniel, Andrew, Martin, Warren and Benjamin) also scored at the average for, or just above, their chronological non-disabled peers on standardized testing. Although in this study these skills were also rated as Prodigious or Savant II skills, they may not rate as being spectacular when compared to the normal person. The inclusion of another level in between Treffert's (1989) Level I and Level II classification, for skills that are average or several percentile ranks above the fiftieth percentile of the non-disabled chronological peer group, would be inclusive of the skills of this group. Perhaps a classification that included four different levels may assist in the future assessment of savant abilities.

The need to expand the range of levels in the classification of savant performance for this study may have been due to the age and intellectual functioning of the children. To date, no study has focused on such a young group of savants. The children ranged in age from four to sixteen years of age, with some being referred initially to the study whilst still attending pre-schools. Yet, in spite of their youth, all presented with a variety of savant abilities that are representative of Hill's (1974) original list of savant skills, with the added inclusion of hyperlexic and athletic skills. The skills of the children also meet the classification criterion in Treffert's (1989) definition of savant syndrome.

Finally, the level of intellectual functioning of the children in this study may have also influenced the need for a re-consideration of additional levels of savant performance. Few studies to date have included savants who have a mild level of intellectual delay. Although many historical cases of savants cited in the literature fail to mention the intellectual functioning of the savant, it is assumed from the in-depth descriptions of these cases that they suffered from severe delays in cognitive functioning (Tredgold, 1914; Treffert, 1989, 2012). Although the term 'idiot-savant' (Down, 1887), from which 'savant syndrome' has been derived, originally referred to persons with severe intellectual handicap but above-average skills in one particular domain, it is now widely accepted that savant abilities have been identified across all levels of intellectual ability (Treffert, 1989). This study may in fact be the first study of a group of autistic savants who display higher levels of intellectual ability. Perhaps previous conceptions of savant syndrome may need to be adjusted to accommodate more intellectually able savants and their characteristics.

Although not directly included as a focus of research in this study, it should be noted that, for some children, their ability to perform well on standardized measures, and to be assessed as displaying Prodigious Level II skills (Treffert, 1989), may have been linked both to their intellectual and linguistic abilities. Several children who were assessed as having borderline or average language ability (Terry, Bradley, and Joseph), and with an average or borderline IQ, performed relatively better on some standardized measures than other children with lower linguistic and cognitive ability (Benjamin, Martin and Patrick). This observation warrants future investigation, as it may be directly associated with the savant's ability to perform on standardized tests and to apply their skills for adaptive functioning.

The issue of single or multiple savant skills exhibited by the children was explored also. All subjects in both the treatment and control groups displayed multiple savant skills. This finding supports Treffert's (1989) observation that it is not uncommon for multiple skills to be exhibited by the savant. It should be noted that the savant skills exhibited by the children in this study also fall within a relatively small range of activities or abilities (Hill, 1974), and this therefore further validates Anderson's (1992) view that these skills are not a result of random occurrences.

The children all displayed memory savant abilities. Although the majority did not perform well on the *WRAML* (wide range assessment of memory and learning) (Scheslow and Adams, 1990) standardized test of memory or learning, information from the *Family and Teacher Savant Skill Questionnaires* (Clark, 2011; Appendix 2 and 3) indicated all subjects had exceptional recall for facts and items of individual interest. The poor performances by the subjects on the standardized memory test may have been due to the complexity of the language of the *WRAML*. It is of interest to note that the highest scoring subjects on the memory test (Terry and Bradley) language skills were assessed by the *CELF-3* as being in the average range. The overall poor results by children in this study on the standardized memory test is similar to findings of Howe (1989) and Young and Nettelbeck (1994), who also found that savants in their studies performed poorly on standardized tests of memory.

Although beyond the scope of this study, the fact that all children displayed aspects of exceptionally good memory supports the view that memory itself may be involved in the development of other savant skills. No matter the savant skill, the children displayed exceptional recall related to their specific skill areas. Patrick, with mathematical and calendar savant skills, displayed exceptional recall for mathematical facts and figures as well as calendar dates. Bradley and Christopher, with mechanical savant skills, could name and recall information about all things electrical, and Daniel, with music savant ability, was able to recall the names and compositions of many famous composers. Again, the use of memory skills by the children in their savant skill areas reinforces the association of good memory skills with savant skills, which has been noted by Goldberg (1987), Hermelin and O'Connor (1989), Hermelin and O'Connor (1987), Stevens and Moffit (1988), Treffert (1989, 2012) and Young and Nettelbeck (1994, 1995).

Given the debate in the field of savant syndrome as to whether savants employ imaginative and creative methods in the expression of their savant abilities, the study sought to elucidate this issue. Findings for the treatment and control groups indicated that the parents generally agreed with the descriptor in the *Savant Skill Family/Teacher Questionnaires* (Appendix 2 and 3), 'uses imaginative and creative methods to accomplish savant skill tasks'. However, teachers of both groups tended to indicate either disagreement with the statement or ambivalence. A significant difference was found between the ratings of the teachers and parents in the treatment group. As discussed earlier, this difference may be attributed to a difference in the home and school settings. With more time available in the home for the children to explore and engage in their savant skill activities than in the classroom, they may have the opportunity to demonstrate greater levels of imagination and creativity, which in turn is noticed by their families. Lower levels of imagination and creativity would be expected in the class setting if little time is allocated for students to engage in their savant activities. No significant differences were found in the teacher and parent ratings of the levels of agreement/disagreement of the use of imagination and creativity in savant skill tasks between the treatment and control groups.

Whether or not savants display creativity and imagination in their fields of endeavour is an issue that is widely debated. The responses of the teachers and parents of this study to this issue are themselves a reflection of the two sides of this debate. The positive perceptions of the parents tend to support the view that some savants display creative elements in their savant domains (Selfe, 1977; Treffert, 1989, 2012 and Sacks,1995).

Behaviour and savant skills

Evidence for increased levels of challenging behaviours or otherwise was sought from parents and teachers of the children. The responses to the statement in the *Savant Skill Family/Teacher Questionnaires* (Appendix 2 and 3), with regard to the children displaying much negative behaviour, were similar for both the parents and teachers of the treatment and control groups, and also between the two groups. The mean scores for the teacher and parent responses for both groups indicated a general level of either ambivalence to the statement and/or low level agreement.

However, the results of the pre-curriculum *Developmental Behaviour Checklist* indicated that the majority of both the treatment and control children exhibited such high levels of challenging behaviours as to warrant the classification of severe behavioural/emotional disturbance. It should be noted that the parents rated their children as displaying higher levels of behavioural disturbance than did the teachers, which again may be due to the children having more time, and therefore greater opportunities, to engage in difficult behaviours in the home than in the more restrictive school setting. My teaching experience of autistic savants has reinforced my belief that autistic savants display particularly high levels of challenging behaviour, and that this perception has most certainly been borne out by the findings of this study.

Change for the better

Data in response to the research questions in this section *Change for the Better* were acquired from the *Savant Skill Post-Study Family/Teacher Questionnaire* (Clark, 2011; Appendix 5), interviews, monitoring documents, artefacts and standardized tests of language (*CELF-3*), behaviour (*Developmental Behaviour Checklist*) and self-esteem (*BASE Rating Scale*). The *Autism Behaviour Checklist* was used to determine any change in level of autism.

The functional application of skills

The major point of inquiry of this study relates to whether or not the often unproductive savant/splinter skills found in the autistic population have 'been applied' in a functional manner, through the implementation of a differentiated curriculum. The parents of the treatment children in this study noted a substantial improvement in the functional application of their children's savant skills over the course of the *Savant Skill Curriculum*. No change in the functional application of the control group subjects was noted over the period of the *Curriculum*.

Although the teachers of the children failed to report an improvement in the functional use of their student's savant skills, as discussed previously, these results may well have been influenced by the changes in teachers for each child that occurred during the *Curriculum*. It should also be noted that, due to time constraints, the initial information and training undertaken with each child's teacher, by the author at the commencement of each child's program, may not have been as thorough as for teachers who participated in the later stages of the study. In other words, the teachers responsible for the implementation of the *Savant Skill Curriculum* at the conclusion of the study may not have been as committed to, or have a comprehensive understanding of, the nature of the differentiated educational program. However, it should be noted that 62 per cent of teachers did in fact report qualitative examples of the functional application of savant skills by the treatment children. Examples of the functional use of savant skills by the treatment children are outlined in Table 3.3.

The data from Table 3.4 also indicated the successful use of savant skills in a teaching/mentoring educational program. All the savant skills of subjects were incorporated into the individual teaching programs and were implemented by the teachers or mentors. A considerable percentage of Curriculum Teaching Strategies

TABLE 3.3 Parents' and teachers' responses, comments and examples of the functional application of savant skills by treatment subjects as a result of the *Savant Skill Curriculum*

Child	Functional Application of Skills Yes/No (Home/School)	Comments/Examples (Home/School)
Patrick	Yes/Yes	Is able to use the computer at home independently. Keeps class calendar, operates class weekly shopping list, types school newsletter, takes class roll.
Christopher	Yes/Yes	Uses library weekly with low support. Can now cook following written instructions. More awareness of C.'s skills by service providers, community and family to be used functionally and not just 'Christopher's obsessions'.
Benjamin	No/Yes	School thinks B. is a 'problem' without much 'potential'. Was unable to carry out mentor program as it's been a 'tough time' in our lives during the study. I would like to 'try again'. Is using computer skills at school for news, social stories and maths programs (with support).
Natasha	No/No	Her behaviours get in the way of her learning and her schooling has stressed her very much lately. More interested in joining in class activities now we include her savant tasks.
Bradley	Yes/Yes	Encourages school work completion. Peers at school very interested in his electrical inventions. Makes up fan games that classmates enjoy. He is growing socially and education wise through this study. He is a happier child at getting access to his interests and using them in his life. Monitors all the school electricals for the General Caretaker. His skills can be worked into the normal curriculum at school. Has made us very 'aware' of the 'potential' of these skills and how to use functionally.
Terry	Nil response/ No	Navigates with the street directory when we travel places. His skills would have increased had it not been for the illness and death of his father several months ago. The computer has been a very successful motivator for appropriate behaviour. The study has given us insight into what can possibly be achieved. I plan to pursue options for my son once our lives settle again. Skills have been used to some degree but Terry has had a very difficult first year in mainstream because his father passed away. He is becoming more settled and is doing some tasks. If circumstances had been different, the program would have helped.

TABLE 3.3 —*continued*

Child	Functional Application of Skills Yes/No (Home/School)	Comments/Examples (Home/School)
Anthony	Yes/No	Uses skills functionally at school but not at home, i.e. rings bell, keeps time for activities independently. Skills given a significance and dignity. Memory for train stations resulted in 'travel-training' and 'librarian work experience'.
John	Yes/Yes	Now uses spreadsheets, types personal lists and uses web on the computer. Highlighted skills for assimilation into general employment and the community. Able to use skills at school with support. Helps others with their computer work. Enjoys peer adulation of his skills. Is motivated to learn if activities involve his skills.
Jeremy	Yes/No	Using computer independently. Jeremy has had a difficult year which has impacted on his acceleration. Types his diary appropriately. Previous class 'too academic/abstract'. A good beginning to focus staff on his skills.
Warren	Yes/Yes	Writes out recipes, shopping lists, is typing and sending email letters. Is able to phone and talk to his father independently. Has been a good 'motivator' in all areas of his life. Is more compliant and will try things if promised his interests as rewards. Uses the computer independently at school and reads to acquire information on his interests. Using memory skill to rote learn maths tables.
Timothy	Yes/Yes	Writes his own stories to make books, writes list of instructions and communicates his feelings with stories. The functional use of his skills still unknown to me (mother). Now completes reading and writing tasks in an age-appropriate manner. Enjoys writing/reading across the curriculum.
Zane	No/No	He doesn't allow these skills to dominate his life. Communication, social and behaviour have all improved through the guidelines offered by the study. Explores the computer to a greater detail. Has highlighted Zane's skills to others and together we are able to nurture these abilities. Skills are within the class 'norms' and hyperlexic skills are catered for by regular classroom activities.
Joseph	No/No	Joseph just goes along as Joseph goes along. Can't say if I've seen a lot of change. We tried art lessons but only did what was expected and then he did his 'own thing'. His abilities are 'not present' at the moment. It has been his teacher's skill in developing his academic tasks and

TABLE 3.3 —*continued*

Child	Functional Application of Skills Yes/No (Home/School)	Comments/Examples (Home/School)
		behaviour management that have led to his overall improvement. I don't think it assisted too much but he enjoyed one-to-one craft lessons.
Martin	No/Yes	I am not sure how his skills can be put to functional use. By writing his own books his comprehension has increased. His drawing skills are continually improving. The study has helped his teachers find new ways to motivate and keep his interest. Martin is expressing himself through his drawing and writing, he is broadening his interests. He is more motivated to do regular school work. Martin is a 'changed person', he is happy and willing to work and I feel much of this change is due to letting him improve his skills in his favourite activities.
Simon	No/Yes	Resists doing things at home that he will do at school and his group home. Willing to help with the shopping. Keeps the class roll, receipts of class purchases, tallies monies required for community access programs, e.g. train travel. Has more functional use of the community, i.e. the library, internet, reading materials, etc. Becoming proficient at word processing. He needs to be helped to use his skills functionally.
Jack	Yes/Yes	This study is very beneficial for children with savant skills, he is doing very well in mainstream class now. He may develop into someone very important in his special field, e.g. an aeronautical engineer, which would be a big use for himself and society. Is teaching his classmates how to make simple constructions and also makes constructions for their play activities. His independent work skills have improved.
Percentage of positive responses	Home – 56.25% School – 65%	

TABLE 3.4 Level of achievement of *Savant Skill Curriculum* teaching strategies and functional application of *Curriculum* savant skills as rated by teachers/mentors

Child	Total Number of Curriculum Strategies Taught	Percentage of Curriculum Strategies Achieved	Percentage of Functional Application of Curriculum Strategy Savant Skill
Patrick	17	76	58
Christopher	23	52	91
Benjamin	Missing data		
Natasha	14	57	50
Bradley	28	60	60
Terry	9	77	77
Anthony	14	78	92
John	18	72	55
Jeremy	16	37.5	6.25
Warren	13	76	46
Timothy	10	80	100
Zane	13	69	61
Joseph	9	66	77
Martin	20	55	40
Simon	14	100	100
Jack	11	63	54
Mean		67.9	64.4
Range		37.5–100	6.25–100

were achieved (mean percentage 67.9 per cent) along with the functional application of the Curriculum Strategy Savant Skills (mean percentage 64.4 per cent).

The successful functional application of savant skills by the treatment children in this study may be attributed to the use of a differentiated educational program for autistic savants, which incorporated a range of educational strategies currently in use for the non-disabled gifted student, and also the student with autism. The interaction of the four *Savant Skill Curriculum* strategies – acceleration, enrichment, mentorships, and the facilitation of adaptive communication, social skills and appropriate behaviours using savant skills and interests – has resulted in a degree of productive talent for many of the children. Although for some their savant skills were not applied functionally, possibly due to the rigidity of their autistic behaviours and extremely obsessive nature of their savant interests (Rimland, 1978; Howe,

1989), many children achieved the functional application of their often 'non-functional' savant skills in the home, school and community.

The functional use of savant skills by individual savants has been achieved and reported upon in the past (Treffert, 1989, 2012). However, this is the first study of a differentiated program for a group of savants which has resulted in the successful functional application of savant skills.

Communication skills

The control group made significantly greater quantitative gains with their communication skills, when compared to the treatment group, over the period of the *Savant Skill Curriculum*. In spite of the inclusion of communication skills strategies involving each treatment child's savant interests in their Individual Savant Skill Programs, a significant improvement in communicative adaptive behaviours did not occur. Several factors may have contributed to this apparent poor result as measured by the *CELF-3*. Firstly, the fact that 83 per cent of the control group were attending mainstream regular education classes by the completion of the *Savant Skill Program*, compared to only 31 per cent of the treatment subjects, and may have helped to further facilitate the communication skills of the control children. It is assumed that the regular education mainstream classroom would provide more communication models and partners for students suffering communication impairments than an autism-specific classroom which the majority of the treatment children attended. Secondly, as the facilitation of adaptive communication, social and behaviour skills was a secondary aim of this study – the functional application of savant skills being the primary aim – fewer communication skills teaching strategies were designed and included in each child's individual program. On average, fewer than 25 per cent of each child's individual teaching goals were communication skills goals or activities. Should this study have included a greater number of communication teaching goals in each treatment child's program, greater gains in quantitative communication skills may have occurred.

Although qualitative gains in communication skills were reported by parents and teachers of the treatment group, these gains may not have been attributed to the *Savant Skill Curriculum*. The majority of subjects also received intensive communication skills teaching through their Individual Education Programs, and some children received additional speech therapy tutoring outside of school hours. However, it should be noted that the qualitative gains in communication skills of the treatment group in this study lends support to previous anecdotal reports of communicative adaptive functioning using savant abilities (Bryant, 1993; Sacks, 1995; Treffert, 1989, 2012).

The use of savant skills to facilitate the communication skills of autistic savants warrants further investigation. The lack of significant quantitative communication gains of the treatment children in this study, compared to the control children, may have in fact been due to the possible factors or variables outlined above, and not any failure of the *Savant Skill Curriculum* strategy to harness the motivation of the savant interests to teach adaptive behaviours.

Behaviour and social skills

The level of behavioural/emotional disturbance, as measured by the *Developmental Behaviour Checklist*, of both the treatment and control groups over the course of the *Savant Skill Curriculum* showed no significant degree of change. Again, this quantitative lack of change in the levels of behaviour/emotional disturbance may have been attributed to the fact that less than 25 per cent of each treatment child's *Savant Skill Program* goals were behaviour/social goals. As for the inclusion of the small number of communication goals, the teaching of behavioural and social skills was secondary to the functional application of savant skills, which formed over 50 per cent of each child's total number of teaching goals.

The lack of quantitative change in behaviours may also be attributed to the fact that the majority of the children in this study were indeed classified as being severely behaviourally/emotionally disturbed. To attempt to reduce the level of severe behavioural/emotional disturbance of the savant, a more intensive program of positive behaviour support than that included in the *Savant Skill Curriculum* would be required.

However, in spite of this reported lack of significant change in levels of behavioural/emotional disturbance of the subjects in this study at the conclusion of the *Savant Skill Curriculum*, the parents of the treatment group reported fewer children as reaching the clinical cut-off score for classification in the severe behaviour/emotional disturbance range. It should be noted that the teachers rated a greater percentage of the treatment group as being severely behaviourally/emotionally disturbed at the end of the *Curriculum*. Again, this difference in the responses between the parents and teachers may have been due to the fact that the parents, and not the teachers, were the stable reporting research partners, due to the many changes of teacher over the period of the *Curriculum*.

Parents and teachers also reported qualitative improvements in social skills and behaviour by treatment children over the course of the *Savant Skill Curriculum*. These qualitative improvements may have resulted from the inclusion of each child's savant obsessions or interests as reinforcers for appropriate social skills and behaviour. As for the facilitation of communication skills, the intense interest and intrinsic motivation demonstrated by autistic savants in their savant tasks was borrowed to facilitate the teaching of appropriate behaviours and social skills, the fourth component of the *Savant Skill Curriculum*. The use of obsessional skills and interests as reinforcers for behaviour change – noted by Kanner (1973), Hung (1978), Wolery et al. (1985), Howlin and Rutter (1987), Treffert (1989, 2012), Grandin (1992) and Charlop-Christy and Haymes (1996) – appears to be supported by the qualitative gains in behaviour and social interactions of the treatment children in this study.

Self-esteem

Although no significant change in levels of academic self-esteem were found using directional t-tests for dependent samples, for either the treatment or control groups over the course of the *Curriculum*, the observational data indicates some changes in the overall self-esteem levels of the treatment group. More than 25 per cent of the treatment children displayed gains, resulting in a change from a low to a moderate level of academic self-esteem, over the period of the *Curriculum*. No improvements in overall levels of academic self-esteem were observed for the control group. As mentioned in the previous chapter, the differences observed between the quantitative and observational data is very probably due to the small *n* resulting from the prevalence of the same rankings.

As no gains in self-esteem were observed in the control group (who were not exposed to a differentiated program related to their savant skills) and positive improvements in self-esteem were observed in the treatment subjects, these gains in self-esteem may be viewed as an outcome of the *Savant Skill Curriculum*. Although there have been no previous studies of the self-esteem of autistic savants, the gains in self-esteem of the treatment children who received a differentiated program may be equated to the positive shifts in self-esteem noted by Gross (1997), in her comparison of non-disabled gifted students in differing ability groups. She concluded that the students who received an accelerated differentiated program related to their abilities displayed the greatest gains in overall levels of self-esteem. Further, the positive shifts in academic self-esteem by the treatment children in this study supports the anecdotal evidence of positive expressions of self-esteem by savants whilst engaged in their individual savant pursuits, noted previously (Grandin, 1992; Miller, 1989; Treffert, 2012; Sacks, 1995).

Degree of autism

Over the course of the *Curriculum*, a definite reduction in the degree or level of autism was reported by the parents of the treatment group using the *Autism Behaviour Checklist*. No significant change in degree of autism was observed for the control group. By using observational data, that is, the mean standard scores for both groups, in fact, the overall mean scores for the control group increased, which implies an increase in the degree of level of autistic behaviours.

It should be noted that the *Autism Behaviour Checklist* would rarely be used today, as it has been replaced by other more comprehensive diagnostic instruments, including the *Childhood Autism Rating Scale* (Schopler et al., 1986), the *Autism Diagnostic Observation Schedule* (Lord et al., 2000) and the *Autism Diagnostic Interview – Revised* (Rutter et al., 2003).

Although, on the basis of the above results, it would appear that the *Savant Skill Curriculum* has impacted positively in diminishing the level of autism in the treatment children, it would be naïve to conclude that the *Curriculum* alone is responsible for this reduction. As well as the *Curriculum*, all children were involved in a variety of educational and/or therapeutic interventions with the aim of reducing the level of each child's autism. Given the complex nature of autism and the multi-faceted levels of impairment across behavioural, social, communication and sensory domains, a very thorough analysis of all aspects of gains in adaptive functioning, in relation to the multi-faced interventions and programs currently in place for each child, would be required. Such an analysis is beyond the scope of this study.

However, it is of interest to note that, for those subjects whose overall level of autism improved significantly, significant gains also occurred in adaptive functioning. For example, Anthony, whose autism level was greatly reduced over the course of the *Curriculum*, showed gains in the functional application of his savant skills, behaviour and social skills. Christopher, whose level of autism was also reduced, demonstrated similar gains in the functional application of his savant skills, qualitative gains in communication, quantitative and qualitative gains in behaviour, and an improvement in self-esteem. For subjects whose level of autism appeared to increase or worsen, fewer gains in adaptive functioning were observed. Jeremy, whose level of autism almost doubled over the period of the *Curriculum*, failed to demonstrate gains in self-esteem and communication skills, his level of behaviour/emotional disturbance greatly increased, and he achieved the least amount of functional application of his savant skills of all subjects.

Changes in the level of autism observed by parents of the treatment children appear to reflect quantitative and qualitative improvements in adaptive communication, behaviour and social skills, as well as the functional application of savant skills – the major aim of this study. This differentiated program for a group of autistic savants, the *Savant Skill Curriculum*, has therefore proven to be successful in reducing the impact of autism on the lives of many of the children who were the subjects of the study.

Change for the worse or no change

The majority of both parents and teachers reported no significant reduction or loss of savant skills over the course of the *Savant Skill Curriculum*. However, for a small number of children, a reduction or loss of skill was indeed noted (15.4 per cent). Where the loss or reduction of skill occurred, comments or possible reasons for the change were proffered by the parent or teacher – see Table 3.5. Several parents reported a qualitative reduction in skill, e.g. 'she used to draw in more detail' and 'the extraordinariness may have decreased', whilst others attributed a change to a 'difficult phase', or to 'fluctuating interests'. It should be noted that in no case was a complete loss of savant skill reported. Only one parent reported her son could no longer recall 'post-codes' but had not lost all of his memory savant ability.

As outlined in Chapter 2, Nadia the autistic savant artist was reported to have lost her drawing skills (Selfe, 1977; 2011) as her language and social skills increased. Nadia's reported loss of skills may have been due to a lack of differentiated programming related to her savant drawing skills, rather than being a consequence

TABLE 3.5 Reduction or loss of savant skills by treatment subjects during the *Savant Skill Curriculum*

Child	Savant Skills Diminished/Lost Yes/No (Home/School)	Comments	
		Family	School
Patrick	No/No		
Christopher	No/No		
Benjamin	No/No	He resists encouragement with his music.	
Natasha	Yes/No	She used to draw in more detail.	About the same.
Bradley	No/No		
Terry	Unsure/No	Maybe the calendar calculation because I haven't followed up with him at all.	
Anthony	Yes/No	Needs to refresh himself on his post-codes.	
John	Unsure/No	Fluctuates – seems to depend upon what is his latest 'interest'.	
Jeremy	No/Yes	Only when he has a difficult phase.	Unsure as new to class but expected skills to be higher.
Warren	No/No		
Timothy	Unsure/No	The 'extraordinariness' may have decreased but the skill may still be increasing.	Comprehension may be increasing.
Zane	No/No		
Joseph	No/No		
Martin	No/No		
Simon	No/No		
Jack	No/No	They are not diminishing and we should not let them.	

of an improvement in adaptive functioning. It is also unclear as to whether Nadia suffered a complete loss of drawing ability or rather, as for several subjects in this study, a qualitative loss only. An improvement in comprehension as being causal to the reduction of a savant skill (hyperlexia) was attributed to only one child in this study. Again this reduction of skill was a qualitative and not quantitative loss of ability.

Although Grandin (1992) is of the belief that savants may lose their savant abilities as they develop socially, the actual loss of skill may in fact be a relative rather than a total loss, as was the experience of a minority of children in this study. Grandin also attributed gains in social adaptive functioning to an actual loss or reduction of obsessive behaviours. Perhaps it is the reduction of the obsessive nature of savant activity, and not the actual skill itself, that leads to improvements in adaptive functioning. This view is further supported by Grandin's own personal experience in which she experienced a reduction in obsessive behaviours due to the use of anti-depressant medication whilst not losing any of her visualization or draughting skills.

To examine more fully the degree of qualitative loss of savant skill reported by a minority of parents in this study, a complete re-assessment of savant skills using both standardized and non-standardized measures would be necessary. As the primary purpose of the *Savant Skill Curriculum* was to apply savant and/or splinter skills in functional ways, an in-depth re-assessment and analysis of these skills was beyond the scope of this study.

References

American Psychiatric Association (2013). *Diagnostic and Statistical Manual of Mental Disorders* (5th Ed.). Arlington, VA: American Psychiatric Publishing.

Anastasi, A., and Levee, R. (1960). Intellectual defect and musical talent: A case report. *American Journal of Mental Deficiency, 64,* 695–703.

Anderson, M. (1992). *Intelligence and Development: A Cognitive Theory.* Oxford: Blackwell.

Angell, M.E., Nicholson, J.K., Watts, E.H., and Blum, C. (2011). Using a multicomponent adapted power card strategy to decrease latency during interactivity transitions for three children with developmental disabilities. *Focus on Autism and Other Developmental Disabilities, 26(4),* 206–217.

Applebaum, E., Egel, A.L., Koegel, R.L., and Imhoff, B. (1979). Measuring musical abilities of autistic children. *Journal of Autism and Developmental Disorders, 9,* 279–285.

Aspect. (2012). *Aspect Comprehensive Approach for Education: Action Research Study and Development of a User Manual.* Retrieved from www.autismspectrum.org.au/content/aspect-comprehensive-approach-education-action-research-study-and-development-user-manual.

Barry, L.M., and Burlew, S.B. (2004). Using social stories to teach choice and play skills to children with autism. *Focus on Autism and Other Developmental Disabilities, 19(1),* 45–51.

Bell, J. (1987). *Doing Your Research Project. A Guide for the First-Time Researchers in Education and Social Science.* Philadelphia: Open University Press.

Blum-Dimaya, A., Reever, S.A., Reever, K.F., and Hoch, H. (2010). Teaching children with autism to play a video game using activity schedules and game-embedded simultaneous video modelling. *Education and Treatment of Children, 33(3),* 351–370.

Brink, T.L. (1980). Idiot savant with unusual mechanical ability: An organic explanation. *American Journal of Psychiatry*, *137*, 250–251.

Bryant, J. (1993). *The Opening Door*. South Australia: Swift.

Campbell, A., and Tincani, M. (2011). The power card strategy: Strength-based intervention to increase direction following of children with autism spectrum disorder. *Journal of Positive Behavioural Interventions*, *13(4)*, 240–249.

Carter, M., Stephenson, J., Clark, T., Costley, D., Martin, J., Williams, K., Browne, L., Davies, L., and Bruck, S. (2014). Perspectives on regular and support class placement and factors that contribute to success of inclusion for children with ASD. *Journal of International Special Needs Education*, *17(2)*, 60–69.

Charlop-Christy, M.H., and Haymes, L.K. (1996). Using obsessions as reinforcers with and without mild reductive procedures to decrease inappropriate behaviours of children with autism. *Journal of Autism and Developmental Disorders*, *26(5)*, 527–546.

Charness, N., Clifton, J., and MacDonald, L. (1988). Case study of a musical 'mono-savant': A cognitive-psychological focus. In L. Obler and D.A. Fein (Eds.), *The Exceptional Brain* (pp. 277–293). New York: Guilford Press.

Cohen, L. and Marion, L. (1989). *Research Methods in Education. 3rd Edition.* New York: Routledge.

Comer, D. (1985). Musical talent brightens life in a blind severely retarded man. *The Toronto Star*, 16 May, p. 6.

Coopersmith, S., and Gilberts, R. (1982). *BASE. Behavioural Academic Self-Esteem. A Rating Scale.* CA: Consulting Psychologists Press, Inc.

Costley, D., Keane, E., Clark, T. and Lane, K. (2012). *A Practical Guide for Students with an Autism Spectrum Disorder in Secondary School.* London: Jessica Kingsley.

Davis, G.A., and Rimm, S.B. (2004). *Education of the Gifted and Talented (5th Ed.).* Boston, MA: Pearson Education.

DeHaan, R.F. and Havighurst, R.J. (1961). *Educating Gifted Children.* Chicago: University of Chicago Press.

Denzin, N.K. (1970). *The Research Act: A Theoretical Introduction to Sociological Methods.* Chicago: Aldine Press.

Down, J.L. (1887). *On Some of the Mental Affections of Childhood and Youth.* London: Churchill.

Einfield, S.L. (1992). Clinical assessment of psychiatric symptoms in mentally retarded individuals. *Australian and New Zealand Journal of Psychiatry*, *26*, 48–63.

Einfield, S.L., Tonge, B.J., and Parmenter, T. (1998). *Developmental Behaviour Checklist. Teachers Version (DBC-T).* Melbourne and Sydney: University of New South Wales, Monash University, and University of Sydney.

Ericsson, K.A., and Faivre, I. (1988). What's exceptional about exceptional abilities? In L. Obler and D.A. Fein (Eds.), *The Exceptional Brain* (pp. 436–473). New York: Guilford Press.

Ericsson, K., Roring, R., and Nandagopal, K. (2007). Giftedness and evidence for reproducibly superior performance: An account based on the expert performance framework. *High Abilities Studies*, *18*, 3–56.

Fein, D., and Obler, L.K. (1988). Neuropsychological study of talent: A developing field. In L. Obler and D.A. Fein (Eds.), *The Exceptional Brain* (pp. 3–18). New York: Guilford Press.

Feldhusen, J.F. (1986). A conception of giftedness. In R.J. Sternberg and J.E. Davidson (Eds.), *Conceptions of Giftedness* (pp. 112–127). Cambridge: Cambridge University Press.

Feldhusen, J.F., and Baska, L.K. (1989). Identification and assessment of the gifted. In J.F. Feldhusen, J. VanTassel-Baska and K. Seeley (Eds.). *Excellence in Educating the Gifted* (pp. 85–101). Denver: Love.

Foster, W. (1986). The application of single subject research methods to the study of exceptional ability and extraordinary achievement. *Gifted Child Quarterly, 30(1)*, 33–37.

Frey, D. (1978). Science and the single case in counselling research. *Personnel and Guidance Journal, 56*, 263–268.

Gagné, F. (1995). The differentiated nature of giftedness and talent: A model and its impact on the technical vocabulary of gifted and talented education. *Roeper Review, 18*, 103–111.

Gagné, F. (2009). Building gifts into talents: Detailed overview of the DMGT 2.0. In B. MacFarlane and T. Stambaugh (Eds.), *Leading Change in Gifted Education: The Festschrift of Dr Joyce Van Tassel-Baska* (pp. 61–80). Waco, TX: Prurfock Press.

Gardner, H. (1983). *Frames of Mind: The Theory of Multiple Intelligences.* New York: Harper and Row.

Goldberg, T.E. (1987). On hermetic reading abilities. *Journal of Autism and Developmental Disorders, 17*, 29–44.

Grandin, T. (1992). An inside view of autism. In E. Schopler and G. Mesibov (Eds.), *High Functioning Individuals with Autism* (pp. 105–126). New York: Plenum Press.

Grandin, T. (1995). *Thinking in Pictures and Other Reports from My Life with Autism.* New York: Vintage Books.

Gray, C., and Garand, J. (1993). Social stories: Improving responses of students with autism with accurate social information. *Focus on Autistic Behaviour, 8*, 1–10.

Gross, M.U.M. (1989). *Children of exceptional intellectual potential: Their origin and development.* A thesis in partial fulfilment of the Doctor of Philosophy Degree, Purdue University.

Gross, M.U.M. (1993). *Exceptionally Gifted Children. (2nd ed.)*London: Routledge.

Gross, M.U.M. (1997). How ability grouping turns big fish into little fish – or does it? Of optical illusions and optimal environments. *The Australian Journal of Gifted Education, 6(2)*, 18–30.

Gross, M.U.M. (2004). *Exceptionally Gifted Children* (2nd Ed.) London: Routledge.

Hermelin, B., and O'Connor, N. (1989). Intelligence and musical improvisation. *Psychological Medicine, 19*, 497–457.

Hermelin, B., and O'Connor, N. (1990). Factors and primes: A specific numerical ability. *Psychological Medicine, 20*, 163–169.

Hill, A.L. (1974). Idiot savants: A categorization of abilities. *Mental Retardation*, December, 12–13.

Hill, A.L. (1978). Savants: mentally retarded individuals with special skills. In N. Ellis (Ed.), *International Review of Research in Mental Retardation, 9* (pp. 277–298). New York: Academic Press.

Hoffman, E., and Reeves, R. (1979). An idiot savant with unusual mechanical ability. *American Journal of Psychiatry, 136*, 713–714.

Hodgdon, L.A. (1995). *Visual Strategies for Improving Communication. Vol. 1: Practical Supports for Home and School.* Michigan: Quirk Roberts.

Hollingworth, L.S. (1942). *Children above IQ 180.* New York: World Books.

Howe, M.J.A. (1989). *Fragments of Genius: The Strange Feats of Idiot Savants.* London: Routledge.

Howlin, P., Goode, S., Hutton, J., and Rutter, M. (2009). Savant skills in autism: Psychometric approaches and parental reports. *Philosophical Transactions of the Royal Society B, 364*, 1359–1367.

Howlin, P., and Rutter, M. (1987). *Treatment of Autistic Children.* Chichester, UK: Wiley.

Hung, D.W. (1978). Using self-stimulation as reinforcement for autistic children. *Journal of Autism and Childhood Schzophrenia, 8(3)*, 355–366.

Jolliffe, T., Lansdown, R., and Robinson, T. (1992). *Autism: A Personal Account*. London: The National Society.

Kanner, L. (1973). *Childhood Psychosis: Initial Studies and New Insights*. New York: Winston/ Wiley.

Kerlinger, F.N. (1970). *Foundations of Behavioural Research*. New York: Holt, Rinehart and Winston.

Krug, D.A., Arick, J.R., and Almond, P.J. (1988). *ABC. Autism Behavior Checklist. First Edition*. Oregon: ASIEP Education Co.

Lansing, M.D., and Schopler, E. (1978). Individualized education: A public school model. In M. Rutter and E. Schopler (Eds.). *Autism: A Reappraisal of Concepts and Treatment* (pp. 439–453). New York: Plenum Press.

Lord, C., Risi, S., Lambrecht, L., Cook, E.H., Jr, Leventhal, B.L., DiLavore,P.C., et al. (2000). The Autism Diagnostic Observation Schedule-Generic: A standard measure of social and communication deficits associated with autism. *Journal of Autism and Develpmental Disorders, 30*, 205–223.

Maker, C.J. (1982). *Curriculum Development for the Gifted*. Rockville, MD: Aspen Systems.

Marland, S.P. (1972). *Education of the Gifted and Talented, Vol. 1: A Report to the Congress of the United States by the U.S. Commissioner of Education*. Washington, DC: US Government Printing Office.

Merriam. S.B. (1988). *Case Study Research in Education: A Qualitative Approach*. San Francisco: Jossey Bass.

Miller, L.K. (1989). *Musical Savants: Exceptional Skill in the Mentally Retarded*. Hillsdale, NJ: Erlbaum.

Moon, S.M. (1991). Case study research in gifted education. In N.K. Buchanan and J.F. Feldhusen (Eds.), *Conducting Research and Evaluation in Gifted Education*, (pp. 157–178). New York: Teachers College Press.

National Autism Centre. (2009). *National Standards Project Findings and Conclusions*. Randolph, MA: Author.

National Research Council. (2001). *Educating Children with Autism*. Washington, DC: National Academy Press.

O'Connor, N. (1989). The performance of the 'idiot savant': Implicit and explicit. *British Journal of Disorders of Communication, 24*, 1–20.

O'Connor, N., and Hermelin, B. (1987). Visual and graphic abilities of the idiot savant artist. *Psychological Medicine, 17*, 79–90.

Odom, S.L., Boyd, B., Hall, L., and Hume, K. (2010). Evaluation of comprehensive treatment models for individuals with autism spectrum disorders. *Journal of Autism and Developmental Disorders, 40*, 425–436.

Perin, R., Berger, T.K., and Markram, H. (2011). A synaptic organising principle for cortical neuronal groups. *Proceedings of the National Academy of Sciences, 108(13)*, 5419–5424.

Powell, S.D., and Jordan, R.R. (1992). Remediating the thinking of pupils with autism: Principles into practice. *Journal of Developmental Disorders, 22(3)*, 417–453.

Renzulli, J.S. (1977). *The Enrichment Triad Mode: A Guide for Developing Defensible Programs for the Gifted and Talented*. Mansfield Centre, CT: Creative Learning Press.

Renzulli, J.S. (1978). What makes giftedness? Reexamining a definition. *Phi Delta Kappan, 60*, 180–184, 261.

Rimland, B. (1978). Inside the mind of the autistic savant. *Psychology Today, 12*, 68–80.

Roberts, M.A., Keane, E., and Clark, T.R. (2008). Making inclusion work, Autism Spectrum Australia's Satellite Class Project. *TEACHING Exceptional Children, Nov/Dec*. Council for Exceptional Children.

Rosen, A.M. (1981). Adult calendar calculators in a psychiatric OPD: A report of two cases and comparative analysis of abilities. *Journal of Autism and Developmental Disorders, 11*, 285–292.

Rutter, M. (1978). Diagnosis and definition. In M. Rutter and E. Schopler (Eds.), *Autism: A Reappraisal of Concepts and Treatment*. New York: Plenum Press.

Rutter, M. (1998). Autism: Two-way interplay between research and clinical work. The Emanuel Miller Memorial Lecture. *Journal of Child Psychology and Psychiatry, 40(2)*, 169–188.

Rutter, M., Le Couteur, A., and Lord, C. (2003). *Autism Diagnostic Interview – Revised (ADI-R)*. Los Angeles: Western Psychological Services.

Sacks, O. (1995). *An Anthropologist on Mars*. London: Picador.

Sak, U. (2011). An overview and social validity of the education programs for talented students model (EPTS). *Education and Science, 36(161)*, 1–17.

Schopler, E., and Mesibov, G. (1992). High functioning individuals with autism. In E. Schopler and G. Mesibov (Eds.), *Current Issues in Autism*. New York: Plenum.

Schopler, E., Reichler, R.J., and Renner, B.R. (1986). *The Childhood Autism Rating Scale (CARS) for Diagnostic Screening and Classification of Autism*. New York: Irvington Publishers.

Schreibman, L., and Mills, J.I. (1983). Infantile autism. In T.J. Ollendick and M. Hersen (Eds.), *Handbook of Child Psychopathology*. New York: Plenum.

Selfe, L. (1977). *Nadia: A Case of Extraordinary Ability in an Autistic Child*. London: Academic Press.

Selfe, L. (2011). *Nadia Revisited – A Longitudinal Study of an Autistic Savant*. London: Psychology Press.

Semel, L., Wiig, E.H., and Secord, W.A. (1995). *Clinical Evaluation of Language Fundamentals – 3rd Edition*. San Antonio: The Psychological Corporation. Harcourt Brace and Co.

Scheslow, D., and Adams, W. (1990). *WRAML, Wide Range Assessment of Memory and Learning*. Torrance, CA: WPS.

Siegle, D. (2007a). *Developing Mentorship Programs for Gifted Students*. Waco, TX: Prufrock Press, Inc.

Siegle, D. (2007b). Podcasts and blogs: Learning opportunities on the information highway. *Gifted Child Today, 30(3)*, 14–19.

Snyder, A.W., and Mitchell, D.J. (1999). Is integer arithmetic fundamental to mental processing? The mind's secret arithmetic. *Proceedings of the Royal Society. Biological Sciences, 266(1419)*, 537–647.

Sternberg, R.J. (1981). A componential theory of intellectual giftedness. *Gifted Child Quarterly, 25*, 86–93.

Sternberg, R.J., and Davidson, J.E. (Eds.) (2005). *Conceptions of Giftedness* (2nd Ed.). Cambridge, England: Cambridge University Press.

Stevens, D.E., and Moffitt, T.E. (1988). Neuropsychological profile of an Asperger's syndrome case with exceptional calculating ability. *Clinical Neuropsychologist, 2*, 228–238.

Tannenbaum, A.J. (1983). *Gifted Children: Psychological and Educational Perspectives*. New York: Macmillan.

Tredgold, A.F. (1914). *Mental Deficiency*. New York: William Wood.

Treffert, D. (1989). *Extraordinary People*. London: Bantam Press.

Treffert, D. (2012). *Islands of Genius: The Bountiful Mind of the Autistic, Acquired, and Sudden Savant*. London: Jessica Kingsley Publishers.

VanTassel-Baska, J., and Wood, S.M. (2009). The integrated curriculum model. In J.S. Renzulli, F.J. Gubbins, K.S. McMillen, R.D. Eckert and C.A. Little (Eds.), *Systems and Models for Developing Programs for the Gifted and Talented.* Mansfield Centre, CT: Creative Learning Press.

Wallace, G.L. (2008). Neuropsychological studies of savant skills: Can they inform the neuroscience of giftedness? *Roeper Review, 30,* 229–246.

Wing, L. (1976). Diagnosis, clinical description, and prognosis. In L. Wing (Ed.), *Early Childhood Autism: Clinical, Educational and Social Aspects* (2nd Ed.). Oxford: Pergamon Press.

Wolery, M., Kirk, K., and Gost, D.L. (1985). Stereotypic behaviour as a reinforcer: Effects and side effects. *Journal of Autism and Developmental Disorders, 15(2),* 35–54.

Wong, C., Odom, S.L., Hume, K., Cox, A., Fettig, A., Kucharczyk,S., Brock, M.E., Plavnick, J.B., Fleury, V.P., and Schultz, T.R. (2013). *Evidence-based Practices for Children, Youth, and Young Adults with Autism Spectrum Disorder.* Chapel Hill: The University of North Carolina, Frank Porter Graham Child Development Institute, Autism Evidence-Based Practice Review Group.

Yin, R.K. (2009). *Case Study Research: Design and Methods* (4th Ed.). Los Angeles, CA: Sage.

Young, R.L. (1995). Savant syndrome: Processes underlying extraordinary abilities. Unpublished doctoral dissertation, University of Adelaide, South Australia.

Young, R.L., and Nettelbeck, T. (1994). The 'intelligence' of calendrical calculators. *American Journal of Mental Retardation, 99,* 186–200.

Young, R.L., and Nettelbeck, T. (1995). The abilities of a musical savant and his family. *Journal of Autism and Developmental Disorders, 25,* 231–248.

4

THE GUIDE TO PRACTICE

How can the Savant Skill Curriculum *be used in daily practice?*

I am a special educator teacher and have taught special education kids for the past 15 years. Unfortunately, I have not had the pleasure of working with any autistic savant children until now. I have no experience with students in this gifted capacity. Please guide me to find resources and strategies to assist my student. He is AMAZING with numbers (math) and calendar math. Thank you for your time.

(Email correspondence special needs teacher,
21 September 2015)

I would appreciate some guidance in thinking about a student who has just applied to undertake an advanced secondary school music course. The student was diagnosed with autism at 4 years of age, and although he has difficulty communicating with people, his family discovered a special talent in music when he was young and have worked consistently to help him develop that ability. He is an extraordinary musician who clearly has savant skills. He also has an exceptional memory which enables him to read and recall text perfectly. Unfortunately, I am concerned that he may not have the higher order thinking skills to engage in the critical writing and complex assignments required for the advanced music course. Could you possibly offer any guidance or suggestions so that we may be able to help this young student?

(Email correspondence from teacher of
secondary student, November 2013)

Today, my almost 4 year old son's doctor told my husband and me about savant and splinter skills and I'm greatly considering implementing a Savant Skill Curriculum for her at home. Although she is only in pre-school, her phonics skills tests are at a 72–85 month old level. She enjoys listening to composers of classical music, learning new visuals, and he has a love for smart-devices such as tablets and iPhones. Any additional help you can share would be greatly appreciated.

> (Email correspondence from mother of three-year-old boy, 16 September 2014)

These emails are examples of the requests for support I regularly receive from teachers and families, and which highlights the need for differentiated programs for these exceptional children. Until now, my response to these requests has usually been to forward the teacher or parents a copy of the *Savant Skill Nomination Form* (Clark, 2011), which was originally developed to identify savant skills in children who were referred to this study. On completion of the form, I would then recommend a number of teaching goals for school and home, using the educational strategies from the *Savant Skill Curriculum* outlined in Chapter 3. By writing this book, this differentiated educational program for autistic savants is now available to all.

This chapter is primarily written for teachers, but will also be of interest to allied health professionals working with students with autism in schools: psychologists, speech and occupational therapists. It will also be of interest to the parents of the 'paradox children', given the numbers of parents who regularly seek support for their children who display these special skills. Research and practice in the field of autism supports the view that the best possible outcomes for students with autism are achieved when educational and behavioural strategies are implemented across all of the child's environments: the school, the home and the community. Given that many of the students' *Savant Skill Curriculum* individual teaching goals were developed for use across school and community environments, it is important that all of those supporting the autistic savant understand how to implement this differentiated educational program.

The chapter will include a step-by-step guide to the implementation of the *Savant Skill Curriculum* through the journey of one child, who participated in the study: from referral and identification, through to the final evaluation. Supporting materials are included in either the appendices, or are available as eResources on the Routledge website.

Steps to the implementation of the *Savant Skill Curriculum*

The steps to the development and implementation of the Curriculum are summarized in Figure 4.1. Each step will be further illustrated through the case of Jeremy.

Jeremy's journey

Jeremy was diagnosed at the age of three with autism and was assessed as having a mild or borderline intellectual delay. Jeremy was eight years of age at the time

Steps to developing the *Savant Skill Curriculum* – Clark, 2011

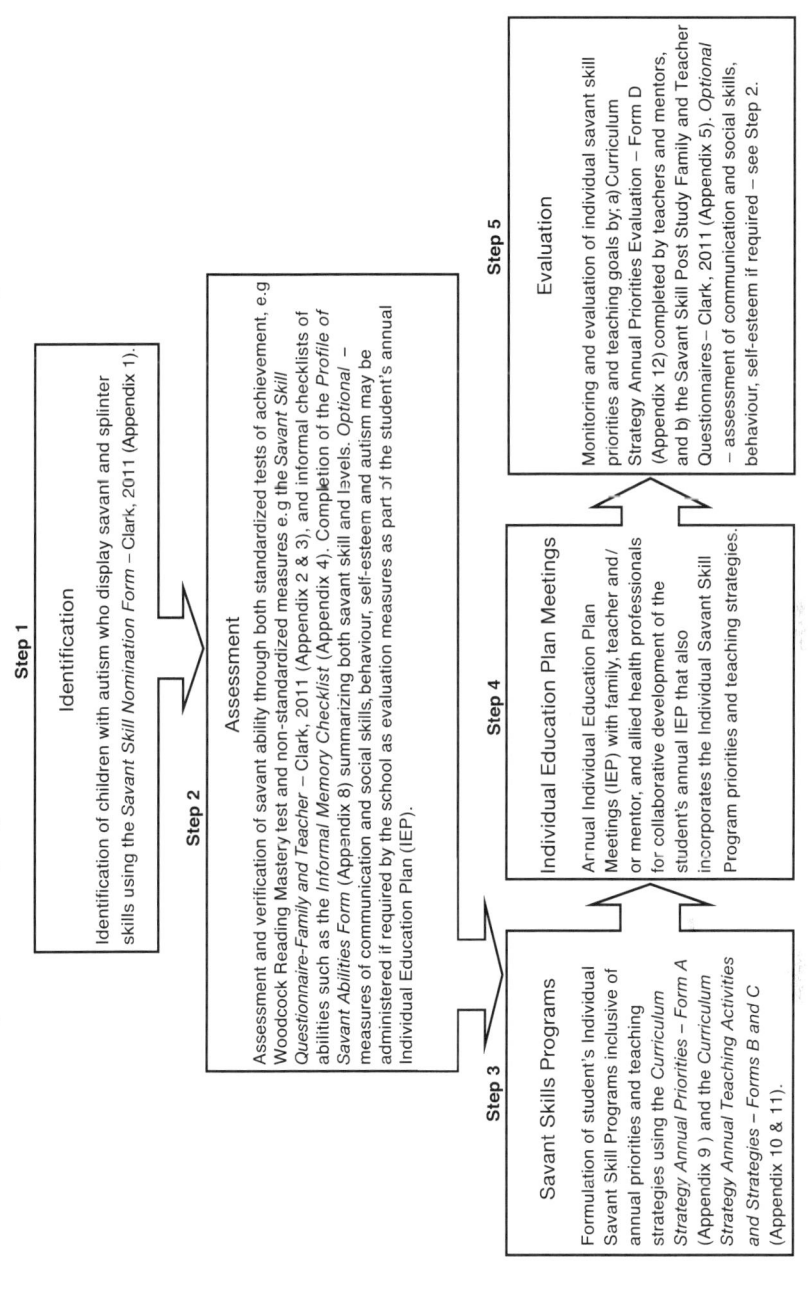

Step 1

Identification

Identification of children with autism who display savant and splinter skills using the *Savant Skill Nomination Form* – Clark, 2011 (Appendix 1).

Step 2

Assessment

Assessment and verification of savant ability through both standardized tests of achievement, e.g Woodcock Reading Mastery test and non-standardized measures e.g the *Savant Skill Questionnaire–Family and Teacher* – Clark, 2011 (Appendix 2 & 3), and informal checklists of abilities such as the *Informal Memory Checklist* (Appendix 4). Completion of the *Profile of Savant Abilities Form* (Appendix 8) summarizing both savant skill and levels. *Optional* – measures of communication and social skills, behaviour, self-esteem and autism may be administered if required by the school as evaluation measures as part of the student's annual Individual Education Plan (IEP).

Step 3

Savant Skills Programs

Formulation of student's Individual Savant Skill Programs inclusive of annual priorities and teaching strategies using the *Curriculum Strategy Annual Priorities – Form A* (Appendix 9) and the *Curriculum Strategy Annual Teaching Activities and Strategies – Forms B and C* (Appendix 10 & 11).

Step 4

Individual Education Plan Meetings

Annual Individual Education Plan Meetings (IEP) with family, teacher and/ or mentor, and allied health professionals for collaborative development of the student's annual IEP that also incorporates the Individual Savant Skill Program priorities and teaching strategies.

Step 5

Evaluation

Monitoring and evaluation of individual savant skill priorities and teaching goals by; a) Curriculum Strategy Annual Priorities Evaluation – Form D (Appendix 12) completed by teachers and mentors, and b) the Savant Skill Post Study Family and Teacher Questionnaires– Clark, 2011 (Appendix 5). *Optional* – assessment of communication and social skills, behaviour, self-esteem if required – see Step 2.

FIGURE 4.1 Steps to the implementation of the *Savant Skill Curriculum*

of this study. Having spent several years attending an autism-specific special school, he recently transferred to one of the school's satellite classes for more able students, which is located in a mainstream setting. His current Individual Education Program (IEP) is focused upon the development of communication and social skills, appropriate behaviours, the mainstream curriculum and gradual integration into mainstream classes. Given Jeremy's placement in a satellite class located in a mainstream school, his journey through the *Curriculum* will serve to provide a model of support for mainstream teachers of autistic savants.

Step 1: Identification of children with autism who display savant and splinter skills

Jeremy's teacher and parents completed the *Savant Skill Nomination Form* (Appendix 1), which was designed to identify whether a student exhibited one or more of the discrete list of savant skills: memory, hyperlexia, maths/number, drawing/art, music, mechanical/spatial, calendar calculation, sensory sensitivity, athletic/ball skills, or other.

Teachers and parents were asked to respond to the question below:

> Does your child show an unusual degree of skill in any or all of the following areas?
>
> *If the answer is YES to any of the following skills, please rate the skill level as either:*
>
> 1 only special in relation to his/her overall ability
> 2 special in comparison to other individuals of similar age
> 3 would be considered EXCEPTIONAL in the normal population
>
> Circle the appropriate number associated with that particular ability. Furthermore, you may like to provide examples of the ability.

The *Savant Skill Nomination Form* also seeks information regarding the child's savant skills, such as level of interest, time spent on interests, if there is evidence of challenging behaviours, if the skill is being used in functional and meaningful ways, and if other family members are gifted or talented.

Jeremy was reported by both his teacher and parents as displaying the following savant or splinter skills, along with their associated ratings: memory (3); hyperlexic (3); mechanical/spatial skills (2); and music (2). He was also reported to display athletic ability (excellent balance and climbing skills), and some sensory sensitivities (can tune TV to correct sound and picture).

Step 2: Assessment and verification of savant ability and level through both standardized and non-standardized measures. Completion of the Profile of Savant Abilities Form

Following his initial identification as outlined above, a complete profile was developed of Jeremy's disabilities, level of cognitive ability, communication skills, behaviour and social functioning, academic self-esteem, savant abilities, age of onset of abilities, familiar background, pregnancy and birth details and educational placement at the commencement of the *Savant Skill Curriculum*. A combination of standardized and non-standardized measures was undertaken of his savant abilities: memory (*Wide Range Assessment of Memory and Learning*, informal memory check-lists); hyperlexia (*Westwood Test of Spelling* and *Woodcock Reading Mastery Tests*); mechanical/spatial skills (*Wide Range Assessment of Visual Motor Abilities*), informal measures such as assembling/disassembling objects – e.g. clocks, radios, construction games; and art/drawing (*Clark's Drawing Abilities Test*). A complete list of the savant skill assessments and their descriptions are available on the Routledge website at Summary and Description of Savant Skill Assessments – Table 2.8. Both the *Savant Skill Questionnaires – Family and Teacher* (Clark, 2011; Appendix 2 and 3) were used for informal non-standardized information in relation to Jeremy's savant abilities. The level of each of Jeremy's savant skills (Treffert, 1989) was then assessed as being a Savant I/S, I or II skill. Where a savant or splinter skill appeared to be less highly developed than a Talented Savant (I) level skill, but is apparent or emerging, the classification of Talented/Splinter skill (I/S) is appropriate. When skills were assessed using standardized measures and Jeremy performed above his chronological age level, the Savant II level skill was awarded. For those skills that did not reach levels of performance equivalent for his chronological age, a Savant I classification was awarded. As mentioned previously, it is not necessary to undertake assessments of communication skills, behaviour and social functioning, academic self-esteem, to develop the Individual Savant Skill Programs. This information may however be required by the school and so would therefore form part of the student's annual individual education plan. The information derived from the assessments and the questionnaires was then used to complete the student's *Profile of Savant Abilities* – template available in Appendix 8. A copy of Jeremy's profile at the time of the study is presented in Table 4.1 along with a descriptive overview of his disabilities and abilities.

Jeremy is the younger of two children and lives at home with his family in Sydney. Jeremy is eight years of age. His teenage sister displays excellent computer skills. Both parents hold university qualifications. Although no other family member has been known to suffer from autism, Jeremy's grandmother was dyslexic. Jeremy was diagnosed with significant autism at the age of two years as a result of delayed language, social skills and obsessive behaviours. It was noted he displayed a keen interest in TV adverts, doing puzzles, exploring how to use the video player, and typing letters on the computer. He displayed little pretend play, tended to line up objects, and was considered inflexible, 'living life to his agenda'. At three years and six months he was referred to an autism-specific early intervention service. Initially assessed as functioning in the globally moderate range of intellectual disability, his most recent psychological assessment (Stanford-Binet IV) placed him in the borderline mild range of intellectual disability.

At the age of three years Jeremy was typing the alphabet independently on the computer. Without formal training, he can use the word processor, use graphic

TABLE 4.1 Profile of Jeremy's savant abilities

PROFILE OF JEREMY'S SAVANT ABILITIES		
NAME: Jeremy *AGE*: 8		
RESULTS OF PRE-TESTS		
PROFILE OF SAVANT SKILLS		
SAVANT ABILITY AND LEVEL	**STANDARDIZED MEASURES**	**NON-STANDARDIZED MEASURES/INFORMATION**
Memory **Savant II** **Hyperlexia (Reading/ Spelling/Writing)** **Savant I**	**WRAML – Wide Range Assessment of Memory and Learning** J. performed in the average range for short term memory (91). There was no discrepancy between verbal and non-verbal memory skills. Results Included; Bead Memory – 46, Memory for Sentences – 45, Memory for digits – 48 (50 being an average score, 94 to 100 being the average total range). Although J. appeared to achieve a higher overall memory score on the Stanford-Binet than the WRAML he was below average on both tests. **The Westwood Spelling Test** **Results:** J. has a spelling age of approximately 9 years, 3 months – 9 years, 6 months i.e. a result approximately 1½ years in advance of his chronological age. **The Woodcock Reading Mastery Tests** (i) Word Identification Age Equivalent = 8 years, 5 months Grade Equivalent = 3:3 Percentile Rank = 81	**Family/Teacher Savant Skill Questionnaire & Informal Tests of Memory Designed for the Study** J. can recall some local post codes of suburbs, some birthdays of familiar persons and some phone numbers associated with commercials (e.g. Pizza Hut – 9498 8211). He has an exceptional memory for directions/routes travelled and TV commercials and songs. J. has a highly selective memory – if not somewhat restricted in repertoire. **Family/Teacher Savant Skill Questionnaire** J. developed an interest in letters and words at an early age. By the age of three, he could type the alphabet on the computer, read TV commercials, street and suburb names i.e. topics of high interest. It would appear that J. taught himself to read.

Mechanical or Spatial Skill **Computer Savant II**	(ii) Passage Comprehension Age Equivalent = 7 years, 2 months Grade Equivalent = 1:9 Percentile Rank = 29 In both spelling and word identification, J. performed above his chronological age (spelling 1½ years and word identification skills 6 months in advance of his chronological age). **A. WRAVMA – Wide Range Assessment of Visual Motor Abilities** The WRAVMA assesses aspects of visual-motor functioning. The Matching Subtest measures 'visual-spatial' skill. **Results :** (i) Matching Subtest (Nov,98) Standard Score = 96 Percentile = 39th Age Equivalent = 7 years. 8 months J's performance on the WRAVMA indicates a nine-month delay	
	B. Differential Aptitude Tests (DAT) ACER Space Relations (Form V, Book 4) Measures a student's ability to visualize and to imagine the shape and surfaces of an object. **Test Date:** **Results:** Raw Score – 22/60 Percentile – 35 Note: The percentile score, although below 50, is an indication that J. does in fact demonstrate spatial ability as the youngest year group on which the scores are normed is Year 9. J. is approximately Year 2 grade.	**Family/Teacher Savant Skill Questionnaire** His family observed J. build a replica of the M2 motorway in the garden. Eventually his construction extended onto the neighbour's yard also. No other evidence of Mechanical/Spatial skill has been observed.

TABLE 4.1 *—continued*

SAVANT ABILITY AND LEVEL	STANDARDIZED MEASURES	NON-STANDARDIZED MEASURES/INFORMATION
Computer **Savant II**	No formal standardized computer tests available at time of testing.	J. has taught himself to use the computer at home. He has received only basic instructions at school. He can: - open and close his saved work - use graphics functions to draw diagrams - resize and delete illustrations - use the word processor for copying information, e.g. lists of street names, etc. - use the printer - type with one finger He also enjoys many computer games at which he is both accurate and fast. He has an excellent ability to remember 'moves' within games. At school he works independently on the computer, operates the mouse and selects his own software. It would appear J. has prodigious computer ability based upon high interest and self-learning.
Athletic Performance	Formal testing not undertaken, as teachers reported that J's athletic skills are equivalent to those of his autistic peers.	Although not tested formally, it would appear that from the Family/Teacher Questionnaire, J. also displays athletic ability. His parents report that he has excellent balance and running ability. He recently went rock climbing and achieved a moderate level of difficulty with ease.
Art **Savant I/Splinter**	Formal testing not administered as artistic skill was not detected until mid-way through the treatment program. J's drawing skills were not included in his savant program.	Teacher reports he has excellent drawing ability – his drawing being graphic and correct.

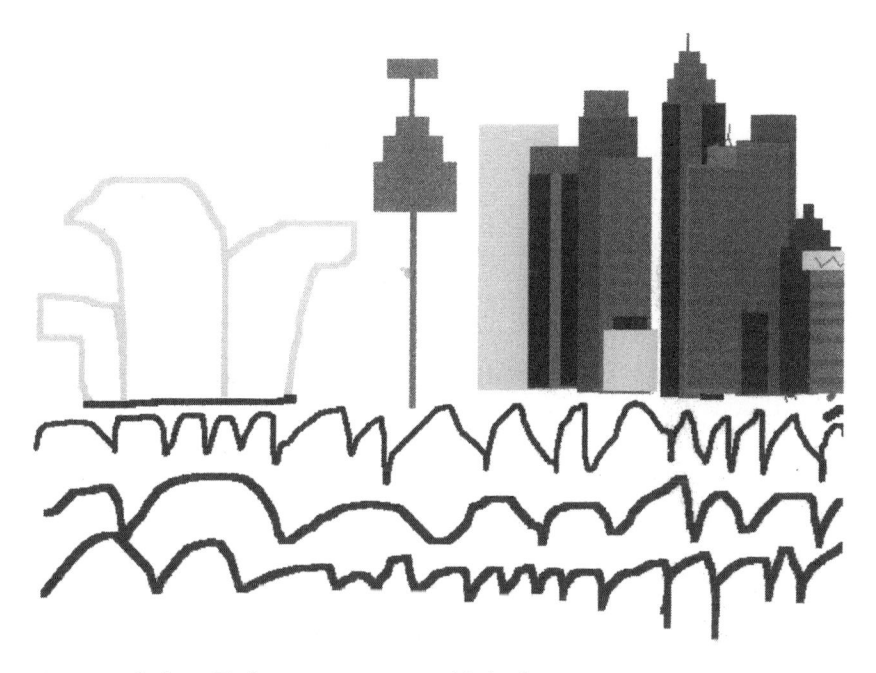

FIGURE 4.2 Sydney Skyline – computer graphic by Jeremy

functions to draw pictures and diagrams, and can accurately play a variety of complex computer games. He has an exceptional memory for directions and a route travelled, and spends many hours studying the street directory. He recalls many TV commercials and favourite songs. He loves to draw buildings and cityscapes, which he translates to computer graphics – see Figure 4.2.

Jeremy's language skills are significantly delayed as assessed on the *CELF-3*. His language skills are equivalent to those of a five-year-old. His performance on the *Word Classes* subtest, however, indicated a relative strength in the ability to associate related words, which is important for making predictions, inferences and creating meaning from spoken language. He is able to use language to communicate his needs and wants. His teacher reports his expressive language can be appropriate when related to a personal interest, which determines his willingness to participate in class conversations and discussions.

Jeremy experiences a great deal of difficulty coping with social situations and also managing his own behaviour. He is considered to be severely behaviourally and emotionally disturbed, as assessed by the *Developmental Behaviour Checklist*. He is socially very aloof and isolated from his peers and will not participate in group social sessions unless prompted to do so. He is often non-compliant at school and home, and requires a great deal of assistance to manage his own behaviour. If not carefully supervised he can place himself in life-threatening situations, which includes running onto roads to gain attention. Although his teacher reports he spends about 75 per cent of his class time in productive learning, he does require a great deal of teacher attention. His academic self-esteem is low as assessed by the *BASE* rating scale.

As mentioned previously, Jeremy was recently transferred to one of his school's satellite classes in a mainstream setting. His current IEP is focused upon the development of adaptive functioning – communication and social skills, appropriate behaviours, and gradual integration into mainstream classes. His savant abilities are not addressed in his class program.

It can be seen from Jeremy's profile that a great deal of information can be gathered on each child using standardized assessments, combined with the qualitative *Savant Skill Questionnaires*. This rich information then allows the teacher to develop the child's differentiated program with confidence.

Step 3: Development of Individual Savant Skill Program

Using the information from the profile of Jeremy's savant abilities, his Individual Savant Skill Program was then developed. Teaching priorities and activities were designed to facilitate the functional application of Jeremy's individual savant skills, incorporating successful and evidence-based strategies currently used in both gifted and autism education. Gifted education strategies included the use of enrichment, acceleration and mentorships. The autism intervention strategies included social stories, visual supports for communication, and positive behaviour support. A variety of communication, social and behavioural priorities were also developed based upon his current school Individual Education Program (IEP) and using his savant interests and skills.

Jeremy's Savant Skill Program is divided into three separate sections:

1 *Curriculum Strategy Annual Priorities – Form A* (Appendix 9), which outlines the twelve-month broad teaching priorities or goals.
2 *Curriculum Teaching Activities and Strategies – Form B* (Appendix 10), which contains the specific teaching activities that relate to each of the Annual Priorities (Form A).
3 *Curriculum Teaching Activities – Form C* (Appendix 11), which incorporates the communication, social or behavioural priorities/goals to be taught.

Jeremy's program contained a 'smorgasbord' of teaching activities for his teacher to select from, and a copy is included in Table 4.2. His Individual Savant Skill Program served as 'working documents' for his family and teachers and were presented at his Individual Annual Education Plan meeting. To further support his computer skills, a teacher assistant from his school with a high-level computer knowledge and ability mentored Jeremy for the two years over the course of the *Savant Skill Curriculum*.

TABLE 4.2 Jeremy's Individual Savant Skill Program

JEREMY'S CURRICULUM STRATEGY ANNUAL PRIORITIES - FORM A						
NAME: Jeremy		*AGE*: 8				
CURRICULUM ANNUAL PRIORITIES						
SAVANT SKILL AND LEVEL (I OR II)	H/ S	ENRICHMENT	ACCELERATION	MENTORSHIP	COMMUNICATION/ SOCIAL	COMMENTS
Memory (Savant II)	H & S	**Geography** To use local and national knowledge i.e. suburbs, capital cities, etc. for individual project/ research work e.g. compile directories for different excursions.	**Comprehension** To use J's interest in commercials to improve reading comprehension.		Refer to Form C.	
Memory (Savant II)	H & S	**Drawing** To use J's interest in commercials to improve artistic skill.				
Memory (Savant II)	H & S	**Memory Games** To develop games e.g. Bingo using memory interests.				
Memory (Savant II)	H & S	**Personal Diary** To develop a personal diary of daily events, visits, etc. at home or school.				

TABLE 4.2—*continued*

JEREMY'S CURRICULUM STRATEGY ANNUAL PRIORITIES – FORM A						
NAME: Jeremy			*AGE*: 8			
CURRICULUM ANNUAL PRIORITIES						
SAVANT SKILL AND LEVEL (I OR II)	H/ S	ENRICHMENT	ACCELERATION	MENTORSHIP	COMMUNICATION / SOCIAL	COMMENTS
Hyperlexia **(Savant I)**	H & S	**Language** To compile word lists (categories) for personal and peer group written language work.	**Reading** To use his interest in words to further increase his vocabulary and comprehension skills e.g. to compile word lists and meanings associated with home and school events i.e. research topics of interest.		Refer to Form C	
Hyperlexia **(Savant I)**	H & S	**Language** To teach J. word games such as Word Lotto and Bingo, which further develop language concepts e.g. bingo of antonyms, synonyms, word meanings.				
Computer **(Savant II)**	H & S	**Computer Software** To introduce different types of software (home/school) that relate to J's interests e.g. games, graphics programs, World Atlas, etc.	**Computer Operations** To teach more advanced computer operations i.e. advanced graphics programs (Mentor Program).	**Mentor** To obtain a mentor to expand J's knowledge and use of more complex computer operations (as for Accelerations).	Refer to Form C	

TABLE 4.2—*continued*

JEREMY'S CURRICULUM STRATEGY ANNUAL PRIORITIES - FORM B						
NAME: Jeremy			*AGE*: 8			
CURRICULUM ANNUAL PRIORITIES						
SAVANT SKILL (I or II)	**H/ S**	**ENRICHMENT**	**ACCELERATION**	**MENTOR**		**COMMENTS**
Memory (Savant II)	H & S	**Knowledge of Geography** J. to compile directory of school/home excursions. Write out directions on his own map.	**Comprehension** J. to write/list familiar, and unfamiliar commercials. Teacher to develop comprehension questions related to commercials.			
Memory (Savant II)	H & S	**Drawing** J. to paint, draw, colour familiar and unfamiliar commercials. Design new commercials also.				
Memory (Savant II)	H & S	**Personal Diary** J. to write out events and activities following home/school excursions (Computer).				
Memory (Savant II)	H & S	**Memory Games** To learn games e.g. Bingo, Happy Families, Swap, etc. (Home/ School) using memory topics.				

TABLE 4.2—*continued*

JEREMY'S CURRICULUM STRATEGY ANNUAL PRIORITIES – FORM B						
NAME: Jeremy		*AGE:* 8				
CURRICULUM ANNUAL PRIORITIES						
SAVANT SKILL (I or II)	**H/ S**	**ENRICHMENT**	**ACCELERATION**	**MENTOR**		**COMMENTS**
Hyperlexia (Savant II)	H & S	**Vocabulary and Comprehension** J. to research interest areas i.e. special buildings, capital cities, places etc.	**Research Skills** Teach 'research skills' to use the school/local library (home/school).			
Hyperlexia (Savant II)	S	**Language** To compile spelling lists, individual topic books of information researched, etc.				
Hyperlexia (Savant II)	S	**Language** Teach J. word games – Lotto, Bingo, crosswords based on language concepts, e.g. antonyms, synonyms, word meanings and introduce unfamiliar words and concepts.				

TABLE 4.2—*continued*

SAVANT SKILL (I or II)	H/ S	ENRICHMENT	ACCELERATION	MENTOR		COMMENTS
Computer (Savant II)	H & S	**Computer Software** Introduce J. to the following programs: World Atlas, World Encyclopaedia, Where in the World is Carmen Santiago?	**Computer Operations** Teach J. the following advanced programs: Microsoft Word, Microsoft Excel, etc.	**Mentor** (As for enrichment and acceleration)		
Computer (Savant II)	H & S	J. to use the computer to keep a personal diary of life events and topics of interest e.g. "My places of interest"	"I want to travel to…"			

TABLE 4.2—*continued*

JEREMY'S CURRICULUM STRATEGY TEACHING ACTIVITIES - FORM C				
NAME: Jeremy		*AGE*: 8		
ANNUAL PRIORITY	**E/ment H/S**	**MUSIC**	**HYPERLEXIA**	**COMPUTER**
COMMUNICATION				
To answer 'why' questions	S	Ask why questions related to interests in commercials and directions for outings (upon return), etc.		Introduce language software that includes the use of questions.
To ask where, what and why questions	S	Include why, what, where comprehension questions for his research topics. Include discussion with adults following research activities.		Include why, what, where questions for his research topics.
To hold a conversation with an adult/peer	S	J. to present research topics to class group. J. to show/tell class of 'where going and how' before class outing.		Mentor to engage J. in conversation (i.e. question him) on programs/topics, etc.
To initiate greetings (open and closure)	S	J. to greet/farewell adult/peers at the start and finish of every conversation.		Report/discuss personal diary with teacher/parents.

TABLE 4.2—*continued*

SOCIAL SKILLS / BEHAVIOUR				
To play with and share equipment with a peer for a brief period of time (ie 10 minutes)	S	J. to play memory/interest games with adults/peers.	J. to play word games with adults/peers i.e. bingo	To play turn-taking computer games with adults/peers.
J. to increase the length of time on work tasks to 12.20 pm	S	Teacher – Write a social story for length of time on task. Type on computer. Reward with a choice of savant interests e.g. dictionary, books, computer/drawing time, etc.		To share the computer with peers (use of a roster).
J. to overcome phobias (i.e. flooring, shopping centres, etc.)	S	Use de-sensitisation programs and again build in 'savant-interest choices/rewards' at different stages through these programs.		
J. to join in group work independently	S	Teacher – to select some tasks/activities that involve J's savant interests to use as a group task. Praise and reinforce him for joining in. Gradually fade to more general topics but offer a savant-activity to reinforce appropriate 'joining in with the group.		

A comprehensive overview of the gifted education teaching strategies – enrichment, acceleration and mentorships – and also the autism educational strategies – social stories, visual supports for communication, and positive behaviour support – are available on the Routledge website – Gifted and Autism Educational Strategies: Individual Savant Skill Programs.

Step 4: Annual Individual Education Plan Meetings (IEP)

Working with his teacher, therapists and parents, Jeremy's Individual Savant Skill Program and teaching strategies were then incorporated into his school IEP at his annual IEP meeting.

Depending on the nature and type of each school's educational programs for students with disabilities, the differentiated Individual Savant Program could, alternatively, be implemented in parallel to the usual program. However, the merging of the two programs into the single educational program (IEP) increases the chances that the implementation of the *Curriculum* will take place, and result in positive educational outcomes for the child.

Step 5: Monitoring and evaluation of an Individual Savant Skill Program

As for any educational program, continual monitoring and evaluation of student progress is the usual business of all schools, no matter the type of program. Jeremy's progress was monitored at two major time-intervals during the course of the *Curriculum*, using the *Curriculum Strategy Annual Priorities Evaluation – Form D* (Appendix 12). His teacher and mentor were asked to rate both the level of skill achievement, and the functional application of skills, on a scale of 1–11; STRONGLY DISAGREE (SD) rated as 1, with STRONGLY AGREE (SA) rating 11. A copy of Jeremy's evaluation form, which includes a sample only of the evaluation of his Annual Priorities, is provided in Table 4.3.

To explore more fully if the functional application of Jeremy's savant skills had been achieved, the *Savant Skill Post-Study Family/Teacher Questionnaire* (Clark, 2011; Appendix 5) was also completed. Assessment of communication and social skills, behaviour, self-esteem can also be completed if required by the school for the students' IEP – see Step 2.

Jeremy's results

Jeremy's parents and mentor reported positive outcomes during the course of the *Curriculum*. They felt he had made more functional use of his computer skills and was using the computer independently. Prior to the *Curriculum*, the computer was a great source of frustration for him; not understanding how to use the computer effectively. He was now recording his daily work schedules appropriately and without a prompt to do so. His parents also reported an improvement in his verbal

TABLE 4.3 Jeremy's Curriculum Strategy Annual Priorities Evaluation Form D

CURRICULUM STRATEGY ANNUAL PRIORITIES EVALUATION – FORM D

NAME: Jeremy AGE: _____ A: 1st Evaluation Date: __ / __ / ____

SCHOOL: _____ TEACHER/MENTOR: _____ B: 2nd Evaluation Date: __ / __ / ____

Annual Priority	Savant Skill	Curriculum Strategy	SKILL ACHIEVEMENT Circle Strongly Agree (SA) to Strongly Disagree (SD) with the appropriate number in relation to the statement: 'the annual priority has been achieved'.	FUNCTIONAL APPLICATION Circle Strongly Agree (SA) to Strongly Disagree (SD) with the appropriate number in relation to the statement: 'the skill is being applied in a functional and meaningful manner to some degree with or without support'.
To develop a 'personal diary' of daily events/visits at home and school	MEMORY (Savant II)	Enrichment	SD　　　　　　　　　　SA A:　1　2　3　**4**　5　6　7　8　9　10　11 B:　1　2　3　4　5　6　7　8　9　10　11	SD　　　　　　　　　　SA A:　1　2　3　4　**5**　6　7　8　9　10　11 B:　1　2　3　4　5　6　7　8　9　10　11
To introduce different types of software (home/school/computer) that relate to J's interests, e.g. games, graphics programs, World Atlas	COMPUTER (Savant II)	Enrichment	SD　　　　　　　　　　SA A:　1　2　3　4　5　**6**　7　8　9　10　11 B:　1　2　3　4　5　6　7　8　9　10　11	SD　　　　　　　　　　SA A:　1　2　3　4　5　**6**　7　8　9　10　11 B:　1　2　3　4　5　6　7　8　9　10　11
To obtain a mentor to expand J's knowledge and use of more complex computer operations	COMPUTER (Savant II)	Mentorship	SD　　　　　　　　　　SA A:　1　2　3　4　5　6　7　**8**　9　10　11 B:　1　2　3　4　5　6　7　8　9　10　11	SD　　　　　　　　　　SA A:　1　2　3　4　5　6　7　**8**　9　10　11 B:　1　2　3　4　5　6　7　8　9　10　11
Ask 'why' questions related to interests in TV commercials and directions for outings (upon return)	MEMORY (Savant II)	Communication	SD　　　　　　　　　　SA A:　1　2　3　4　5　6　**7**　8　9　10　11 B:　1　2　3　4　5　6　7　8　9　10　11	SD　　　　　　　　　　SA A:　1　2　3　**4**　5　6　7　8　9　10　11 B:　1　2　3　4　5　6　7　8　9　10　11

and written communication skills. It should be noted that, following Jeremy's relocation to a satellite class in a mainstream school, which was in the last year of the *Savant Skill Curriculum*, his teacher reported his behaviour deteriorated, which impacted his learning and progress generally. It was felt that he may not have been ready to make the move to a mainstream class environment. Children with autism often experience difficulties in coping with changes in their environment, which can in turn lead to problems with regulating or managing their own behaviours. This is one of the many challenges facing students with autism in schools today, and serves to highlight the need for more educational research in autism, and for a differentiated approach to their education.

The following *Savant Skill Curriculum* planning templates and questionnaires are also available as eResources on Routledge website www.routledge.com/978113 8839540:

- *Savant Skill Nomination Form* Appendix 1
- *Savant Skill Questionnaires – Family and Teacher* – Clark, 2011 Appendix 2 and 3
- *Informal Savant Skill Memory Assessment* Appendix 4
- *Savant Skill Post-Study Family/Teacher Questionnaire* Appendix 5
- *Christopher's Curriculum Strategy Annual Priorities Evaluation – Form D* Appendix 6
- Family Interview (*Pre-Treatment*) Appendix 7
- *Profile of Savant Abilities* Appendix 8
- *Curriculum Strategy Annual Priorities – Form A* Appendix 9
- *Curriculum Teaching Activities and Strategies – Form B* Appendix 10
- *Curriculum Teaching Activities – Form C* Appendix 11
- *Curriculum Strategies Annual Priorities Evaluation – Form D* Appendix 12

Reference

Treffert, D. (1989). *Extraordinary People*. London: Bantam Press.

5

THE VISION FOR THE FUTURE

The 'paradox children' and differentiated programs revisited – what lies ahead for autistic savants?

The focus children revisited

Patrick, Bradley and Terry, the three focus 'paradox children' who you met in the opening chapter of this book, will now be revisited, to see what, if any, changes have taken place for them as a result of the *Savant Skill Curriculum*. How were they helped? What worked? What did not? What do they need going forward? To recap, the differentiated program was primarily developed to assist a group of young autistic savants, to make functional use of their often non-functional savant or splinter skills at home, at school and in the community. By harnessing the high levels of motivation and interest that these children have in their savant areas of interest, the program also sought to make adaptive improvements with the children's communication and social skills, and in behaviour. By doing so, it was hoped for a reduction in the overall impact of autism on their lives. The outcomes for these three children will help to illustrate the major results of the study, and to give clues as to what lies ahead for these extraordinary children, and what I believe should be the vision for the future thinking and practice, in the education of the savant. The children's outcomes presented below are those reported at the conclusion of the study.

Patrick is now sixteen years of age. He continues to display a range of savant skills, many rated as being at the Prodigious Savant II level. They include: memory, hyperlexic, mechanical/spatial (computer), music, calendar calculation, arithmetic calculation and sensory abilities. No reduction or loss of his savant skills were reported during, or as a result of, the program. At home, Patrick is now using the computer (mechanical/spatial skills) appropriately and independently. At his current special school for students with intellectual impairment, he is using his calendar calculation and number savant skills, keeping the class calendar, operating his class weekly shopping list and accounts, tracking student absences, attendances and birthdays using the class daily roll. He is also responsible for typing the school newsletter. Although significant gains did not result in his quantitative communication skills, his teacher noted some improvement in his qualitative communication skills at school. He is beginning to use appropriate language in the community, for example, when ordering food, and appears generally to be more aware of his peers and teachers. Some quantitative and qualitative gains in Patrick's behaviour and social skills have also been noted in the home and at school. His family reported he was better able to manage his own behaviour, and his teacher considers Patrick to now be more interested in interacting with others, and better able to accept change. Although no quantitative gains in academic self-esteem resulted, his family reported a significant reduction in observable autistic behaviours.

Bradley, like Patrick, continues to display an obsessive interest in his savant skill areas which include: memory, hyperlexic, mechanical/spatial, arithmetic calculation and sensory skills. In spite of his move to rural New South Wales, and a change from an autism-specific school to a regular mainstream school during the study, his family reports significant functional application of his savant skills. His teacher reports that at school his work completion improved after she introduced savant skill activity rewards, and his peers became very interested in his electronic inventions. Both his popularity and social skills improved greatly through the inclusion of his savant activities in his class program. Although now only seven years of age, under the careful mentorship and supervision of the school caretaker, he helps to monitor his school's electronic systems. Although on testing, his overall communication skills indicated a slight reduction over the two-year period, they were still in the average range. His social language was reported to have improved, which may be attributed to his new-found popularity at his new school. He now greets his teacher and classmates by name, and takes part in group activities and joins in games in the playground. Although on testing there appeared to be no change in his self-esteem, it remains in the moderate range. His new-found interest in socializing does suggest a possible positive change in his overall confidence. Like Patrick, Bradley's parents reported a significant reduction in observable autistic behaviours.

Terry is now seven years of age. Like Patrick and Bradley, his multiple savant skills did not disappear or reduce over the two-year period. They continue to include: memory, hyperlexic, mechanical/spatial (computer), calendar calculation and arithmetic calculation. His mother did comment that his calendar calculation skills were not as apparent, but that they had not followed this up with him lately. Terry's father passed away in the second year of the study, which his mother felt had a significant negative impact on him, and made his transition to a mainstream class more difficult. Functional application of his skills was, however, reported. He now navigates places and routes of travel for his mother using the street directory. The use of his computer interest and skill, as a positive reward for appropriate behaviour, has seen an improvement in his overall behaviour, although he continues to display high levels of anxiety in some situations. He is becoming more settled and is doing a wider variety of tasks on the computer. Although a slight reduction in his overall communication skills was reported (*CELF-3*), they were still above average. There was no change in Terry's reported level of self-esteem which was rated in the moderate range. In spite of the death of his father, and difficulties transitioning into his mainstream school, a slight reduction in observable autistic behaviours was observed by his mother. Terry's mother felt that, in spite of the difficulties surrounding the death of Terry's father, the *Curriculum* had given her an insight into what could be achieved in the future for her son.

In summary, the *Savant Skill Curriculum* proved beneficial in the functional application of savant skills, not only for Patrick, Bradley and Terry but also for many of the other young autistic savant children in this study. It is safe to say that 'change for the better', which was the second major area of inquiry of this study, has taken place as a result of this differentiated program. An overall reduction in the level of autism was noted for many of the subjects, including a significant change for both Patrick and Bradley, with a smaller change for Terry. Again, these results must be treated with caution. As well as receiving the *Savant Skill Curriculum*, all of the children in the study were involved in a variety of educational and/or therapeutic interventions that also sought to overcome the impairments associated with autism. Given the complex nature of the disability of autism, involving multi-faceted levels of impairment across behavioural, social, communication and sensory domains, it is usual for parents to enlist a range of interventions and programs to help their children. From a research perspective, it is therefore challenging to evaluate the efficacy of one program alone, when subjects may be exposed to several programs simultaneously. However, as outlined in the results in Chapter 3, there was no similar overall significant reduction in observable autistic behaviours in the control group children, who did not receive this differentiated program.

Vision for the future

> It is important that children with autism have time to think about their special interests. If they don't have special time and maybe someone to talk to about it they can get cross. They could even have a meltdown. They concentrate best when learning stuff about their special interests.
>
> (Asha Tulloch-Hoskins, 2013, pp. 5–7)

Wise words indeed from a young fourteen-year-old Australian student with autism who wrote a book for mainstream teachers, *You Can Know Us: Information About Children with Autism for Mainstream Teachers That Don't Understand Us* (2013). Asha advocates that teachers should include the special interests of children with autism in their lessons, the central tenet of the *Savant Skill Curriculum*, and this study. The voice of students with autism, with or without savant skills, is critical to the design and implementation of appropriate differentiated educational programs. My vision for the education of the autistic savant is shared by Asha, which is that all teachers should include the special interests of children with autism in their class lessons, and that, as a result, the students will no longer feel frustrated and feel the need to resort to outbursts of challenging behaviour. In her book, Asha describes how her own special interest in air conditioners was included in her class lessons and group work by her teacher, and the positive effect it had on her learning. Her teacher even developed a class air-conditioner quiz, which she naturally won. She reports with great delight that the school principal, who also joined in the quiz, was awarded the 'last' sticker certificate.

For our shared vision to be achieved, there are a number of changes in our thinking and practice around the education of the 'paradox children' that will need to take place.

Implications for thinking and practice

Researchers in the field have suggested for some time that it is important to cater to the educational needs of the savant, and to assist savants to develop their skills to the fullest extent possible (Cheatham et al., 1995; Treffert, 1989, 2012, 2013; Wehmeyer, 1992; Yewchuk, 1990). As this study represents the only example, until now, of a successful differentiated educational program for autistic savants, the *Savant Skill Curriculum* has an important role to play in our future thinking and educational practice.

I believe we need to re-evaluate the long-held view that savant skills are merely 'freak talents', and rigid and obsessive skills that are resistant to change, or have little, if any, functional use. The view that savant skills are merely anomalous talents, and that 'investment in talent will not generalise to broader areas of functioning' (Nettlebeck and Young, 1999, p. 172), has been brought into question by this study. Many of the subjects did in fact achieve a level of functional application of their savant skills, in the home, the school and in the community. The functional use of savant skills by individual savants has been reported anecdotally in the past (Treffert, 1989, 2012).

As mentioned previously, to understand the thinking behind the adoption of the gifted education strategies used in the *Curriculum*, we need to view these 'paradox children' as gifted students who have a disability – they are 'twice-exceptional' gifted students with autism. At the commencement of my *Savant Skill Curriculum* training workshops, I invite the participants (teachers, therapists, psychologists, or parents), to 'suspend your current thinking that these children are disabled, and instead to view them as gifted children who have the disability of autism'. It is by merging the two distinct fields of gifted and autism education that we can then see the possibilities of what might be achieved in the education of these students. The strategies of acceleration, enrichment and mentorships, widely employed in the education of the gifted non-disabled student, appear to be equally successful in the education of the autistic savant.

It is important that we also develop better identification and differentiated programs for the growing numbers of 'twice-exceptional' intellectually gifted students with autism. To date, there have been only a few studies of this cohort of gifted autistic children, and the findings of these studies highlight the confusion that exists among teachers and school psychologists with respect to their identification, and their educational needs (Nicpon et al., 2011). Given that autistic savants are a cohort of the broader 'twice-exceptional' autistic group, this is an emerging field of inquiry that encompasses both gifted and autism education, and one in which more research is required to advance our thinking and our practice.

Moving forward, it is important that teachers, allied health professionals and parents learn how to identify young children with autism who display savant skills, and how they can cater to their specific educational needs. Differentiated programs should be rolled out across special education and mainstream classrooms, in government and non-government schools wherever the child is enrolled. These programs should be designed not only for the school setting, but also the child's home and community environments. It should be noted that my call for differentiated programs for autistic savants is in keeping with the views of the Australian Advisory Board on Autism Spectrum Disorders, as outlined in their February 2012 Education Position paper, *Education and Autism Spectrum Disorders in Australia. The Provision of Appropriate Educational Services for School-Age Students with Autism Spectrum Disorders in Australia* (p. 2). Two of the key governing principles outlined are particularly relevant to the education of autistic savants:

1. Every child and adolescent with an ASD should have access to an educational service appropriate to his her/needs.
2. All government and non-government educational sectors should provide educational services that cater to the needs of children and adolescents with an ASD.

The introduction of appropriate differentiated programs for the 'twice-exceptional' student with autism, including the autistic savant, is essential if we are to truly provide an appropriate education for all students with autism. Existing gifted and talented programs in schools need to be reviewed and broadened to ensure they cater to all 'twice-exceptional' students with autism, including the autistic savant. As Dr Treffert so wisely concluded in his book, *Islands of Genius. The Bountiful Mind of the Autistic, Acquired, and Sudden Savant* (2012, p. 281), 'the trail ahead for savants will see the expansion of the numbers and types of programs, some will be schools especially targeted to "twice-exceptional" students including savants; and some will be vocational programs designed to match the savant skills in association with willing employees'. I trust that Dr Treffert's prediction, Asha's and my shared vision will become a reality. No more should the needs of the autistic savant be put on the 'back-burner', or in the 'too hard' basket.

I previously touched upon the need for teachers, allied health professionals (speech and occupational therapists, school psychologists) and families to be trained in the field of savant syndrome. Such training would need to be delivered primarily by tertiary institutions that provide courses in education, psychology, speech and occupational therapies. Tertiary courses in the education of the gifted and talented child should also include a topic related to the 'twice-exceptional' student with autism, and which includes the autistic savant. Course content should include: an

FIGURE 5.1 Cartoon of teacher and young savant playing

overview of savant syndrome; the nature of savant skills; the 'twice-exceptional' intellectually gifted student with autism, and the autistic savant; the identification and assessment of savant abilities; the conceptual framework for development of the differentiated program; the design, implementation and evaluation of differentiated educational programs; and post-school transition programs and supports. Education sector teacher training institutes could also link this training to their teacher accreditation and registration requirements. Organizations that support those with autism should also provide courses for families which are related to the educational needs of the 'twice-exceptional' student with autism. The need for increased training of teachers, and for the development of differentiated educational programs for this group, is cleverly portrayed in the cartoon in Figure 5.1. The cartoon was drawn by a young teacher of students with autism at the conclusion of one of my savant skill teacher training workshops.

There are some further implications of the *Curriculum* and this study for the wider field of autism. The fact that there are many more people with autism who display savant skills (30 per cent of adults with autism – Howlin et al., 2009) is not yet widely known or understood by many professionals and parents in the field of autism today. The more we come to understand and appreciate the very special skills of the autistic savant, and through differentiated educational programs, such as this *Curriculum*, the greater will be their chances of achieving improved life-long outcomes.

Given that research is highlighting the poor outcomes post-school for many on the autism spectrum, including those with savant skills, there is an urgent need for autism-related service organizations to adopt differentiated programs, which address the specific needs of this group. One such example is that of Autism Spectrum Australia (Aspect), which is now Australia's largest national autism-specific service provider. Aspect has fully embedded the principle of 'person-centred' approaches in all of its programs and services. The individual needs of the person with autism, including their strengths and interests, are placed at the very centre of service provision. The 'strengths-based' approach to working with all people with autism, including autistic savants, is one of the key directions and drivers of Aspect's current strategic and business plans. The educational approach developed by Aspect (the Aspect Comprehensive Approach for Education), which underpins the education of all students with autism in the organization's eight schools, now also includes a guide for teachers on how to implement a differentiated program for students who display savant skills.

Future research – what lies ahead for autistic savants?

We are only at the forefront of understanding how to best support children and adults with autism who also display savant abilities. Although it is important to continue to increase our knowledge and understanding of the nature of savant skills, I believe it is time that we gave equal priority to the exploration of the 'human side' of this extraordinary condition. To do so will increase the range and types of evidence-based programs that are directed toward supporting the Patricks, Bradleys and Terrys of this world, to make functional use of their special gifts or skills.

Given that this was the very first exploratory study of its kind, a replication study of the *Savant Skill Curriculum* should be considered. As I write, it is indeed promising to report that interest is growing for the development of such a new study in Australia, which will involve a number of Australian universities, leaders in the fields of autism and gifted education, autism service providers and several educational sectors.

As positive outcomes were observed in adaptive functioning in some children in the study, a further exploration of the use of savant skills to facilitate communication, social skills and behaviour would be an important future project. As the improvement of adaptive functioning in those with autism is pivotal to their future life-long outcomes, such a project should be fast-tracked.

In relation to the nature of savant skills, further examination of the familial links in giftedness and savant abilities should be undertaken. Given that 72 per cent of the families of the children who received the *Curriculum* either displayed a similar skill to the area of their child's savant ability, or were considered to be gifted themselves, this would suggest further research is warranted. A closer examination of the relationship between giftedness, autism and savant syndrome may shed further insight into our understanding of these different areas of the human condition. This view is shared by Wallace (2008), who concluded that from the growing literature in the fields of savant syndrome and giftedness, further research of savant skills may not only lead to better understanding talent and skill development in general, but also to elucidate models of intelligence, learning and memory, and the etiological mechanisms in autism. Given also that mechanistic commonalities may underlie savant skills and certain forms of giftedness, the study of savant skills indeed may inform our understanding of the neuroscience of giftedness.

A closer examination of the influence of memory skill on the development of all savant skills should be the subject of future research. The fact that all of the children displayed savant memory ability in this study is an important finding and should be examined more fully. This important finding was the direct result of using a wide range of quantitative and qualitative measures to assess the skills of the children (triangulation of data). Such mixed method qualitative and quantitative research should be used for future studies of savant skills; standardized measures alone fail to fully identify the savant abilities of subjects. Most of the children in this study failed the standardized memory tests; however, on informal tests of memory related to their areas of personal interest, they all displayed high-level memory ability.

The link between the functional application of savant skills, and the savants' cognitive and language ability, is another important area of future research. For some children in this study, their ability to perform well on standardized measures resulted in their skills being assessed as Prodigious Level II skills (Treffert, 1989). In reality, these results may been linked to both the child's intellectual and linguistic abilities. Several subjects who were assessed as having borderline or average language ability, and an average or borderline IQ (Terry, Bradley and Joseph), performed relatively better on some standardized measures than other subjects, who had lower linguistic and cognitive ability (Benjamin, Martin and Patrick). Further research may unpack whether language ability and IQ level influence the functional application of savant skills.

As discussed above, more differentiated programs and research is needed to grow our knowledge and understanding of the 'twice-exceptional' intellectually gifted student with autism. Some of the children in this study were assessed with above-average intellectual functioning. One of the main issues educators face when working with a gifted student with autism, including the autistic savant, is how to meet their academic needs while accommodating for their behavioural, social and emotional concerns. Many educational professionals have limited knowledge about how to implement the necessary accommodations that address areas of educational talent, let alone for those identified as 'twice-exceptional' (Assouline et al., 2009). Studies exploring better identification, and appropriate differentiated programs for these gifted students with autism, should be prioritized.

Finally, and quite possibly the most important area for future research, and the next big area of discovery in savant syndrome and autism, is the development and evaluation of post-school programs and strategies, that better assist students to transition from school to adulthood. Research into the outcomes for adults on the spectrum universally show poor employment, social and life outcomes. This is not an acceptable outcome for the students we support with autism. We must do more in our collective endeavours to develop evidence-based differentiated programs that will truly result in an improvement in adult outcomes. It is my hope and belief that this study, and the *Savant Skill Curriculum*, will provide an important model for future differentiated educational programs, which aim to support the successful transition of young autistic savants to post-school life.

References

Assouline, S.G., Foley-Nicpon, M., and Doobay, A. (2009). Profoundly gifted girls and autism spectrum disorder: A psychometric case study comparison. *Gifted Child Quarterly, 53*, 89–105.

Australian Advisory Board on Autism Spectrum Disorders. (2012). *Education and Autism Spectrum Disorders in Australia. The Provision of Appropriate Educational Services for School-Age Students with Autism Spectrum Disorders in Australia.* www.autismadvisoryboard. org.au.

Cheatham, S.K., Rucker, H.N., Polloway, E.A., Smith, J.D., and Lewis, G.W. (1995). Savant Syndrome: Case studies, hypotheses, and implications for special education. *Education and Training in Mental Retardation and Developmental Disabilities, 30*, 243–253.

Howlin, P., Goode, S., Hutton, J., and Rutter, M. (2009). Savant skills in autism: Psychometric approaches and parental reports. *Philosophical Transactions of the Royal Society B, 364*, 1359–1367.

Nettlebeck, T., and Young, R.L. (1999). Savant Syndrome. In L. Masters Glidden (Ed.), *International Review of Research in Mental Retardation, 22*, 137–173.

Nicpon, M.F., Allmon, A., Seick, B. and Stinson, R.D. (2011). Empirical investigation of twice-exceptionality: Where have we been and where are we going? *Gifted Child Quarterly, 55(1)*, 3–17.

Treffert, D. (1989). *Extraordinary People.* London: Bantam Press.

Treffert, D. (2012). *Islands of Genius: The Bountiful Mind of the Autistic, Acquired, and Sudden Savant.* London: Jessica Kingsley Publishers.

Treffert, D. (2013). Savant Syndrome. A compelling case for innate talent. In S.B. Kaufman (Ed.), *The Complexity of Greatness: Beyond Talent or Practice* (pp. 103–118). New York: Oxford University Press.

Tulloch-Hoskins, A. (2013). *You Can Know Us.* Flinders Park, SA. Our Lady of La Vang.

Wallace, G.L. (2008). Neuropsychological studies of savant skills: Can they inform the neuroscience of giftedness? *Roeper Review, 30*, 229–246.

Wehmeyer, M.L. (1992). Developmental and psychological aspects of the savant syndrome. *Journal of Disability, Development and Education, 39*, 153–163.

Yewchuk, C. (1990). Idiot savants: Can retarded individuals be gifted? *Gifted Education International, 17*, 16–18.

6

CONCLUSION

Summary of the study and update of 'where are the children now?'

In the field of giftedness and talent, one of the catalysts that contribute to transforming a natural gift or aptitude into a fully fledged talent is 'chance' (Gagné, 2009). 'Chance' played an important role in the development of this study and the *Savant Skill Curriculum*. The 'chance' that I had the good fortune to be Patrick's teacher whilst also studying a unit of gifted education, as part of my university degree. And 'chance', that I also should meet Emeritus Professor Miraca Gross, the convenor of my course. I will never forget her feedback on one of my assignments, which was based on the development of a differentiated program for Patrick. In her very strong Scottish accent she declared, 'My god, you are onto something here!' Given his seven savant abilities, some at the prodigious level, Patrick was 'out-of-sync' with his autistic peers. Patrick needed much more than the usual autism Individual Education Program that I was able to offer him as his teacher. To put it simply, he was bored.

The study and *Savant Skill Curriculum* reviewed

Before we explore further the value of this study to the children, their teachers and families, and its place in the research and our knowledge of savant syndrome, let us briefly revisit the study. 'What was the scope of the problem? What did the study and the *Savant Skill Curriculum* aim to achieve? What did we find?'

The purpose of this study, as outlined in the preceding chapters, was threefold. The primary aim of the study was to assess whether, over a two-year period, the development of a differentiated curriculum could assist a group of autistic savants, the 'paradox children', to make functional use of their often non-functional savant or splinter skills at home, school and in the community. A combination of educational strategies used in the fields of gifted and autism education were merged to form the educational strategies employed in the *Savant Skill Curriculum*.

The *Curriculum* also attempted to harness the motivation and interest displayed by the children, in their savant fields or domains, in order to teach adaptive behaviours – communication and social skills, and appropriate behaviours. Should improvement in these adaptive behaviours have occurred, a change in the degree or impact of autism on the lives of the subjects was also expected.

The third and final aim of this study was to gather further information on the development and nature of savant skills, and to add to the current literature on savant syndrome. A variety of research questions (19) were developed to explore whether the above aims of the study would be achieved. The questions were divided into three distinct areas of inquiry: a) the nature of savant skills, b) change for the better, and c) change for the worse or no change.

Restatement of the problem

There are children with disabilities in our schools today who are both gifted and disabled; they are referred to as 'twice-exceptional' students. 'Autistic savant' is the term used to refer to children and adults who have been diagnosed with autism, and who also display savant skills or abilities. Savant skills are restricted to Hill's (1974) list of discrete savant abilities: memory, art, music, mechanical, calendar, calculation, arithmetic calculation, athletic skill, sensory sensitivity and hyperlexic skills (the ability to read, write and spell). Just as there exist many levels of giftedness in the non-disabled population, savant abilities may also be classified at different levels; either a lower-level Savant I (Talented) skill, or a higher-level Savant II (Prodigious) skill (Treffert, 1989; 2012).

The profiles and stories of Patrick, Bradley and Terry, three of the twenty-two children who participated in this study and the *Curriculum*, were told to illustrate their abilities, and their disabilities, along with the many challenges they face daily at school, at home and in the community. All of the children displayed multiple savant skills at either the Savant I or Savant II level. As a result of the frustration of not having their special learning needs met in the classroom, and the impact of their autism, they all displayed challenging behaviours. The children were not receiving any form of differentiated educational programs. They remain the least recognized and underserved minority of all gifted students. Their savant skills or gifts have largely been ignored, put on the 'back-burner', or seen only as useless obsessions.

The problem is further compounded by the fact that there are many more autistic savants in the overall autistic population than were first thought (Howlin et al., 2009). Although we do not know the exact numbers across the autism spectrum, what we do know is that there are increasing numbers of children and adults being diagnosed with autism world-wide, so it follows that there must be an associated increase in the number of autistic savants.

Looking beyond the school years, research is showing that post-school life and employment outcomes for people with autism are poor. Poor post-school outcomes were also reported for the group of adult autistic savants who participated in the study exploring the rates of savant skills in adults with autism (Howlin et al., 2009); only five of the 137 individuals were employed. For the majority, the skills remained isolated, leading to neither employment nor social integration. There is, therefore, a growing need to do more to support these young students. To ignore the exceptional skills of autistic savants is no longer an option. Just as gifted students without disabilities require support to transform their gifts into productive talents (Gagné, 2009), autistic savants require specialized educational support to apply their savant skills.

A solution – the Savant Skill Curriculum

The *Savant Skill Curriculum* was designed as a solution to the problem of the lack of differentiated educational programs for autistic savants in schools and classrooms today. The conceptual framework for the *Curriculum* and the study is based on the merging of the two fields of gifted and autism education. The definition of giftedness and talent that inclusive of the savant is Gagné's Differentiated Model of Giftedness and Talent (DMGT) (2009). For talent to emerge, causal contributions from many sources are required, among them high natural abilities (gifts), motivation, perseverance, supportive parents and teachers, as well as long-term investment in learning, training and practising. These causal contributions form the basis of Gagne's DMGT, and which equally apply to the case of the autistic savant. To further explain the thinking behind the *Savant Skill Curriculum*, and the facilitation of savant skills into productive talent, a new model was developed – the Model for Savant Skill and Talent Development (Clark, 2011). The model goes further than the DMGT by the inclusion of the disability of autism, its impact on adaptive functioning, and savant skill teaching strategies directed at improved adaptive functioning. The *Savant Skill Curriculum* included a range of educational strategies used to support the non-disabled gifted student – acceleration, enrichment and mentorships. Autism-specific intervention strategies were used in tandem with the gifted education strategies: social stories, visual supports for communication, and the use of obsessions and stereotypes as positive reinforcement and motivators to learning. The merging of the gifted and autism strategies was designed to facilitate the unproductive savant skill, or quasi-talent, into a productive talent.

Methodology and procedures of the study

A longitudinal multiple-replication case study design was used to evaluate the *Savant Skill Curriculum*. The study sought to also explore key issues related to the savant syndrome and the nature of savant skills, and included: memory ability; the role of practice, motivation, training and creativity; whether skills may be inherited; age of onset; and the extent of challenging behaviours. Standardized and non-standardized measures of each subject's savant abilities and adaptive functioning were taken as pre- and post-measures, to determine the effectiveness of the

Curriculum. The twenty-two subjects, who displayed both autism and savant, or splinter skills, and were between four and sixteen years of age. Subjects formed two groups, one an experimental group, the other a control group, and were tracked over a two-year period during the implementation of the *Curriculum.* A comparison of the pre- and post-measures of the two groups was made. Case study methodology was selected for use in the study, as they are particularly appropriate for advancing knowledge of rare phenomena, and in this case for developing specific knowledge about the savant syndrome in current time. The study also employed aspects of a quantitative quasi-experimental investigation.

The Savant Skill Nomination Form (Appendix 1) was used to identify students for the study, and was completed by both teachers and families. Tests of savant skills were then completed using standardized measures, and non-standardized measures where no tests were available. Additional information on each of the children's savant abilities was gathered using questionnaires *The Savant Skill Questionnaires – Family and Teacher* (Appendix 2 and 3). The results of both the standardized and non-standardized measures were included in the *Profile of Savant Abilities Form* (Appendix 8), which was then used to design each child's Individual Savant Skill teaching program.

Pre- and post-measures of the *Savant Skill Curriculum* were administered to explore if change had resulted in relation to the following: the functional application of the savant skill; communication ability; social skills and behaviour; academic self-esteem; and degree of autism. To increase the internal validity of the research findings, 'triangulation' (Denzin, 1970) of data methodology was used, which combines dissimilar data to study the same topic or unit of measurement. Data included: standardized and non-standardized tests, questionnaires, interviews, observations, documents and artefacts. A variety of non-parametric statistical analyses were used: the Wilcoxin T Test for two dependent samples, the Mann-Whitney U Test for two independent samples, and directional t-tests for dependent samples.

The results

In relation to the first area of inquiry, the 'nature of savant skills', the results highlighted the following: the obsessive nature of savant skills; the high levels of challenging behaviours associated with savants and their interests; the high levels of interest and motivation by the savant in their pursuit of savant activities; the early onset of savant skills in the absence of formal training; the familial link between the subject child's savant abilities and/or giftedness and superior performance; insight into the types and various levels of savant skills; and evidence for the use of imaginative and creative methods in association with savant performance.

The second area of inquiry of the study was to explore if 'change for the better' had resulted for the treatment children following the implementation of the Curriculum. The key findings included the following: the functional application of savant skills by many of the treatment children had taken place; no significant quantitative communication gains resulted, however qualitative gains were reported for some subjects; no significant degree of change took place in the levels of behaviour/emotional disturbance, but for some children qualitative improvements in social skills and behaviour were observed; fewer children were rated at the clinical cut-off score for classification in the severe behaviour/emotional disturbance range following the study; no significant change in levels of academic self-esteem resulted, however 25 per cent of the treatment subjects' self-esteem moved from a low to a moderate-level rating of academic self-esteem; a significant reduction in the degree or level of autism was reported by the parents of the treatment children.

For the final area of inquiry, 'change for the worse or no change', the majority of both parents and teachers of the treatment children reported no reduction or loss of savant skills over the course of the *Savant Skill Curriculum*. However, for a small number of subjects, a partial reduction or loss of skill was noted (15.4 per cent).

The role of the study and its place in world-wide gifted and autism research

As this was the first exploratory study involving a differentiated program for young autistic savants, and one that demonstrated positive outcomes for the children involved, it has an important role to play in the theory development of savant syndrome. The fact that the functional application of savant skills was achieved through the *Savant Skill Curriculum* challenges the preconceptions that savant skills are 'freak talents' only, and are resistant to change or functional application. What this study contributes to our understanding is that, when an intensive differentiated program, such as the *Savant Skill Curriculum*, is implemented over an extended period of time, positive change can take place for young autistic savants. It has to be said that a great deal of support and commitment from teachers and families is critical to the success of any differentiated program. Based on the Model for Savant Skill and Talent Development (Clark, 2011), the natural savant skills can be nurtured by teachers and parents using the *Savant Skill Curriculum*, which acts as an environmental catalyst to facilitate the savant skills into functional or partial talents. The teaching of adaptive behaviours using savant interests also served as an environmental catalyst to support talent and functional savant skill development.

Further, the findings of this study have made a substantial contribution to the existing literature pertaining to the nature and development of savant skills. The findings are both confirmation of our previous understanding of the nature of savant skills, but are also breaking new ground, particularly with reference to several key findings: the fact that there appears to be evidence of a familial link in relation to savant skills, which is further supported by the early onset of the skills without training; that all of the children displayed multiple skills and at various levels (Savant I or II); all children displayed high-level memory skills; and the finding that savant abilities did not diminish as a result of the intervention. These findings combine to add new knowledge to the field.

As mentioned in Chapter 5, this study is on the leading edge of the development of a whole new field of discovery, in relation to the 'twice-exceptional autistic' student. By merging the knowledge of the two fields of giftedness and autism, a new approach to the education of autistic savants, and, possibly, the wider 'twice-exceptional autistic' group, is now possible. A closer examination of the relationship between giftedness, autism and savant syndrome is required to shed further insight into our understanding of these different areas of the human condition.

A key rationale for the design and the implementation of this differentiated program was to better support the children who are autistic savants – that is, to focus on the 'human side' of the condition. Given the lack of research exploring the 'human side' of the condition, this study provides an example of the type of intervention research that is required going forward, and research which is driven by the need to improve the life-long outcomes of autistic savants. This view is supported by Treffert (1989, p. 265) who also believes that 'by training the talents of the savant some of the other deficits would be lessened, albeit not altogether eliminated'. The *Savant Skill Curriculum* has achieved exactly what Treffert considered possible – a reduction in the deficits of the savant.

The lessons learned for the educational practice of autistic savants – 'What has been lost? What has been gained?'

The high level of interest and motivation that the 'paradox children' display for their savant skill areas is a major driving force in the development of savant abilities. The passion they have for their areas of interest and skill result in moments of great joy and happiness, often in a world that is confusing and frightening, and hard to understand as a result of their autism. From the first time I met Patrick, it was clear that his love of words, books, numbers and calendars was a source of immense joy and fun for him. With interest comes motivation. Throughout history, human achievement has been linked to high levels of interest and motivation, no matter the chosen field of endeavour. It is by harnessing the motivation and interest that these children have for their savant areas of interest that teachers and parents can borrow or apply this motivation to increase learning in other areas, and to improve adaptive functioning.

Autistic savants are gifted; however, their ability to perform higher cognitive functions is masked by their autism impairments, which are pervasive. This view is further supported by the number of characteristic traits that the highly gifted non-disabled student and the autistic savant have in common. These shared characteristics include: the early onset of skills; the familial link; an obsessive motivation in areas of interest and skill; and high memory ability. It could be said that, in fact, many of the findings from this study, related to the nature of savant skills, may be also assigned to the young highly gifted non-disabled student.

As we develop differentiated educational programs for the autistic savant, we must listen to the voice of these children and their parents. It was indeed rare to find any parents involved in this study who over-rated their own child's savant abilities. I believe parents are the best identifiers of their children's abilities. Parent and teacher/professional partnerships are the core to the success of any differentiated program. The wise words of fourteen-year-old Asha, who wrote about her special interests, are without doubt extremely insightful. Our challenge is to find ways that our students with autism can share their thoughts and feelings, and to become partners in the design and development of their educational programs.

If there was one thing I consider to be a loss in the field of savant syndrome, and in the education of autistic savants, it is the failure in the past to identify this group of twice-exceptional students with autism, and the missed opportunities to include them in appropriate differentiated educational programs. With the advent of the *Savant Skill Curriculum*, there now exists a model for such programs to be developed in the future. They will no longer be the most unrecognized and underserved minority of 'twice-exceptional' gifted disabled students.

Finally, the major outcome of this study for me, personally, has been to be witness to the incredible dedication, commitment and support of the teachers and the parents of these remarkable children, in helping them make the most of their special skills. Without this support, I do not believe that 'change for the better' would have been the outcome for many of the children. It can be said with confidence that, yes, the savant skills of young autistic savants can be applied in functional and purposeful ways, as a result of the *Savant Skill Curriculum*. The story does not, however, end here. I do not want to finish, leaving the impression that by merely adopting the *Savant Skill Curriculum* the future will be bright and a miracle will result for all young autistic savants. What is required for these 'paradox children' is the long-term sustained differentiated support by teachers, mentors and families for the early gains in the functional application of savant skills to endure, and to truly make a difference to their life-long outcomes. The next part of our journey in the understanding of savant syndrome, and the impact of the functional application of savant skills on post-school outcomes, begins below with an update of 'where are the "paradox children" now?'

Where are the 'paradox children' now?

As I started writing this book, I made contact with the original children in the study and their families, to learn 'where are they now?' I was keen to know if they were still using their savant or splinter skills and abilities in functional ways, as young adults with autism, and of their education and post-school outcomes. Of those I succeeded in contacting, their journeys have been marked with stories of both success and failure. Although the inclusion of all of their stories is beyond the brief of this book, I will continue to document the experiences and life-journeys of this group of young 'paradox adults', who, in spite of their ups and downs, continue to display extraordinary savant skills. By sharing this study now, and in the future the unfolding life stories of this exceptional group of people, many other autistic savants may be supported to enjoy the quality of life that is their right.

Patrick

Now thirty-four years of age, Patrick is living at home in the western suburbs of Sydney with his mother and five brothers. He continues to display all seven of his savant abilities, which include: memory, hyperlexic, calendar calculation, mathematics calculation, mechanical/spatial, music and computer skills. The majority of his skills remain exceptional; he continues to be quite possibly one of the world's most prodigious savants.

Since leaving his special education school at the age of eighteen, Patrick has not had a job. His family made the decision that they did not want him to attend a post-school options program for young adults with a disability, most of these programs at this time operating as nothing more than 'sheltered workshops', and which provided limited activities and opportunities for Patrick to make use of his savant abilities. He would have been extremely bored. Instead, his family decided it would be best to engage him in activities at home that could make better use of his skills and interests. Patrick has his own home office and uses this relatively independently. The majority of his savant skills are used for leisure and recreation activities, as he prefers not to work. He uses his prodigious memory to remind his brothers of their work schedules, and the family of upcoming social events. His ability to hold a conversation on topics that interest him has improved greatly and he is now less obsessive or repetitive in these discussions. His communication overall has improved and he no longer uses language on a 'needs-only' basis. Patrick's eye-contact has also improved and his interactions with people appear more mature.

Patrick's use of the computer remains a high-level interest activity and his skills are now more functional. At the moment, he enjoys using Wikipedia and Google for advanced searches on topics that interest him – history, music, newspapers from the 1980s, old commercials and, recently, television shows. Because of Patrick's obsessive interest in the computer, his family have needed to place restrictions on the amount of time he spends on this interest, a not uncommon issue in many households today. He continues his great love of dates and numbers, and enjoys nothing better than to calculate the day of the week of any date in history and to calculate advanced arithmetic calculations. With supervision, he does the family grocery shopping each week and has the responsibility for paying for them correctly. He is 95 per cent self-sufficient and only requires support with sharing with others, road-crossing and with cooking.

Although Patrick is reported by his brother to be 'happy in his environment', his family are concerned that he needs more social experiences. They believe he needs something more to look forward to other than his life at home. With this in mind, his family are now exploring alternate options for Patrick with a number of disability service providers in Sydney. With a recent change in the way disability government funding is administered in Australia, funding is now available for individualized funding packages, which can be designed to meet the person with a disability's own interests and needs. Given that Patrick continues to display high-level savant skills, this person-centred funding support may hold new possibilities for him to be engaged in a wider variety of activities that are related to his abilities. This will also provide Patrick with a wider social network and, importantly, reduce his boredom, and further increase his feelings of happiness.

Christopher

Christopher is now thirty-one years of age. He lives with his mother and brother in the western suburbs of Sydney, his father having passed away several years ago. As mentioned previously, Christopher is unique in that he was the only non-verbal participant in the study. He provides a role model for teachers and parents of other non-verbal savants as to what can be achieved through the identification of their savant abilities and inclusion in a differentiated educational program.

Each of his previously identified savant abilities – memory, hyperlexic and computer skills – not only remain intact today, but are used functionally by Christopher. Christopher loves to travel and can independently navigate anywhere he needs to go by train or by bus in Sydney, without the use of directories. The functional application of his remarkable memory skills, which are mostly related to his childhood interest in train and bus routes, has given Christopher a great deal of pleasure as a form of leisure and recreation, and also his independence in spite of his disability. Although his mother trusts him, as a precaution, she has a tracking device installed on her phone for safety should Christopher get into difficulties while travelling. His interest in travel is also related to his interest in shopping centres and, in particular, their different corporate names. He enjoys nothing better than studying street directories of cities in other Australian states, which he has started to visit, accompanied by his mother. They have been to Brisbane, Melbourne, Canberra and Adelaide, and now Christopher is planning trips to Perth, every four years. On arrival in these cities, Christopher uses his tablet to plan his bus travel to visit shopping centres, and the exact time he needs to return to meet his mother before their flight home.

During a recent terrorist-related hostage siege in Sydney, all train travel was stopped throughout the centre of the city. Christopher, who was travelling on a train at this time, was able to use his iPhone travel application to redirect his trip home by way of bus. He has also become highly skilled at texting, a skill that relies on his advanced ability to read, write and spell words – his hyperlexic savant abilities. It has been many years since he last absconded or got lost.

After leaving school at the age of eighteen, Christopher transitioned to a post-school day options program for adults with a disability in Western Sydney. At this time, he was assessed as not being eligible for an employment program due to his high support needs. Although he continues to be involved in this program, he only attends the program's weekly shopping days, which is linked to his great love of shopping centres.

Although Christopher does not have a job, he has achieved a great deal. When not travelling, he is engaged in a range of community-based activities. He visits a lot of different libraries throughout Sydney, using their computers and reading newspapers. He orders his favourite pizzas online, accesses the ATM for the money he needs, and then travels independently to collect them. His days are filled with travelling, watching musical programs, walking bus routes, exploring the internet, reading magazines, and buying street directories, which he then stores, and gives to himself as a Christmas present each year. He uses his iPhone to communicate by exploring the meaning of words and concepts, then typing his communication messages. He continues to experience anxiety and becomes upset when there are changes to his routines or schedules.

The functional use of Chrostopher's savant skills has given him an enormous amount of confidence. He is now a very able young man. Craig's mother believes that the *Savant Skill Curriculum* has also given her enormous confidence to grow with him as well. Christopher's journey is best summarized by his mother: 'above all else, Christopher gets a great deal of enjoyment from these activities'.

Jeremy

Jeremy is now twenty-seven years old. Jeremy's journey through the *Savant Skill Curriculum* was outlined in Chapter 4 – the Guide to Practice. On entry to the study, Jeremy's savant skills included memory, hyperlexic and computer (mechanical/spatial) skills. All of these skills are still evident today, although his parents have observed that the greater number of activities Jeremy is involved with, his savant skills are less obvious. The broadening of his horizons may have diminished somewhat his strong focal attention for detail, a common characteristic of people with autism and savants.

Like the stories of Patrick and Christopher, Jeremy's is marked by successes and challenges. Following his transition from his autism-specific special school to a mainstream school in 2000, he adapted very well to this change with support from his teachers, made progress, and was happy. He attended a special education support class in a mainstream secondary school which his parents describe as 'the best days of his life'. He continued to use his advanced computer skills, although attempts to integrate him into a mainstream computer class were not successful due to a lack of one-to-one teaching support, and he found the noise levels in the computer class distressing. He was also introduced to drama at this school, which he enjoyed a great deal, and which resulted in improvements in his communication and confidence. In spite of several incidents of bullying, and which were effectively managed by his teachers, Jeremy has continued to visit the school every Thursday since 2010, where he 'pretends' to be a teacher's assistant by helping out the staff where he can.

On leaving school, Jeremy participated in a transition to work program for two years, which proved challenging. Rather than focusing on employment opportunities related to his strengths and abilities, he spent most of his time in community outings. His peer group were mostly severely physically and intellectually disabled. An employment opportunity was eventually found for Jeremy, but failed due to the need for a lengthy train journey to the work-site, which proved too stressful for him.

Jeremy then transferred to a different transition-to-work program, which was more successful, as all of the participants had autism. Following the publication of an article in a Sydney major newspaper, which highlighted Jeremy's difficulties in finding a job, he secured a permanent part-time position with a national measurement organization. He worked four hours, two days per week, doing data entry tasks. Unfortunately, the job only lasted for six months, as the company experienced financial difficulties, and cut Jeremy's position. He became very depressed as a result, as he enjoyed this job, which he found very stimulating.

Jeremy has attempted many technical and further education courses over recent years. He has always been willing to participate in these courses, but they were used mostly as a means of keeping him interested and engaged, rather than to educate for an end goal. In the words of his mother, 'the courses were to fend off his boredom'. The courses included: employment skills, social and communication skills, visual arts and contemporary craft, Life Skills High Certificate, computing, cooking, personal hygiene, stress management, tourism and hospitality.

By cold-canvassing local businesses, Jeremy's mother managed to find him his next job at a recycling company. Once again, the job was short-lived, as the company experienced financial problems and was forced into liquidation.

In 2009, he managed to get a small part-time position in a local Neighbourhood Centre doing data entry work, but due to their very limited budget they are only able to pay him for two hours of work each month. Jeremy continues to do this job today. His parents report that he is very good at this work, and has coped with a number of changes to role. His accuracy and speed of working is often acknowledged by his work colleagues.

In 2013, with the support of his parents, Jeremy moved into his own apartment in a northern suburb of Sydney. He is close to public transport and has adapted remarkably well to the freedom of getting about on his own. He undertakes all his own cleaning, shopping and cooking. His weekly schedule includes: personal training, drama sessions, his work at the Neighbourhood Centre, social outings and clubs with his disability support agency, and autism social club group. He continues to volunteer at Chatswood High School each week as outlined previously. He sees a psychiatrist several times a year or when he feels he is not coping. He is on medication to assist with his ongoing anxiety. His parents are both retired but continue to offer Jeremy a high level of support. Like Patrick and Christopher, his story is one of both success and failure, but, importantly, he is happy and engaged in his community.

The post-school journeys of these 'paradox children', on their way to being adults, is accurately described by the father of one of these young people: 'So, overall, some challenges and some successes!' The focus of any program, or services for people with autism, including those who display savant skills, should be to strive to increase their levels of happiness and independence. This is no different from what we all strive for in life, no matter our skills and talents, our deficits and challenges.

The emerging focus on using the strengths and interests of those with autism is driving new possiblities in research and intervention. Stephen Shore, a person with autism who is an assistant professor at the Ammon School of Education at Adelphi University, highlights the positive outcomes that are now possible for people with autism.

> We are on the edge of going beyond just acceptance of people on the autism spectrum to a society appreciating and valuing people on the spectrum for who they are. As time goes on we will see more people on the spectrum being hired, included, and otherwise integrated into society as they are as opposed to how much they are unlike someone else. The future is bright.
>
> (Stephen Shore, 2012, p. 14)

My hope for the future of every young autistic savant is that their skills will be identified in their early years of schooling, and that they are then provided with an appropriate differentiated educational program, so they can be supported to become valued and happy members of society.

References

Denzin, N.K. (1970). *The Research Act: A Theoretical Introduction to Sociological Methods*. Chicago: Aldine Press.

Gagné, F. (2009). Building gifts into talents: Detailed overview of the DMGT 2.0. In B. MacFarlane and T. Stambaugh (Eds.), *Leading Change in Gifted Education: The Festschrift of Dr. Joyce VanTassel-Baska* (pp. 61–80). Waco, TX: Prufrock Press.

Hill, A.L. (1974) Idiot savants: A categorization of abilities. *Mental Retardation*, December, 12–13.

Howlin, P., Goode, S., Hutton, J., and Rutter, M. (2009). Savant skills in autism: psychometric approaches and parental reports. *Philosophical Transactions of the Royal Society B, 364*, 1359–1367.

Shore, S. (2012). Observations on education from within the autism spectrum. In L. Perner (Ed.), *Scholars with Autism. Achieving Dreams*. Arizona: Auricle Books.

Treffert, D. (1989). *Extraordinary People*. London: Bantam Press.

Treffert, D. (2012). *Islands of Genius: The Bountiful Mind of the Autistic, Acquired, and Sudden Savant*. London: Jessica Kingsley Publishers.

FIGURE 6.1 'The Orchestra' by Daniel. A ten-year-old musical and artistic savant with a prodigious memory for composers and their music.

Acknowledgements

Patrick, one of the remarkable young autistic savants whom you meet in this book, was the inspiration and the catalyst for the development of the *Savant Skill Curriculum*. I dedicate this book to Patrick and his family, which includes his caring and supportive brother, who acted as Patrick's mentor throughout the course of the study, and who continues to do so today. I would like to express my gratitude to all of the twenty-two remarkably gifted autistic children who participated in the study. And to their devoted and loving families, who, in pursuit of an educational program that was inclusive of their children's special skills, were so willing to join me on this journey of discovery. To the forty-four dedicated teachers who delivered the differentiated educational program in their classrooms, I say thank you. I also would like to acknowledge the long-term support and encouragement I received from both Emeritus Professor Miraca Gross and Dr Darold Treffert – without their belief in this project, it would not have come to fruition. Finally, I must thank my support crew – the significant others in my life, both professionally and personally, including Charlie and Hayley. I would also like to acknowledge Routledge for their guidance and support, and for making this differentiated educational program available worldwide, for teachers and the families of school-age children with autism who display savant skills.

APPENDIX 1

SAVANT SKILL NOMINATION FORM

Child's name: .... *D.O.B.:* ....

School: ....

Name of person completing this form: ....

Relationship to nominated child: ....

Child's address: .... *Postcode:* ....

INSTRUCTIONS

Place a ✓ in the box next to the most applicable response.
Please feel free to add comments when appropriate.
Thank you.

A DIAGNOSIS

1   Has he/she ever had a diagnosis of autism?   NO [ ]   YES [ ]
    If YES, what was the diagnosis? ....
    At what *age* was this given?   __ years __ months

2   Is he/she presently receiving a *service* related to
    his/her autism?   NO [ ]   YES [ ]
    If YES, what service? ....

3   If he/she *verbal?*   NO [ ]   YES [ ]
    If non-verbal, what is his/her main means of
    communication?...

B SKILLS

1 Does your child show an unusual degree of skill in any or all of the following areas?

If the answer is YES to any of the following skills, please rate the skill level as either:

1 only special in relation to his/her overall ability
2 special in comparison to other individuals of similar age
3 would be considered EXCEPTIONAL in the normal population

Circle the appropriate number associated with that particular ability. Furthermore, you may like to provide examples of the ability.

a) *Memory (e.g. telephone numbers, songs, TV commercials, places, events, birthdates, Presidents, capital cities, etc.).*

No special skill [ ]   Yes, demonstrates skill [ ]   1   2   3

Examples: ....

b) *Hyperlexia (unusual ability in reading)*

No special skill [ ]   Yes, demonstrates skill [ ]   1   2   3

Examples: ....

c) *Mathematics/numbers*

No special skill [ ]   Yes, demonstrates skill [ ]   1   2   3

Examples: ....

d) *Drawing/art*

No special skill [ ]   Yes, demonstrates skill [ ]   1   2   3

Examples: ....

e) *Musical ability*

No special skill [ ]   Yes, demonstrates skill [ ]   1   2   3

Examples: ....

f) *Good pitch*

No special skill [ ]   Yes, demonstrates skill [ ]   1   2   3

Examples: ....

g) *Spatial skills (e.g. puzzles, mechanics)*

No special skill [ ]   Yes, demonstrates skill [ ]   1   2   3

Examples: ....

h) *Calendar calculation (i.e. ability to tell you on what day of the week a day will fall)*

No special skill [ ]   Yes, demonstrates skill [ ]   1   2   3

Examples: ....

i) *Sensory sensitivity (sound, touch, etc.)*

No special skill [ ]   Yes, demonstrates skill [ ]   1   2   3

Examples: ....

j) *Ball skills or other athletic performance*

No special skill [ ]   Yes, demonstrates skill [ ]   1   2   3

Examples: ....

k) *Other skills*

No special skill [ ]   Yes, demonstrates skill [ ]   1   2   3

Examples: ....

2 Does he/she display an *interest* in these areas of special
ability?   NO [ ]   YES [ ]

If YES, would you consider this interest *intense?*   NO [ ]   YES [ ]

3 Does he/she spend a *great deal of time* involved in these areas
of special skill?   NO [ ]   YES [ ]

If YES, how much time?   ___ hours per day   ___ hours per week

4 Has he/she ever received *training* in the areas(s)
of special skill?   NO [ ]   YES [ ]

If YES, describe the training ....

5 Would you consider he/she has a *narrow range of
interests?*   NO [ ]   YES [ ]

If YES, what are these interests?

6 Does his/her special skill(s) create *problems* at home or
school?   NO [ ]   YES [ ]

If YES, what problems? ....

7 Does he/she display *difficult behaviours* at home or
school?   NO [ ]   YES [ ]

If YES, please explain ....

8 From the list of skills, is there any one skill you consider to be
exceptionally advanced or prodigious?   NO [ ]   YES [ ]

If YES, which skill? ....

9 Do you feel he/she is *presently* using the special skill(s) in
functional and meaningful ways?   NO [ ]   YES [ ]

If YES, please indicate the *level of usefulness* or *functional value* of the skill at
present. *Circle* the number that best illustrates this.

1	2	3
of very little use	of some use	a great deal of use

10 Would you like your child to make *full use* of his/her special skills,
i.e. be of *practical* value to him/her on a regular basis? NO [ ]   YES [ ]

11 Are there any *members* of his/her immediate family who
demonstrate any of the above skills *or* might be considered
gifted or talented in any other way?   NO [ ]   YES [ ]

If so, provide details ....

12 Are there any *members* of his/her family who are also known
to suffer from *autism* or a *communication disorder?*   NO [ ]   YES [ ]

If YES, provide details ....

THANK YOU FOR YOUR CO-OPERATION

APPENDIX **2**

SAVANT SKILL TEACHER QUESTIONNAIRE

Some children and adults with autism appear to display special high level skills, sometimes referred to as savant skills or gifts, in one or more areas, e.g. number calculation, reading and spelling, drawing, singing, playing an instrument, etc.

A child in your class has been identified as displaying such skills. This questionnaire is designed to find the degree and stage of development of the child's savant skills, form a complete profile of their skills, and establish the current functional use to the child of these skills.

Your answers to the questionnaire will help us to find out more about savant skills in the autistic population and to develop ways to put these skills to functional use and help reduce the impact of autism on the life of the child and others who display savant skills or gifts.

This questionnaire can be completed by a teacher or teacher's aide.

The information that you disclose will be used for research and/or program development purposes and will therefore be *CONFIDENTIAL*.

Child's name: .... Sex: ....

Date of birth: .... Today's date: ....

School: ....

Name of person completing this questionnaire: ....

        Teacher   *Teacher's Aide*

(please circle 1)

> **Please *circle* the *YES* or *NO* to indicate your answer.**
> **Please add comments if you would like.** *Thank you.*

A EDUCATIONAL PLACEMENT:

1 Is he/she presently receiving a *service* related to
   his/her autism?   YES   NO

   If *YES,* what service? ....

   If *NO,* describe the child's *present educational placement* ....

2 Is he/she *verbal?*   YES   NO

   If *non-verbal,* what is his/her main means of communication? ....

B SKILLS:

The following is a list of savant skills or gifts and examples of each. Decide if the child displays each skill and indicate *how much* you think the child's skill *is like* the item by using the scale to the right of each item.

Mark on the scale of 1 to 11 whether you *STRONGLY AGREE (SA)* to *STRONGLY DISAGREE (SD).* Circle *the appropriate number.* If you are unclear or haven't observed the skill in the child, put a tick (✓) in the *UNSURE* or *DON'T KNOW* box. Use the space below the item for examples concerning the child's skill(s).

*   The child displays a high level of skill or ability above that expected of a child with autism, or even a non-disabled child in:

1 *Recall of Information/Memory:*   SA   SD
   (e.g. remembers complex details and   11 10 9 8 7 6 5 4 3 2 1
   happenings, i.e. telephone numbers,
   songs, TV commercials, places events,
   birth dates, capital cities, postcodes, etc.).   [ ] UNSURE OR DON'T KNOW

   A personal example: ....

   ....

2 *Reading/Spelling/Writing (Hyperlexia):*   SA   SD
   (e.g. can read, spell and/or write a lot   11 10 9 8 7 6 5 4 3 2 1
   of words, some of which are relatively
   complex)   [ ] UNSURE OR DON'T KNOW

   A personal example: ....

   ....

3 *Art (Drawing or Painting):*   SA   SD
   (e.g. can draw/paint detailed and   11 10 9 8 7 6 5 4 3 2 1
   complex representations of objects,
   people, places, etc.)   [ ] UNSURE OR DON'T KNOW

A personal example: ....
....

4   *Music:*   SA   SD
     (e.g. can play an instrument or sing with   11 10 9 8 7 6 5 4 3 2 1
     relative ease, can play/sing melodies upon
     a single hearing, has very good pitch, etc.)   [ ] UNSURE OR DON'T KNOW

     A personal example: ....
     ....

5   *Mechanical or Spatial Skill:*   SA   SD
     (e.g. can complete complex puzzles   11 10 9 8 7 6 5 4 3 2 1
     quickly, assembles or disassembles
     electronic equipment, deciphers   [ ] UNSURE OR DON'T KNOW
     mechanical manuals/diagrams,
     i.e. car repair guides, etc.)

     A personal example: ....
     ....

6   *Calendar Calculation:*   SA   SD
     (e.g. can tell you the exact day of the   11 10 9 8 7 6 5 4 3 2 1
     week a date in history will fall,
     correctly names ages of people once   [ ] UNSURE OR DON'T KNOW
     birth dates are known, correctly recalls
     or predicts scheduled events with dates,
     etc.)

     A personal example: ....
     ....

7   *Calculation of Numbers/Mathematic Skill:*   SA   SD
     (e.g. can calculate many equations,   11 10 9 8 7 6 5 4 3 2 1
     i.e. multiplies, divides, subtracts, gives
     square roots of numbers, identifies   [ ] UNSURE OR DON'T KNOW
     prime numbers, etc., rapidly)

     A personal example: ....
     ....

8   *Sensory Sensitivity:*   SA   SD
     (e.g. a highly developed sense of smell,   11 10 9 8 7 6 5 4 3 2 1
     taste, touch, sight, hearing, etc. May
     also display an accurate sense of time   [ ] UNSURE OR DON'T KNOW
     and direction)

     A personal example: ....
     ....

9 *Athletic Performance:*   SA   SD

   (e.g. has highly developed sense of   11 10 9 8 7 6 5 4 3 2 1

   balance, climbing, running or jumping

   ability, etc.)   [ ] UNSURE OR DON'T KNOW

   A personal example: ....

   ....

10 *Other Skills:*   SA   SD

   (e.g. ability in using and deciphering   11 10 9 8 7 6 5 4 3 2 1

   complex computer programs and

   functions)   [ ] UNSURE OR DON'T KNOW

   A personal example: ....

   ....

C PROFILE OF SKILL(S):

To explore more *fully* the child's savant skills or gifts, please indicate *how much* you think the child *is like* the item by using the scale to the right of each item as before.

Circle *STRONGLY AGREE (SA)* to *STRONGLY DISAGREE (SD)* and circle *the appropriate number.* If you are unsure or don't know, please put a (✓) in the *UNSURE* or *DON'T KNOW* box.

*   THE CHILD:

                            SA   SD

1 Displays a *great deal of interest* in   11 10 9 8 7 6 5 4 3 2 1

   his/her area(s) of skill, i.e. spends a

   great deal of time thinking,

   talking, working on the skill area   [ ] UNSURE OR DON'T KNOW

   (e.g. counting and writing numbers

   constantly)

   A personal example: ....

   ....

                            SA   SD

2 Spends a *great deal of time* involved in   11 10 9 8 7 6 5 4 3 2 1

   his/her area(s) of skill

   (i.e. can spend hours at a time

   drawing/singing, etc. to the exclusion   [ ] UNSURE OR DON'T KNOW

   of others)

   An example of how much time per day, per week ....

   ....

		SA										SD

3 Is *easily upset* if unable to have access
   SA   SD
11 10 9 8 7 6 5 4 3 2 1
to *high interest tasks* and becomes
difficult to manage (e.g. will tantrum   [ ] UNSURE OR DON'T KNOW
if not able to play/sing songs)

Some examples: ....
....

4 Displays many *negative or inappropriate*
   SA   SD
11 10 9 8 7 6 5 4 3 2 1
behaviours and is *difficult to manage*
(e.g. throws severe tantrums that are   [ ] UNSURE OR DON'T KNOW
long-lasting)

List negative behaviours:...
....

5 Appears to be *more highly sensitive or*
   SA   SD
11 10 9 8 7 6 5 4 3 2 1
aware of other people compared with
other autistic or non-autistic children   [ ] UNSURE OR DON'T KNOW
(e.g. purposely avoids/seeks out contact
with other adults and children,
easily upset or over-stimulated by others)

Describe some examples: ....
....

6 Is highly *motivated* when working on
   SA   SD
11 10 9 8 7 6 5 4 3 2 1
their skills (i.e. is enthusiastic, excited
and concentrates on skill activities)   [ ] UNSURE OR DON'T KNOW

A personal example: ....
....

7 Uses *imaginative or creative methods* to
   SA   SD
11 10 9 8 7 6 5 4 3 2 1
accomplish tasks (e.g. changes tunes/words
of songs, shows imaginative ways of   [ ] UNSURE OR DON'T KNOW
seeking out tasks)

Some examples: ....
....

		SA										SD

8 Has received some *formal training* in his/her skill area(s) at school (e.g. has piano or extra art lessons, etc.)

SA   SD
11 10 9 8 7 6 5 4 3 2 1

[ ] UNSURE OR DON'T KNOW

An example of the type and amount of training: ....

....

9 Has *fully developed* gift or skill, i.e. has developed to its fullest potential (e.g. the child plays Grade 8 level on the piano and is only 10 years of age)

SA   SD
11 10 9 8 7 6 5 4 3 2 1

[ ] UNSURE OR DON'T KNOW

Please elaborate: ....

....

10 Is making the *fullest functional use of the skills* at school i.e. the skill is being applied fully in a meaningful and purposeful manner for the child (e.g. the number calculation ability is being used by the child to add up the school roll and accounts)

SA   SD
11 10 9 8 7 6 5 4 3 2 1

[ ] UNSURE OR DON'T KNOW

List examples of their functional use: ....

....

11 Has *one* area of skill which appears to be *more highly developed and advanced* than his/her other skill

SA   SD
11 10 9 8 7 6 5 4 3 2 1

[ ] UNSURE OR DON'T KNOW

A personal example: ....

....

Please describe in as much detail as you can, *over the page,* the child's *present* savant skills. Select no more than 2 skills to describe fully, ensuring you include the child's *most highly and advanced* skill (as outlined in the previous question no. 11).

Musical Skill includes detail such as:

- can play tunes or melodies on the piano/instrument with relative ease (examples)
- learned to play the piano/instrument with no training
- can sing/play melodies upon a single hearing (examples)

- plays the following pieces of music (list them)
- spends a great deal of time listening/playing music (amount)
- has perfect pitch
- sensitive to rhythm

SKILL DESCRIPTION:
THE MOST HIGHLY DEVELOPED
and ADVANCED SKILL

Area of skill: ....

Skill description: ....

SKILL DESCRIPTION:
OTHER SKILLS

Area of skill: ....

Skill description: ....

Do the child's savant skills create
problems for you or the child in
the school environment?   YES   NO

If *YES*, provide details:

....

....

*Are there any other comments you would like to make regarding
the child's savant skills, their development, or functional application?*

....

....

THANK YOU FOR YOUR CO-OPERATION

APPENDIX 3

SAVANT SKILL FAMILY QUESTIONNAIRE

Some children and adults with autism appear to display special high level skills, sometimes referred to as savant skills or gifts, in one or more areas, e.g. number calculation, reading and spelling, drawing, singing, playing an instrument, etc.

Your child has been identified as displaying such skills. This questionnaire is designed to find the degree and stage of development of your child's savant skills, form a complete profile of their skills, and establish the current functional use to your child of these skills.

Your answers to the questionnaire will help us to find out more about savant skills in the autistic population and to develop ways to put these skills to functional use and help reduce the impact of autism on the life of your child and others who display savant skills or gifts.

This questionnaire can be completed by the individual concerned,
or, if unable to answer the questions without help,
by a family member or another individual who knows the family well.

The information that you disclose will be used for research and/or program cevelopment purposes only and will be *CONFIDENTIAL.*

Child's name: .... Date of birth: ....

School: .... Today's date: ....

Name of person completing this questionnaire: ....

Relationship to child: ....

Child's address: ....

Telephone: .... Postcode: ....

**Please *circle* the *YES* or *NO* to indicate your answer
and add comments if you would like. *Thank you.***

A PERSONAL DETAILS:

1   Was pregnancy normal and *delivery normal?*   YES   NO
    If NO, provide details ....

2   What week of gestation was your child delivered? .... weeks

3   Did your child ever receive oxygen?   YES   NO
    If *YES*, when? ....

B DIAGNOSIS:

1   Has he/she ever had a *diagnosis of autism?*   YES   NO
    If *YES*, what was the diagnosis? ....
    At *what age* was this given?   __ years __ months

2   Is he/she presently receiving a *service* related to
    his/her autism?   YES   NO
    If *YES*, what service? ....
    If *NO*, describe your child's *present educational placement* ....
    ....

3   Is he/she *verbal?*   YES   NO
    If *non-verbal*, what is his/her main means of communication? ....

C SKILLS:

The following is a list of savant skills or gifts and examples of each. Decide if your child displays each skill and indicate *how much* you think your child's skill *is like* the item by using the scale to the right of each item.

Mark on the scale of 1 to 11 whether you *STRONGLY AGREE (SA)* to *STRONGLY DISAGREE (SD)*. Circle *the appropriate number*. If you are unclear or haven't observed the skill in your child, put a tick (✓) in the *UNSURE* or *DON'T KNOW* box. Use the space below the item for examples concerning your child's skill(s).

- My child displays a high level of skill or ability above that expected of a child with autism or even a non-disabled child in:

1 *Recall of Information/Memory:* SA SD
   (e.g. remembers complex details and 11 10 9 8 7 6 5 4 3 2 1
   happenings, i.e. telephone numbers,
   songs, TV commercials, places, events, [ ] UNSURE OR DON'T KNOW
   birth dates, capital cities, postcodes,
   etc.)
   A personal example: ....
   ....

2 *Reading/Spelling/Writing (Hyperlexia):* SA SD
   (e.g. can read, spell and/or write a lot of 11 10 9 8 7 6 5 4 3 2 1
   words, some of which are relatively
   complex) [ ] UNSURE OR DON'T KNOW
   A personal example: ....
   ....

3 *Art (Drawing or Painting):* SA SD
   (e.g. can draw/paint detailed and 11 10 9 8 7 6 5 4 3 2 1
   complex representations of objects,
   people, places, etc.) [ ] UNSURE OR DON'T KNOW
   A personal example: ....
   ....

4 *Music:* SA SD
   (e.g. can play an instrument or sing with 11 10 9 8 7 6 5 4 3 2 1
   relative ease, can play/sing melodies upon
   a single hearing, has very good pitch, etc.) [ ] UNSURE OR DON'T KNOW
   A personal example: ....
   ....

5 *Mechanical or Spatial Skill:* SA SD
   (e.g. can complete complex puzzles 11 10 9 8 7 6 5 4 3 2 1
   quickly, assembles or disassembles
   electronic equipment, deciphers
   mechanical manuals/diagrams, [ ] UNSURE OR DON'T KNOW
   i.e. car repair guides, etc.)
   A personal example: ....
   ....

6 *Calendar Calculation:*   SA   SD
(e.g. can tell you the exact day of the   11 10 9 8 7 6 5 4 3 2 1
week a date in history will fall,
correctly names ages of people once   [ ] UNSURE OR DON'T KNOW
birth dates are known, correctly recalls
or predicts scheduled events with dates, etc.)

A personal example: ....

....

7 *Calculation of Numbers/Mathematic Skill:*   SA   SD
(e.g. can calculate many equations,   11 10 9 8 7 6 5 4 3 2 1
i.e. multiplies, divides, subtracts, gives
square roots of numbers, identifies prime   [ ] UNSURE OR DON'T KNOW
numbers, etc., rapidly)

A personal example: ....

....

8 *Sensory Sensitivity:*   SA   SD
(e.g. a highly developed sense of smell,   11 10 9 8 7 6 5 4 3 2 1
taste, touch, sight, hearing, etc. May
also display an accurate sense of time   [ ] UNSURE OR DON'T KNOW
and direction)

A personal example: ....

....

9 *Athletic Performance:*   SA   SD
(e.g. has highly developed sense of   11 10 9 8 7 6 5 4 3 2 1
balance, climbing, running or jumping
ability, etc.)   [ ] UNSURE OR DON'T KNOW

A personal example: ....

....

10 *Other Skills:*   SA   SD
(e.g. ability in using and deciphering   11 10 9 8 7 6 5 4 3 2 1
complex computer programs and
functions)   [ ] UNSURE OR DON'T KNOW

A personal example: ....

....

D PROFILE OF SKILL(S):

To explore more *fully* your child's savant skills or gifts, please indicate *how much* you think your child *is like* the item by using the scale to the right of each item as before.

Circle *STRONGLY AGREE (SA)* to *STRONGLY DISAGREE (SD)* and circle *the appropriate number.* If you are unsure or don't know, please put a (✓) in the *UNSURE* or *DON'T KNOW* box.

- My child:

		SA										SD

1 Developed an interest and showed some   11 10 9 8 7 6 5 4 3 2 1
early signs of ability in the skill(s)
at an early age   [ ] UNSURE OR DON'T KNOW

A personal example and age of child at the time: ....

....

                             SA   SD

2 Displays a *great deal of interest* in   11 10 9 8 7 6 5 4 3 2 1
his/her area(s) of skill, i.e. spends a
great deal of time thinking,
talking, working on the skill area (e.g.   [ ] UNSURE OR DON'T KNOW
counting and writing numbers constantly)

A personal example: ....

....

                             SA   SD

3 Spends a *great deal of time* involved in   11 10 9 8 7 6 5 4 3 2 1
his/her area(s) of skill
(i.e. can spend hours at a time
drawing/singing to the exclusion   [ ] UNSURE OR DON'T KNOW
of others)

An example of how much time per day, per week ....

....

                             SA   SD

4 Is *easily upset* if unable to have access   11 10 9 8 7 6 5 4 3 2 1
to *high interest tasks* and becomes
difficult to manage (e.g. will tantrum if
not able to play/sing songs)   [ ] UNSURE OR DON'T KNOW

Some personal examples: ....

....

                             SA   SD

5 Displays *many negative behaviours* and is   11 10 9 8 7 6 5 4 3 2 1
difficult to manage (e.g. throws severe
tantrums that last a long time)   [ ] UNSURE OR DON'T KNOW

List negative behaviours: ....

....

6 Appears to be *more highly sensitive* or *aware of other people* compared with other autistic and non-autistic children (e.g. purposely avoids/seeks out contact with other family members or friends, easily upset or over-stimulated by other people, etc.)

SA   SD
11 10 9 8 7 6 5 4 3 2 1

[ ] UNSURE OR DON'T KNOW

Describe some examples: ....

....

7 Is highly *motivated* when working on his/her skills (i.e. is enthusiastic, excited and concentrates on skill activities)

SA   SD
11 10 9 8 7 6 5 4 3 2 1

[ ] UNSURE OR DON'T KNOW

A personal example: ....

....

8 Uses *imaginative or creative methods* to accomplish tasks (e.g. changes tunes/ words of songs, shows imaginative ways of seeking out favourite tasks)

SA   SD
11 10 9 8 7 6 5 4 3 2 1

[ ] UNSURE OR DON'T KNOW

Some examples: ....

....

9 Has received some *formal training* in the skill area(s) (e.g. has piano or art lessons)

SA   SD
11 10 9 8 7 6 5 4 3 2 1

[ ] UNSURE OR DON'T KNOW

An example of the type and amount of training: ....

....

10 Skill or gift is *fully developed*, i.e. has developed to its *fullest* potential (e.g. my child plays Grade 8 level on the piano at 10 years of age)

SA   SD
11 10 9 8 7 6 5 4 3 2 1

[ ] UNSURE OR DON'T KNOW

Please elaborate: ....

....

		SA	SD

11 Is making the *fullest functional*   SA   SD
     use of the skills at home, school   11 10 9 8 7 6 5 4 3 2 1
     and in the community, i.e. the skill
     is being applied fully in a meaningful   [ ] UNSURE OR DON'T KNOW
     and purposeful manner for my child
     (e.g. my child displays art works in
     the local art gallery)

List examples of their functional use: ....

....

12 Has *one* area of skill which appears   SA   SD
     to be *more highly developed and advanced*   11 10 9 8 7 6 5 4 3 2 1
     than his/her other skills   [ ] UNSURE OR DON'T KNOW

A personal example: ....

....

Please describe in as much detail as you can, *over the page,* your child's *present* savant skills. Select no more than 2 skills to describe fully, ensuring you include your child's *most highly and advanced skill* (as outlined in the previous question no. 12).

e.g. Musical Skill includes detail such as:

- can play tunes or melodies on the piano/instrument with relative ease (examples)
- learned to play the piano/instrument with no training (age)
- can sing/play melodies upon a single hearing (examples)
- plays the following pieces of music (list them)
- spends a great deal of time listening/playing music (amount)
- has perfect pitch
- sensitive to rhythm

SKILL DESCRIPTION:
THE MOST HIGHLY DEVELOPED
and ADVANCED SKILL

Area of skill: ....

Skill description: ....

SKILL DESCRIPTION:
OTHER SKILLS

Area of skill: ....

Skill description: ....

Please circle the *YES* or *NO* to indicate your answer.

E FAMILY BACKGROUND:

1 Are there *any members of your child's immediate*
   family who demonstrate any of the skills listed
   above or might be considered *gifted or talented*
   (i.e. performs significantly beyond his/her age peers)   YES   NO

   If YES, provide details: ....

   ....

2 Are there *any members of your child's family*
   who are also known to suffer from
   autism or a communication disorder?   YES   NO

   If *YES,* provide details: ....

   ....

3 Do your child's savant skills *create problems*
   for both your child and family?   YES   NO

   If *YES,* provide details: ....

   ....

4 Are there any other comments you would like to add regarding your child's
   savant skills, their development, or functional application?

   ....

   ....

   ....

THANK YOU FOR YOUR CO-OPERATION

APPENDIX 4

INFORMAL SAVANT SKILL MEMORY ASSESSMENT

MEMORY

Savant Skill Research Project

Name: Example Case 1: Timothy   **Date:** _____

Memory Items (from *Savant Skill Questionnaires – Family and Teacher*, T.R. Clark)

Car Information

Name of Person	*Car Registration Number*	*Model of Car*
e.g. Mother	RYF 153	Toyota

Time/Life Events

Family Event or Activity	*Time of day*	*Day of the Week*
McDonald's	5.00pm	Saturday

Commercials

Name of Commercial	Words/lines recalled from Commercial
e.g. Pizza Hut	'Dial 1311, Pizza Hut Delivery'

Mapping/Directional Recall

Location of Place Visited (family/friends, house, school, shopping centre, etc.)	*Route Travelled*
e.g. Chatswood Chase Shopping Centre	Willoughby Rd, Kenthurst St, then Victoria Rd

Other
(Items recalled with ease)

e.g. Songs (names and artists)	Jewel – 'Foolish Game'

....

....

....

MEMORY

Savant Skill Research Project

Name: Example Case 2: Christopher (Non-verbal)   **Date:** _____

Memory Items

CARS

Point to which 'model' of car matches the 'make' (brand)

MODEL	MAKE
Barina	Holden
Laser	Ford
Lantra	Hyundai
Magna	Mitsubishi
Cielo	Daewoo
Pulsar	Nissan
Lexcen	Toyota
MX5	Mazda

TRAIN STATIONS AND LINES

Which station is on which train line?

STATION	LINE
Allawah	Cronulla
Martin Place	Bondi Junction
Campsie	Liverpool via Bankstown
Holsworthy	Macarthur via East Hills
Dundas	Carlingford
Gordon	Emu Plains
Turrella	Lithgow
Riverstone	Richmond

FOOTBALL TEAMS

Which teams are Super League and which teams are Australian Rugby League?

TEAM	ARL or SUPER LEAGUE
Western Suburbs	ARL
Penrith Panthers	Super League
St. George	ARL
North Sydney	ARL
Cronulla Sutherland	Super League
Western Reds	Super League
Brisbane Broncos	Super League
Parramatta	ARL

OLYMPIC GAMES

Which city held the Olympic Games in which year?

YEAR	CITY
1908	London
1996	Atlanta
1960	Rome
1956	Melbourne
1984	Los Angeles
1988	Sole
1972	Munich
2000	Sydney

APPENDIX 5

SAVANT SKILL POST-STUDY FAMILY/TEACHER QUESTIONNAIRE

Your child/student has participated in the 'Savant Skill Curriculum Program' for the past two years. During this time strategies to facilitate the functional use of your child's/student's savant skills at home and school have been trialled by families, teacher and/or mentors. By using these savant skills as *motivators to learning*, activities were also trialled to improve communication, social skills, self-esteem and behaviour.

To assist us to find out whether or not your child/student has made gains in the functional application of savant skills, in communication, social skills and behaviour, please answer the following questions. The information you give will in turn help us to assist other children with autism displaying savant skills. Some questions remain the same as those in the Pre-Study Family/Teacher Savant Skill Questionnaire.

This questionnaire can be completed by the individual concerned, or, if unable to answer the questions without help, by a family member or another individual who knows the family well.

The information that you disclose will be used for research and/or program development purposes only and will be *CONFIDENTIAL*.

Child's name: .... *Date of birth:* ....

School: .... *Today's date:* ....

Name of person completing this questionnaire: ....

Relationship to child: ....

Child's address: ....

Telephone: .... *Postcode:* ....

A SAVANT SKILLS:

The following is a list of savant skills or gifts and examples of each. Decide if your child displays each skill and indicate *how much* you think your child's skill *is like* the item by using the scale to the right of each item.

Mark on the scale of 1 to 11 whether you *STRONGLY AGREE (SA)* to *STRONGLY DISAGREE (SD)*. Circle *the appropriate number.* If you are unclear or haven't observed the skill in your child, put a tick (✓) in the *UNSURE* or *DON'T KNOW* box. Use the space below the item for examples concerning your child's skill(s).

My child displays a high level of skill or ability above that expected of a child with autism or even a non-disabled child in:

1 *Recall of Information/Memory:*   SA   SD
(e.g. remembers complex details and 11 10 9 8 7 6 5 4 3 2 1
happenings, i.e. telephone numbers,
songs, TV commercials, places, events, [ ] UNSURE OR DON'T KNOW
birth dates, capital cities, postcodes,
etc.)

A personal example: ....

....

2 *Reading/Spelling/Writing (Hyperlexia):* SA   SD
(e.g. can read, spell and/or write a lot of 11 10 9 8 7 6 5 4 3 2 1
words, some of which are relatively
complex)   [ ] UNSURE OR DON'T KNOW

A personal example: ....

....

3 *Art, i.e. Drawing or Painting:*   SA   SD
(e.g. can draw/paint detailed and 11 10 9 8 7 6 5 4 3 2 1
complex representations of objects,
people, places, etc.)   [ ] UNSURE OR DON'T KNOW

A personal example: ....

....

4 *Music:*   SA   SD
   (e.g. can play an instrument or sing with 11 10 9 8 7 6 5 4 3 2 1
   relative ease, can play/sing melodies upon
   a single hearing, has very good pitch, etc.) [ ] UNSURE OR DON'T KNOW

   A personal example: ....

   ....

5 *Mechanical or Spatial Skill:*   SA   SD
   (e.g. can complete complex puzzles   11 10 9 8 7 6 5 4 3 2 1
   quickly, assembles or disassembles
   electronic equipment, deciphers   [ ] UNSURE OR DON'T KNOW
   mechanical manuals/diagrams, i.e.
   car repair guides, etc.)

   A personal example: ....

   ....

6 *Calendar Calculation:*   SA   SD
   (e.g. can tell you the exact day of the   11 10 9 8 7 6 5 4 3 2 1
   week a date in history will fall,
   correctly names ages of people once   [ ] UNSURE OR DON'T KNOW
   birth dates are known, correctly recalls
   or predicts scheduled events with dates, etc.)

   A personal example: ....

   ....

7 *Calculation of Numbers/Mathematic Skill:* SA   SD
   (e.g. can calculate many equations,   11 10 9 8 7 6 5 4 3 2 1
   i.e. multiplies, divides, subtracts, gives
   square roots of numbers, identifies prime [ ] UNSURE OR DON'T KNOW
   numbers, etc., rapidly)

   A personal example: ....

   ....

8 *Sensory Sensitivity:*   SA   SD
   (e.g. a highly developed sense of smell, 11 10 9 8 7 6 5 4 3 2 1
   taste, touch, sight, hearing, etc. May
   also display an accurate sense of time   [ ] UNSURE OR DON'T KNOW
   and direction)

   A personal example: ....

   ....

9   *Athletic Performance:*   SA   SD

(e.g. has highly developed sense of   11 10 9 8 7 6 5 4 3 2 1
balance, climbing, running or jumping
ability, etc.)   [ ] UNSURE OR DON'T KNOW

A personal example: ....

....

10   *Other Skills:*   SA   SD

(e.g. ability in using and deciphering   11 10 9 8 7 6 5 4 3 2 1
complex computer programs and
functions)   [ ] UNSURE OR DON'T KNOW

A personal example: ....

....

B   PROFILE OF SKILL(S):

To explore more *fully* your child's/student's savant skills or gifts, please indicate *how much* you think your child *is like* the item by using the scale to the right of each item as before.

Mark on the scale of 1 to 11 whether you *STRONGLY AGREE (SA)* to *STRONGLY DISAGREE (SD)* with each statement and circle *the appropriate number.* If you are unsure or don't know, please put a (✓) in the *UNSURE* or *DON'T KNOW* box.

* My child:

                                SA   SD

1   Displays a *great deal of interest* in   11 10 9 8 7 6 5 4 3 2 1
his/her area(s) of skill, i.e. spends a
great deal of time thinking,
talking, working on the skill area (e.g.   [ ] UNSURE OR DON'T KNOW
counting and writing numbers constantly)

A personal example: ....

....

                                SA   SD

2   Spends a *great deal of time* involved in   11 10 9 8 7 6 5 4 3 2 1
his/her area(s) of skill
(i.e. can spend hours at a time
drawing/singing, etc. to the exclusion   [ ] UNSURE OR DON'T KNOW
of others)

An example of how much time per day, per week ....

....

SA   SD

3   Is *easily upset* if unable to have access   11 10 9 8 7 6 5 4 3 2 1
    to *high interest tasks* and becomes
    difficult to manage (e.g. will tantrum if
    not able to play/sing songs)   [ ] UNSURE OR DON'T KNOW

    Some personal examples: ....

    ....

SA   SD

4   Displays *many negative behaviours* and is   11 10 9 8 7 6 5 4 3 2 1
    difficult to manage (e.g. throws severe
    tantrums that last a long time)   [ ] UNSURE OR DON'T KNOW

    List negative behaviours: ....

    ....

SA   SD

5   Appears to be *more highly sensitive* or   11 10 9 8 7 6 5 4 3 2 1
    aware of other people compared with
    other autistic and non-autistic children
    (e.g. purposely avoids/seeks out contact   [ ] UNSURE OR DON'T KNOW
    with other family members or friends,
    easily upset or over-stimulated by
    other people, etc.)

    Describe some examples: ....

    ....

SA   SD

6   Is highly *motivated* when working on   11 10 9 8 7 6 5 4 3 2 1
    his/her skills (i.e. is enthusiastic, excited
    and concentrates on skill activities)   [ ] UNSURE OR DON'T KNOW

    A personal example: ....

    ....

SA   SD

7   Uses *imaginative or creative methods* to   11 10 9 8 7 6 5 4 3 2 1
    accomplish tasks (e.g. changes tunes/
    words of songs, shows imaginative ways
    of seeking out favourite tasks)   [ ] UNSURE OR DON'T KNOW

    Some examples: ....

    ....

		SA		SD

8 Skill or gift is *fully developed,*
i.e. has developed to its *fullest*
potential (e.g. my child plays Grade 8
level on the piano at 10 years of age)

SA   SD
11 10 9 8 7 6 5 4 3 2 1

[ ] UNSURE OR DON'T KNOW

Please elaborate: ....

....

9 Is making the *fullest functional
use of the skills* at home, school
and in the community, i.e. the skill
is being applied fully in a meaningful
and purposeful manner for my child
(e.g. my child displays art works in
the local art gallery)

SA   SD
11 10 9 8 7 6 5 4 3 2 1

[ ] UNSURE OR DON'T KNOW

List examples of their functional use: ....

....

10 Has *one* area of skill which appears
to be *more highly developed and advanced*
than his/her other skills

SA   SD
11 10 9 8 7 6 5 4 3 2 1

[ ] UNSURE OR DON'T KNOW

A personal example: ....

....

C USE OF SAVANT SKILL(S) :

To explore more fully the functional use of your child's savant skills and any improvements in communication, behaviour and social skills, please complete the following questions.

Please circle YES or NO to indicate your answer and add comments if you would like.

1 The aim of this study has been to help your child/student to make *functional use of his/her savant skills in daily activities at home and school.* Do you believe your child/student is *beginning to apply these skills* in functional ways (with or without support) having been on the Program for two years?

YES   NO

If YES, provide details (i.e. functional uses, e.g. keeps class roll, keeps home accounts, level of support, etc.)

....

....

2   *If the answer to the first question is NO, could you give possible reasons* why the skills have not been applied in a functional manner *at home or school?*

....

....

3   Do you feel your child/student has made/is making gains with their *communication, social skills and behaviour* as a result of this study?

                                                                        YES   NO

    If YES, provide details (i.e. in communication, social skills, behaviour)

....

....

4   If the answer to the question above is NO, could you suggest 'why gains have not been made'?

....

....

5   *Have you observed any increase/decrease in* motivation to learning tasks *when teaching or using the* Savant Curriculum Teaching Priorities *at home/school?*

                                                                        YES   NO

    If YES, provide details:

....

....

6   Do you feel some savant skills are *more/less able* to be used in a teaching/mentoring/home program than other savant skills?

                                                                        YES   NO

    If YES, provide details (i.e. which savant skills, why?)

....

....

7   Are there some savant skills you feel *are not able to be applied functionally?*

                                                                        YES   NO

    If YES, provide details:

....

....

8   If the answer to the question above was YES, why do you feel the savant skills you listed *are not able to be applied functionally?*

....

....

9 Are any of the curriculum strategies *more effective in the application of savant skills* i.e. Enrichment, Acceleration, Mentorship, Development of Communication/Social Skills and Behaviour?

YES   NO

If YES, provide details:

....

....

10 Do you feel any of your child's/student's *savant skills are in fact developing further ?*

YES   NO

If YES, provide details:

....

....

11 Do you feel your child's/student's *savant skills are in fact diminishing?*

YES   NO

If YES, provide details:

....

....

12 If gains have been made in the functional use of your child's/student's savant skills, improvement in communication, socialization and *behaviour, will they continue on beyond this study,* with or without support?

YES   NO

If YES, provide details:

....

....

13 What assistance do you believe your child will require to *continue to make functional use of his/her savant skills?*

....

....

14. Finally, what are your views on the *ability of this study to assist your child/student to make functional use of their skills?*

....

....

Thank you for your time and assistance in attempting to help this unique group of children with both autism and savant abilities to apply their skills in meaningful ways. Please return when completed.

THANK YOU FOR YOUR CO-OPERATION

APPENDIX 6

CHRISTOPHER'S CURRICULUM STRATEGY ANNUAL PRIORITIES EVALUATION – FORM D

CURRICULUM STRATEGY ANNUAL PRIORITIES EVALUATION – FORM D

NAME: Christopher AGE: 13 A: 1st Evaluation (1yr) Date: __ / __ / ____

SCHOOL: _____ TEACHER/MENTOR: _____ B: 2nd Evaluation (2yr) Date: __ / __ / ____

Annual Priority	Savant Skill	Curriculum Strategy	SKILL ACHIEVEMENT Circle Strongly Agree (SA) to Strongly Disagree (SD) with the appropriate number in relation to the statement: 'the annual priority has been achieved'.	FUNCTIONAL APPLICATION Circle Strongly Agree (SA) to Strongly Disagree (SD) with the appropriate number in relation to the statement: 'the skill is being applied in a functional and meaningful manner to some degree with or without support'.
To use his interest in trains/buses and cars to develop 'personal train/bus schedules' for himself and others. Compile 'personal' car catalogues.	MEMORY (Savant II)	Enrichment	SD SA A: 1 2 3 4 5 6 7 8 9 10 11 B: 1 2 3 4 5 6 7 8 9 10 11	SD SA A: 1 2 3 4 5 6 7 8 9 10 11 B: 1 2 3 4 5 6 7 8 9 10 11
Apply interest in mapping skills for home/school excursions and holidays e.g. compile travel itineraries, cities, countries, etc.	MEMORY (Savant II)	Enrichment	SD SA A: 1 2 3 4 5 6 7 8 9 10 11 B: 1 2 3 4 5 6 7 8 9 10 11	SD SA A: 1 2 3 4 5 6 7 8 9 10 11 B: 1 2 3 4 5 6 7 8 9 10 11
To use interest in dates and life events to compile school/home historical diaries.	MEMORY (Savant II)	Enrichment	SD SA A: 1 2 3 4 5 6 7 8 9 10 11 B: 1 2 3 4 5 6 7 8 9 10 11	SD SA A: 1 2 3 4 5 6 7 8 9 10 11 B: 1 2 3 4 5 6 7 8 9 10 11
To use knowledge of world geography, i.e. capital cities etc. for individual research/project work.	MEMORY (Savant II)	Acceleration	SD SA A: 1 2 3 4 5 6 7 8 9 10 11 B: 1 2 3 4 5 6 7 8 9 10 11	SD SA A: 1 2 3 4 5 6 7 8 9 10 11 B: 1 2 3 4 5 6 7 8 9 10 11

APPENDIX 7

FAMILY INTERVIEW (PRE-TREATMENT)

PRE-SAVANT SKILL CURRICULUM

Questions

1. The aim of this study is to help your child with savant abilities to apply his/her skills in daily activities at home and school, that is, functionally. Do you believe that your child is currently applying these skills in a functional manner? If YES, please outline some examples and how your child uses his/her savant skills in functional ways.

2. If your child is NOT applying his/her skills in functional ways, could you suggest why this is the case?

3. In the past or currently, has your child been assisted (received training) to make functional use of his/her savant skills?

4. Would you like to see your child's savant skills develop further and be used in functional ways? If YES, why?

5. What effect, if any, do you feel having a child with both autism and savant abilities has on your family? Please outline.

6. In your view, does your child display a poor or positive self-esteem? Can you provide examples?

7. Should it be possible to apply your child's savant skills functionally over the next two years, what effect, if any, do you feel this would have for your child, and your family?

8. What are your views of the ability of this study to help your child apply his/her savant skills in functional and meaningful ways?

9. What are your goals/expectations for your child over the next five years? Ten years?

10. What other programs or interventions, that is, educational, medical or therapeutic, is your child currently receiving?

Thank you for your assistance.
T.R. Clark

APPENDIX 8

PROFILE OF SAVANT ABILITIES

PROFILE OF SAVANT SKILL

NAME: _____   DOB: _____   AGE: _____

SCHOOL: DATE: _____

PROFILE OF SAVANT SKILLS

SAVANT SKILL & LEVEL (LEVEL I & II)	STANDARDIZED MEASURES	NON-STANDARDIZED MEASURES/INFORMATION

APPENDIX 9

CURRICULUM STRATEGY ANNUAL PRIORITIES – FORM A

SAVANT ABILITIES

CURRICULUM STRATEGY ANNUAL PRIORITIES – FORM A

NAME: _____   DOB: _____   AGE: _____

SCHOOL: DATE: _____

PROFILE OF SAVANT SKILLS

SAVANT SKILL & LEVEL (I or II)	HOME OR SCHOOL	ENRICHMENT	ACCELERATION	MENTOR	COMMUNICATION/ SOCIAL SKILLS/ BEHAVIOUR

APPENDIX 10

CURRICULUM TEACHING ACTIVITIES AND STRATEGIES – FORM B

SAVANT ABILITIES

CURRICULUM TEACHING ACTIVITIES AND STRATEGIES – FORM B

NAME: _____   DOB: _____   AGE: _____

SCHOOL: DATE: _____

PROFILE OF SAVANT SKILLS

SAVANT SKILL & LEVEL (I or II)	HOME OR SCHOOL	ENRICHMENT	ACCELERATION	MENTOR	COMMUNICATION/ SOCIAL SKILLS/ BEHAVIOUR

CURRICULUM TEACHING ACTIVITIES – FORM C

CURRICULUM TEACHING ACTIVITIES – FORM C

NAME: _____   DOB: _____   AGE: _____

SCHOOL: DATE: _____

ANNUAL PRIORITY	HOME OR SCHOOL	SAVANT SKILL			
		e.g. Memory	e.g. Calendar	e.g. Music	e.g. Art
COMMUNICATION					
SOCIAL SKILLS					
BEHAVIOUR					

APPENDIX **12**

CURRICULUM STRATEGY ANNUAL PRIORITIES EVALUATION – FORM D

CURRICULUM STRATEGY ANNUAL PRIORITIES EVALUATION – FORM D

NAME: _____   AGE: _____   A: 1st Evaluation   Date: __ / __ / ____

SCHOOL: _____   TEACHER/MENTOR: _____   B: 2nd Evaluation   Date: __ / __ / ____

Annual Priority	Savant Skill	Curriculum Strategy	SKILL ACHIEVEMENT Circle Strongly Agree (SA) to Strongly Disagree (SD) with the appropriate number in relation to the statement: 'the annual priority has been achieved'.	FUNCTIONAL APPLICATION Circle Strongly Agree (SA) to Strongly Disagree (SD) with the appropriate number in relation to the statement: 'the skill is being applied in a functional and meaningful manner to some degree with or without support'.
			SD SA A: 1 2 3 4 5 6 7 8 9 10 11 B: 1 2 3 4 5 6 7 8 9 10 11	SD SA A: 1 2 3 4 5 6 7 8 9 10 11 B: 1 2 3 4 5 6 7 8 9 10 11
			SD SA A: 1 2 3 4 5 6 7 8 9 10 11 B: 1 2 3 4 5 6 7 8 9 10 11	SD SA A: 1 2 3 4 5 6 7 8 9 10 11 B: 1 2 3 4 5 6 7 8 9 10 11
			SD SA A: 1 2 3 4 5 6 7 8 9 10 11 B: 1 2 3 4 5 6 7 8 9 10 11	SD SA A: 1 2 3 4 5 6 7 8 9 10 11 B: 1 2 3 4 5 6 7 8 9 10 11
			SD SA A: 1 2 3 4 5 6 7 8 9 10 11 B: 1 2 3 4 5 6 7 8 9 10 11	SD SA A: 1 2 3 4 5 6 7 8 9 10 11 B: 1 2 3 4 5 6 7 8 9 10 11

INDEX

Note: Page numbers in *italics* indicate figures, forms, and tables.